Innovation and Growth

Innovation and Growth
Schumpeterian Perspectives

F. M. Scherer

The MIT Press
Cambridge, Massachusetts
London, England

Third printing, 1989

This book was set in Times New Roman by Asco Trade Typesetting Ltd.,
Hong Kong and printed and bound by Murray Printing Company in the
United States of America.

Library of Congress Cataloging in Publication Data

Scherer, F. M. (Frederic M.)
  Innovation and growth.

  Includes bibliographical references and index.
  1. Technological innovations.   2. Schumpeter, Joseph Alois, 1883–1950.
I. Title.
HC79.T4S33 1984   338′.06   83-24875
ISBN 0-262-19222-5

MIT Press

0262691027

**SCHERER
INNOVATN GROWTH**

Contents

Introduction

The papers reprinted with minor editorial changes in this volume have as a common theme certain questions concerning technological innovation: what its characteristics are, under what conditions it thrives, and its consequences for economic growth and welfare. The innovation theme has been central to much of my work as an economist. I was started on this course at the age of twenty-one, when I was captivated by the writings of Joseph A. Schumpeter, whose centennial we celebrated in 1983. Three decades later I continue to be a Schumpeterian in the most fundamental sense. That is, I am persuaded that technological change has had, and will continue to have, much more of an impact on material well-being than the niceties of static resource allocation to which microeconomists devote most of their attention.

Three substantive premises in Schumpeter's writings between 1911 and 1942 provided the foundation for much of my research agenda.

One was his notion, elaborated upon from Marx, that innovation, and especially technological innovation, imparts to capitalistic economies their peculiar dynamics through a process of "creative destruction." Old product and industry structures are repeatedly displaced or altered by new forms, and disequilibrium is more prevalent than equilibrium.

Second and without doubt most important, Schumpeter insisted that the dramatic gains in real income per capita experienced by western industrialized nations were not for the most part attributable to increases in population, money supplies, or land resources or to such governmental actions as tariff reform. Technological progress, he argued, was a more plausible explanatory factor, but it alone was insufficient if treated in isolation from the business milieu in which it occurred. "It is therefore quite wrong," he wrote in 1942 (p. 110), "to say . . . that capitalist enterprise was one, and technological progress a second, distinct factor in the observed development of output; they were essentially one and the same thing or . . . the former was the propelling force of the latter."

Schumpeter's third conjecture was more radical. The mainstream of western economic thought from the time of Adam Smith on had extolled the virtues of competitive market processes as the wellspring of prosperity. Schumpeter argued, to the contrary, that the expectation of a monopoly position and perhaps even the possession of one were more conducive to the technological innovation that brought economic progress:

What we have got to accept is that [the large-scale establishment or unit of control] has come to be the most powerful engine of . . . progress and in particular of the long-run expansion of total output not only in spite of, but to a considerable extent through, this strategy which looks so restrictive when viewed in the individual case and from the individual point in time. In this respect, perfect competition is not only impossible, but inferior, and has no title to being set up as a model of ideal efficiency. It is hence a mistake to base the theory of government regulation of industry on the principle that big business should be made to work as the respective industry would work in perfect competition (1942, p. 106).

For reasons I cannot fully reconstruct, this passage and others in Schumpeter kindled a flame when I first read them during my senior year at the University of Michigan in 1954. I had been a mediocre student, more interested in extracurricular activities than academic work. But in my last semester I decided to take advantage of what a great university was all about, enrolling in a writing course taught by Katherine Anne Porter, Shorey Peterson's economics honors seminar, and a graduate business administration seminar on "the economics of the large corporation." The third choice, unusual for a liberal arts undergraduate, suggests that the tinder had been prepared, perhaps because I was contemplating a business career and because my parents had given me a subscription to *Fortune* magazine. Excited by Schumpeter's theses, I wrote my honors paper on how legislated restrictions on atomic energy invention patent rights might affect the development of commercial nuclear power. And from that time on, I was hooked, although it took me a while to recognize the fact.

What we do is shaped by the opportunities we enjoy. My research has been influenced greatly by three special opportunities.

As an MBA student at the Harvard Business School, I enrolled in the most popular second-year course, Georges Doriot's "Manufacturing." The title was misleading but misled no one. Doriot had been deputy director of U.S. Army R & D during World War II and was founding father of the venture capital firm American Research and Development Corporation. The principal message of his lectures was that technological innovation could make innovators wealthy and the nation strong.[1] Doriot's students, working in groups of nine, were required to conduct two on-site company projects and write a long "topic report." Our report dug further into questions I first addressed in my undergraduate honors

---

1. Yes, Doriot lectured, contrary to the Harvard Business School tradition. Had the rest of the faculty lectured, he insisted, he would have taught by the case method.

thesis. In 1956 AT&T and IBM had signed antitrust decrees requiring compulsory licensing of their patents, usually without royalties. Many other corporations had entered similar decrees. What impact did such provisions have on company incentives to perform research and development? To find out, we read voraciously, interviewed executives of twenty-two companies, surveyed many more by mail, and conducted a statistical analysis of patenting trends. The result, along with much new insight for me into how the R&D world worked, was a book, *Patents and the Corporation* (1958), which we published privately and sold successfully in two editions.

In October 1957 the Soviet Union's first successful Sputnik launch precipitated a period of national soul-searching. Why was the United States behind in space? Had U.S. management or governmental institutions failed? The Harvard Business School initiated a Weapons Acquisition Research Project to find out what had gone wrong. I was invited to participate as a junior research assistant and, given my smoldering interest in technological innovation, enthusiastically signed on. It was an extraordinary experience. Our team—a professor of business, an economist (M. J. Peck), a retired Navy captain, a veteran Capitol Hill lawyer, and myself—began by compiling historical case studies of seven technological innovations developed in the private sector. We then studied in detail twelve major weapon systems developments. I have often regretted that the case studies were not published so that others could share, outside the interpretative constraints of books by Peck and myself (1962, 1964), in what we learned about the details of how an ambitious technological development program takes place.

During off moments of what proved to be a five-year weapons project research commitment, I escaped to the other side of the Charles River and acquired a Ph.D. from Harvard's economics department. Graduating in 1963, I embraced my third career-determining opportunity. In an effort to spur studies of technological change, the Ford Foundation (which had also financed the Weapons Acquisition Research Project) granted $150,000 to an interuniversity committee of seven economists, among whom I was the junior member. Our meetings provided among other things an opportunity for intensive discussions with Jacob Schmookler, who was hard at work on his pioneering book, *Invention and Economic Growth* (1966), to which my previous and ongoing work with patent data was complementary. Schmookler's results emphasized the influence of

demand forces on invention; mine were beginning to suggest the importance of what I called "technology push." We debated the merits of our
positions and whether we might both be right, each from a different
perspective. Some of the papers reprinted here stem directly from those
conversations, which also triggered, I believe, the synthesis Schmookler
achieved in chapter 8 of his 1966 book. The Ford Foundation research
program culminated in a March 1966 conference attended by more than
forty economists, including most of those who would prove to be the
next decade's leaders in pushing out the frontiers of knowledge on the
economics of technological innovation.

The imprint of the original Schumpeterian challenge and those three
early opportunities I enjoyed to confront it is seen in every paper published
here. In addition a fourth Schumpeterian trait must be acknowledged.
In his *History of Economic Analysis* (1954, p. 12), Schumpeter claims that
"What distinguishes the 'scientific' economist from all the other people
who think, talk, and write about economic topics is a command of
techniques that we class under three heads: history, statistics, and 'theory.'
The three together make up what we shall call Economic Analysis."
In my work on technological change (and much else) I have tried hard to
keep those three techniques in balance—not because Schumpeter urged
it but because I have always instinctively believed it was the right way
to do economics. Since this approach runs somewhat against the grain
of current fashion, knowing my prejudices may help the reader understand
the peculiar flavor of the papers that follow.

References

Peck, M. J., and F. M. Scherer. *The Weapons Acquisition Process: An Economic Analysis.*
Harvard Business School Division of Research, Boston, 1962.

Scherer, F. M., S. E. Herzstein Jr., A. W. Dreyfoos, W. G. Whitney, O. J. Bachmann,
C. P. Pesek, C. J. Scott, T. G. Kelly, and J. J. Galvin. *Patents and the Corporation.* Private
publication, 1958; 2nd ed., 1959.

Scherer, F. M. *The Weapons Acquisition Process: Economic Incentives.* Harvard Business
School Division of Research, Boston, 1962.

Schmookler, Jacob. *Invention and Economic Growth.* Cambridge: Harvard University Press,
1966.

Schumpeter, Joseph A., *The Theory of Economic Development.* Trans. Redvers Opie.
Cambridge: Harvard University Press, 1934 (orig. German lang. ed., 1911).

Schumpeter, Joseph A. *Capitalism, Socialism, and Democracy.* New York: Harper, 1942.

Schumpeter, Joseph A. *History of Economic Analysis.* New York: Oxford University Press,
1954.

Innovation and Growth

I THE NATURE OF TECHNOLOGICAL INNOVATION

My views on the nature of technological innovation were very much shaped by the nineteen systems development case studies compiled for the Harvard Weapons Acquisition Research Project as well as by reading other scholars' works. When my MBA classmates and I wrote *Patents and the Corporation* in 1958, we did an extensive literature search for a chapter on "Industrial Invention and Innovation." My subsequent case study research left me dissatisfied with that section, and when the first edition sold out in early 1959, I drew upon our early case study experience to rewrite the chapter for a second edition. Chapter 1 is an excerpt dealing with an important insight: how the level of uncertainty faced by decision makers changes over the life of an R & D project and with the rate at which funds are invested. Other parts of the same chapter went on to provide anecdotal evidence, mostly from published sources, on the magnitude of R & D project costs and uncertainties. They are omitted from the selection here because more systematic statistical work has been published on those questions by Edwin Mansfield and associates (1968, pp. 55–62; 1971; 1977, chs. 2, 4, 5).

Chapter 2 attempts to apply concepts articulated by Schumpeter and A. P. Usher to one of the most famous "inventions" of all time—the Watt-Boulton steam engine. Consistent with studies of modern R & D projects, it finds that seminal technical concepts, arising unpredictably when the proper Gestalt materializes, may be quite inexpensive. But before they are ready for commercial application, they require a time-consuming and costly development effort supported by entrepreneurial talents quite different from those giving birth to the original invention.

The third selection was inspired by my exchanges with Jacob Schmookler. Seeking to reconcile "demand pull" and "technology push" theories of invention, Schmookler conceived the idea of an input-output-like matrix tracing new technology from industries performing the R & D to industries using the fruits of that R & D. Tackling the job of actually measuring such a matrix appeared attractive to me only when the Federal Trade Commission's line of business program first made available data on industrial R & D expenditures (for 1974) broken down into narrowly defined performing industries. The resulting "technology flows matrix" provides many new and more precise insights into specialization patterns, degrees of R & D self-sufficiency, and other aspects of industrial R & D. It also sets the stage for productivity studies reported in Part IV.

Looking back, I am impressed at how much we (and I mean especially economists) have learned during the past quarter century about the nature of technological innovation in its modern R & D institutional form. Numerous case studies have illuminated the chain of interrelated events and the flow of decisions leading to new products and processes. Historians and statistical researchers, among whom Edwin Mansfield merits repeated mention, have done much to clarify our understanding of the costs and risks. As I see it, the most important problem on the "nature of innovation" agenda is not advancing our knowledge even further (although gaps remain), but diffusing it. In particular, much needs to be done in our universities to convey to would-be or recycling managers, scientists, and engineers a deep understanding from a social science perspective of what the innovation process is all about. The result, I believe, would be more effective toil in the world's innovation vineyards and greater success in advancing the frontiers of technology.

References

Mansfield, Edwin. *Industrial Research and Technological Innovation*. New York: Norton, 1968.

Mansfield, Edwin, John Rapoport, Jerome Schnee, Samuel Wagner, and Michael Hamburger. *Research and Innovation in the Modern Corporation*. New York: Norton, 1971.

Mansfield, Edwin, John Rapoport, Anthony Romeo, Edmund Villani, Samuel Wagner, and Frank Husic. *The Production and Application of New Industrial Technology*. New York: Norton, 1977.

1 The Investment Decision Phases in Modern Invention and Innovation

It should not be concluded that there is a necessary correlation between the magnitude of research and development expenditures and the importance of inventions produced. Many major advances in science and technology have been brough into the world at relatively little expense. Some, like Dr. Alexander Fleming's discovery of penicillin, originate from an unsolicited accident combined with the rare ability to recognize new possibilities in an event that has happened many times before. Others result from research and development efforts that are modest relative to the importance of the outcome. Lee De Forest's audion, for example— probably the most important invention in electronics—was conceived during the inventor's part-time experiments concurrent with more mundane engineering duties. The General Electric Company spent only $116.856 in its successful efforts to devise a method for producing ductile tungsten, and only $195,000 in developing the gas-filled lamp—trifling sums, considering the importance of the results.[1] The German prototype aircraft which made the world's first jet-propelled flight in 1939 required only $100,000 in developmental expenditures.[2]

On the other hand, the enormous outlays made to create many of our very complex new products and processes frequently contribute little in the way of basically new technology. In much of the work done to design new automobiles, airplanes, guided missiles, electronic data-processing equipment, communications systems, and other complex products, the primary problem is one of integrating already invented components and subcomponents into a system that operates reliably as a whole. This is accomplished through the costly and time-consuming process of trial and error, and during this process wholly new inventions arise more by accident than by requirement or intent.

In this apparent incongruity between the cost of research and development and the importance of technical advances obtained thereby lies the key to understanding the investment decisions made in modern technological invention and innovation. It has already been mentioned that R & D activity can be classified on a spectrum of specificity, and that the more fundamental types of research comprise only a small percentage of R & D activity. More important is the fact that, in the creation of complex

Source: This material is excerpted from a monograph, *Patents and the Corporation*, 2nd ed. (Boston: privately published by James J. Galvin, 1959), coauthored with S. E. Herzstein Jr., A. W. Dreyfoos, W. G. Whitney, O. J. Bachmann, C. P. Pesek, C. J. Scott, T. G. Kelly, and J. J. Galvin, pp. 28–32.

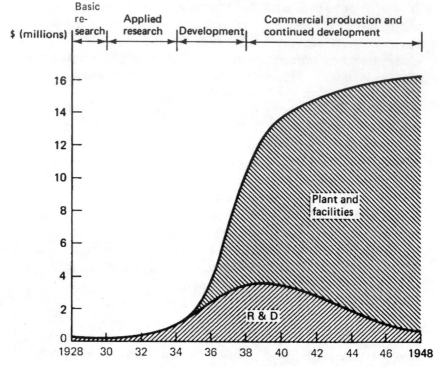

Figure 1.1
DuPont's annual investment in nylon, 1928–1948. The data that permitted the plotting
of this investment curve came from a number of sources, including *U. S.* v. *Imperial
Chemical Industries, Ltd.*, 105 F. Supp. 215, 222 (1952); Mitchell Wilson, *American
Science and Invention*, (New York: Simon and Schuster, 1954), p. 388; and Floyd
L. Vaughan, *The United States Patent System*, (Norman: University of Oklahoma Press,
1956), p. 10. The curves have been somewhat smoothed in construction of the chart.

new products and processes, the various phases of research and development fall into a logical and highly ordered sequence.

This sequence is best illustrated by an actual case example concerning
the development of nylon. It can be expressed in terms of a curve showing
DuPont's investment in the new synthetic fiber as a function of time,
figure 1.1. As the figure shows, the creation of nylon began in 1928 with
the basic research of Wallace H. Carothers. When Carothers' small group
made the initial discovery in 1930 of synthetic fiber possibilities, less than
$50,000 had been spent. By 1934, after research expenditures of $1 million,
the nylon superpolymer was synthesized. Following these fundamental

breakthroughs, the tempo of research increased as basic properties of the new synthetic were analyzed and as alternative approaches were contemplated. When the invention went to DuPont's development sections, an additional $44 million was spent to devise mass production processes, test pilot process models, incorporate manufacturing improvements, and improve the fiber's quality. During these latter phases many more people became involved in the project, expensive equipment had to be fabricated, and improvements had to be tested and revised in a costly process of trial and error. Long before the final improvements were conceived, outlays for manufacturing facilities which dwarfed the expenditures on R & D commenced.

From this investment curve analysis, it is readily seen that DuPont's investment in nylon was not one sweeping decision but a series of related decisions, each requiring a higher rate of investment. But as the rate of investment increased, the amount of technical information for use in the decisions also increased. The question, "Can a synthetic fiber be created?" was answered at a relatively low expenditure level. Answers to "Does the fiber have commercial quality possibilities?" and to "Can the fiber be mass-produced economically?" were secured at higher rates of investment, but before really major outlays for plant and equipment began. With each successive step the technical uncertainties became less fundamental.

The nylon story represents a rather pure case of a complex technological development. In it a basic technical breakthrough was followed fairly quickly by the recognition of possible economic applications, and then by rapidly increasing investment in product and process development and in manufacturing facilities. Nevertheless, it illustrates cogently a principle that has widespread application in the innovation of new products and processes: the concept of confining phases of high technological uncertainty to low-spending-level phases of research, undertaking costly specific development projects only when these basic uncertainties have been sufficiently reduced.

The question then arises, How is it possible to reduce these technical uncertainties sufficiently while maintaining a low spending level? This question is often stated in the more practical terms of, How can we spend so little on basic research?

To answer these questions is to clarify the economic distinction between invention and innovation. The allocation of tangible resources—money, engineers, and materials—is much less important in the securing of invention than it is in the perfection and integration of available inventions into commercially feasible products and processes. In the creation of basic inventions, intangibles such as time, the "flash of genius," and the overall advance of science are equally important. Physical resources allocated to the support of basic research, or simply to bringing scientists and engineers into contact with the unsolved problems of technology, provide the institutional setting where these intangibles operate. But when, where, and how a basic invention will occur is difficult if not impossible to predict.

In contrast, once the necessary inventions are available, the development of new products or processes to the innovation stage depends largely upon the allocation of human and material resources in order to solve through costly trial and error the detailed problems of technical advance.[3] Solving these problems is frequently difficult and takes time. But, as an executive of one leading industrial laboratory stated, the capable scientist or engineer knows that with a hardheaded attack they can in fact be solved. The allocation of resources to solve these problems is one of the principal elements of innovation, and the processes of specific development required for innovation comprise the bulk of U.S. research and development expenditures.

The distinction in an economic sense between invention and the development processes underlying innovation is best summarized in the difference between the two words "predictability" and "describability." Basic invention is truly unpredictable: even the most competent scientist cannot predict when or how it will come, let alone what the solution will resemble. On the other hand, he or she knows in appraising the detailed problems of development that an answer will be obtained and can only not describe what the answer will be.

It must be recognized, however, that invention, like many other things, is a matter of degree. There are highly dramatic breakthroughs and relatively unexciting ones; inventions may be highly complex and sophisticated, or the essence of simplicity. Nevertheless, the concept of confining activities of relatively high technical uncertainty to low-spending-level phases of research and development is applicable equally well to very complex or very plain innovations. It is simply sound management of resources to eliminate as many unpredictables and undescribables as one can before committing substantial investments in prototypes, testing, and manufacturing facilities. As a result the nylon investment curve shown in figure 1.1 is strikingly typical of all cases where new products and new processes are developed for quantity production.[4]

Notes

1. Arthur A. Bright, Jr., *The Electric Lamp Industry* (New York: Macmillan, 1949), pp. 195 and 323.

2. Robert Schlaifer, Big Business and Small Business: A Case Study, *Harvard Business Review* (July 1950): 107.

3. The reader is again warned of the distinction between the economist's definition of invention and that used in patent law. Although the solutions to these detailed technical problems are not considered inventions in the economic sense, they typically possess the inventive qualities required for patentability.

4. See, for example, the diagrams presented by Lawrence H. Hafstad, vice-president of research for General Motors, in "Research or Invention," *Proceedings of the 10th National Conference on the Administration of Research* (University Park, Pa.: Pennsylvania State University Press, 1957), p. 123. This concept is partially rejected in "crash" developments and in the military "weapon system" approach to weapons development. In these cases the pressure of competition forces the developer to sacrifice certainty for lead time. Even in the "weapon system" approach, however, resolution of initial component problems necessitates an investment curve similar to the one present in figure 1.1. See J. S. Butz, Jr., Rivalry Intense in Soviet Weapon Design, *Aviation Week* (November 24, 1958): 91.

2 Invention and Innovation in the Watt-Boulton Steam Engine Venture

It is well known how the Watt-Boulton steam engine freed England and then all nations from the geographic and climatic vagaries of water power and how it permitted enterprises for the first time to concentrate great quantities of efficient motive power in one location. But how did this important transformation come about? What lessons about the economic characteristics of technological invention and innovation can we learn from the steam engine's history?

The terms "invention" and "innovation" suggest the conceptual formulations of Abbott Payson Usher and Joseph A. Schumpeter. Crucial to Usher's conception of invention is an "act of insight" going beyond the exercise of normal technical skill, even though additional activities (perception of a problem, setting the stage, and critical revision) are also recognized.[1] Schumpeter, on the other hand, defined innovation as "the carrying out of new combinations."[2] For the case of new technology this can be identified with reducing an invention to practice and exploiting it commercially. Schumpeter emphatically distinguished his concept of innovation from that of invention:

> Economic leadership in particular must be distinguished from "invention." As long as they are not carried into practice, inventions are economically irrelevant. And to carry any improvement into effect is a task entirely different from the inventing of it, and a task, moreover, requiring entirely different kinds of aptitudes. Although entrepreneurs of course *may* be inventors just as they may be capitalists, they are inventors not by nature of their function but by coincidence and vice versa. . . . It is, therefore, not advisable, and it may be downright misleading, to stress the element of invention as much as many writers do.[3]

Between the Usherian and Schumpeterian conceptions of technological change there are significant differences in emphasis and, to some extent, substance. Unfortunately, a dialogue to resolve or focus these differences did not take place before Schumpeter's death in 1950. Through an analysis of the Watt-Boulton steam engine's history, this paper assesses the ability of the two partly conflicting theories to integrate key behavioral variables in the process of technological change and identifies a sector of the problem underemphasized by both authors. Particular attention will be devoted to the roles played by insight, special aptitudes, risk bearing, and motivation. The impact of the patent system on invention and innovation in the steam engine venture will also be explored. An attempt is made to

Source: *Technology and Culture* 6 (Spring 1965): 165–187.

reiterate familiar historical details only to the extent that they are directly germane to the Usher and Schumpeter schemata.

2.1 The Separate Condenser: A Classic Example of Invention

Let us begin with Watt's first and most fundamental invention in the field of steam engine technology: the separate condenser. We shall find it to be an unusually clear example of Usherian invention.

In 1712 Thomas Newcomen erected a steam engine that combined for the first time a piston-in-cylinder arrangement and a basic motive principle involving the formation of a vacuum within the cylinder through the induced condensation of steam. This "atmospheric" engine saw extensive use, especially for pumping water from the English coal mines. Even though many minor improvements were made in its design during the following fifty years, substantially increasing the engine's operating efficiency, no one successfully challenged Newcomen's general approach.

In the winter of 1763–64 John Anderson, professor of natural philosophy at Glasgow University, brought a small model of the Newcomen engine for repair to James Watt, twenty-eight-year-old mathematical instrument maker to the university. Watt was perplexed by several aspects of the model's operation, especially by the unexpectedly large quantity of steam consumed. At first he attributed this to conduction of heat through the cylinder walls, but tests on a larger model with a wooden cylinder, which conducted less heat than the university model's brass cylinder, showed that to be only a partial explanation. Further experiments occupied most of the time Watt could spare from his regular duties for more than a year and led him to recognize a paradoxical deficiency in the Newcomen engine's operating concept: to utilize steam efficiently, the cylinder had to be kept at 100°C, so there would be no condensation during the piston's unpowered stroke; but to form an effective vacuum for the power stroke, considerable cooling water had to be injected into the cylinder, and this tended to cool the cylinder below 100°.[4] This was, in Usher's terminology, the perception of an unsatisfactory pattern. Then, presumably while Watt was strolling on the Green of Glasgow "on a fine Sabbath afternoon" early in 1765, came his famous insight: he would condense the engine's steam not in the operating cylinder, as Newcomen and all his followers had done, but rather in a separate condensing vessel to which it would be drawn by a pump or by other means.

The following day Watt began work on a small ($1\frac{3}{4}$-inch cylinder diameter) model to test his separate-condenser idea, and in his own words, "in three days, I had a model at work nearly as perfect ... as any which have been made since that time."[5] In another narrative Watt said that with the testing of this model: "excepting the nonapplication of the steam-case and external covering, the invention was complete, in so far as regarded the savings of steam and fuel. A large model, with an outer cylinder and wooden case, was immediately constructed, and the experiments made with it served to verify the expectations I had formed, and to place the advantage of the invention beyond the reach of doubt."[6] There is some reason to question whether Watt actually accomplished decisive results in only three days.[7] We know from a letter written by Watt to Dr. James Lind on April 29, 1765, that he was working on a new engine and soon hoped "to have the decisive trial." The first surviving contemporary reference to successful results is a letter from Watt to Dr. John Roebuck dated August 23, 1765. Nevertheless, there is no doubt that invention of the separate condenser in the Usherian sense had occurred by the summer of 1765, somewhat more than a year after Watt first received the Newcomen engine model for repair. Usher sets the date for Watt's strategic invention more precisely: "There is an unusually clear basis for recognizing that the solution of the problem was achieved during this Sunday afternoon walk. If the concept then achieved had been less adequate, we might properly set a later date for the solution of the problem, but the actual task proved to be the realization in actual mechanism of the apparatus conceived at that time. The concept itself did not require revision."[8]

2.2 The Support of Watt's Work by Roebuck and Boulton: Investment or Schumpeterian Innovation?

When the principle of Watt's separate condenser was successfully demonstrated with a test model, the new steam engine was far from ready for commercial exploitation. There remained much technical effort to scale it up to full size and to make the full-scale version work efficiently and reliably. This effort is logically subsumed under the fourth step —critical revision—of Usher's schema. However, Schumpeter's concept of innovation may also be applied to describe these post-initial-demonstration activities, and here we shall view the steam engine's development initially from the Schumpeterian viewpoint. Let us for the moment ignore the specific technical activities pursued and consider only how these activities were supported.

This support was financial in nature. Watt's funds were quite limited, but he was able to finance several models and experiments during 1765 and 1766 by borrowing from his friend Professor Joseph Black. From the summer of 1766 to January 1768, Watt found it necessary to engage full time in more remunerative activities (mainly surveying) and thus made little progress on his steam-engine experiments. Nevertheless, by the spring of 1768 Watt's debt to Black and a former partner had accumulated to more than £1,000. At that time Watt entered into a partnership with Dr. John Roebuck, who paid off Watt's debts and the cost of a patent, receiving in return a two-thirds share in the invention. There followed a second period of active experimentation, during which an 18-inch cylinder diameter model was erected and, with somewhat disappointing results, tested at Roebuck's Kinneil residence. However, Roebuck, who was experiencing growing financial embarrassment due to other ventures, was unable to pay all of these costs. Instead Watt defrayed them, partly by borrowing from Black, and from early in 1770 to May 1774 he again found it necessary to take up surveying as a nearly full-time occupation. This decision was explained in 1772 by Watt as follows: "I pursued my experiments till I found that the expense and loss of time lying wholly upon me, through the distress of Dr. Roebuck's situation, turned out to be a burthen greater than I could support; and not having conquered all the difficulties that lay in the way of execution, I was obliged for a time to abandon the project."[9] Thus Watt spent not more than three years' time actively pursuing the development of his steam engine in the nine-year period from 1765, when he first conceived the separate-condenser principle, to 1774. During the remaining time, lack of financial support forced him to accept jobs offering more immediate compensation.

In 1773 Roebuck became bankrupt, and in 1774 Matthew Boulton, a Birmingham manufacturer and creditor of Roebuck who for some time had been interested in Watt's engine, acquired Roebuck's two-thirds share in the invention. The firm of Boulton & Watt was established; facilities connected with Boulton's Soho manufactory were occupied; the 18-inch Kinneil engine was rebuilt there; and in May 1774 Watt turned his full-time attention to the engine business. Under their partnership agreement

Boulton financed the firm's developmental expenses and paid Watt an annual salary of £330 plus expenses. From the outset Boulton recognized that the venture would be costly and risky. He wrote to Watt in 1773: "The thing is now a shadow, it is merely ideal, and it will cost money to realize it."[10] Testifying before the House of Commons in 1775, Dr. Roebuck stated that he and Boulton had spent more than £3,000 on early experiments, and that total expenses in view would add at least another £10,000.[11]

This was no small sum, either generally or to Boulton in particular. During the early years of steam engine work at Soho, skilled craftsmen were paid roughly £50 per year; thus the costs already sunk by 1775 were the equivalent of 60 man-years of skilled labor, and 200 more man-year equivalents were contemplated. The manufactory of Boulton & Fothergill, erected at Soho in 1764 and known throughout England as a leading example of the factory system, initially cost only £9,000. Although he had acquired a landed estate of about £28,000 through two marriages, Boulton's financial position in 1774 was by no means strong. The Boulton & Fothergill firm was apparently on the brink of bankruptcy, and only by selling his wives' properties was he able to keep it solvent.[12] The risks of failure were substantial: the tests at Kinneil had not been notably successful, and of the several steam engine projects undertaken during the preceding century, only Newcomen's and some improvements of the Newcomen engine by John Smeaton achieved any lasting economic success.[13] Indeed, Boulton's partner Fothergill would have nothing to do with the new steam engine venture. And with the exception of Boulton, none of Roebuck's creditors placed any value on the engine patent.[14]

What motives led Roebuck and then Boulton to invest in Watt's steam engine project? For Roebuck, the prospect of a new and more efficient steam engine fitted well with his other business interests. He was principal partner in an iron works at Carron, Stirlingshire, that produced major components for Newcomen atmospheric engines. He had also become committed to a coal-mining venture in Borrowstounness (Bo'ness), but the pits had flooded and the atmospheric engines available were not powerful enough to remove the water. If Watt's steam engine were successful, it might, among other things, save Roebuck's otherwise lost investment at Bo'ness.

Boulton's motives centered not so much on saving an enterprise as on creating one. To be sure, Boulton anticipated that Watt's engine could remedy a problem at his Soho manufactory, for summer water shortages made his water wheels inoperative and necessitated the expense of horses to propel the machinery. But Boulton was not interested in just one or a few engines; in the expansive attitude which characterized his ventures, he wanted to produce for the whole world. As he wrote to Watt on February 7, 1769, explaining his decision not to accept a partnership with Roebuck permitting Boulton to manufacture engines only for the midland counties of Warwick, Stafford, and Derby:

> I was excited by two motives to offer you my assistance—which were, love of you, and love of a money-getting, ingenious project. . . . To . . . produce the most profit, my idea was to settle a manufactory near to my own, by the side of our canal, where I would erect all the conveniences necessary for the completion of engines, and from which manufactory we would serve all the world with engines of all sizes. . . . It would not be worth my while to make for three counties only; but I find it very well worth my while to make for all the world.[15]

In any event the availability of financial support was an important determinant of the rate at which Watt perfected his engine. Progress was impeded for long intervals when no investor appeared with the necessary combination of confidence in the engine's principles, available funds, and willingness to bear the risks of development.

The financial support of Watt's work cannot, however, be called an innovative role in the strict Schumpeterian sense. Schumpeter carefully distinguished between the role of the capitalist, or investor of risk capital, and the entrepreneur or innovator. Were Roebuck and (especially) Boulton something more than capitalists in their support of the Watt steam engine project? Schumpeter provided a number of distinguishing characteristics to help identify his entrepreneur-innovator:

1. New combinations are as a rule embodied in new firms which do not arise out of the old ones but start producing beside them.[16]
2. The entrepreneur-innovator is characterized by "initiative," "authority," and "foresight"; he is the "captain of industry" type.[17]
3. The only person the entrepreneur-innovator has to convince is the banker who is to provide the financing.[18]
4. The entrepreneur-innovator retires from the arena only when his or her strength is spent.[19]
5. The entrepreneur-innovator's motivation includes such aspects as the

dream to found a private kingdom, the will to conquer and to succeed for the sake of success itself, and the joy of creating and getting things done.[20]

Examination of the evidence against these characteristics suggests that Boulton and, to a lesser extent, Roebuck rather than Watt occupied the innovator's position during most of the steam-engine development. Boulton clearly qualifies under the first (perhaps least important) condition: he set up a wholly new business for the steam engine venture, since Fothergill would have nothing to do with the scheme.

Classifying the principals under Schumpeter's second criterion is not so simple. Watt's *technical* initiative and foresight were outstanding, particularly in his younger years. Both Roebuck and Boulton also displayed exceptional initiative in establishing several industrial ventures. The quality of their foresight is more debatable, as evidenced by Roebuck's bankruptcy and Boulton's unprofitable experiences in hardware manufacturing, silver mining, canal building, and spelter manufacturing.[21] J. E. Cule has attributed the unprofitability of Boulton's hardware enterprise in part to mismanagement.[22] But skill in performing the day-to-day management function is not a requisite for Schumpeter's entrepreneur-innovator.[23] And the losses of Boulton & Fothergill probably resulted more directly from overexpansion, due in turn to the very megalomania that made Boulton a "captain of industry" type, than from mismanagement.[24]

In contrast to Roebuck and Boulton, Watt demonstrated little zest for business affairs. It was necessary for Roebuck continually to spur him on when they were partners. During the Watt-Boulton partnership Watt typically worked at his home while Boulton managed operations at Soho. Watt was perpetually overloaded with work because he tried to do everything himself and would not delegate to others. His letters repeatedly reveal his fear of managing and dealing with other people. For example, listing reasons why Boulton should be taken in as an active partner, Watt wrote to Roebuck on September 24, 1769: "Consider my uncertain health, my irresolute and inactive disposition, my inability to bargain and struggle for my own with mankind; all which disqualify me for any great undertaking." In similar vein was his letter to Dr. William Small on November 24, 1772: "I am extremely indolent, cannot force workmen to do their duty, have been cheated by undertakers and clerks, and am unlucky enough to know it. . . . I would rather face a loaded cannon than settle an account or make a bargain. In short I find myself out of my sphere when I have anything to do with mankind."

Watt also had no aptitude for dealing with bankers. The firm's borrowing was left to Boulton, but their obligations were still a nightmare to him.[25] For instance, even after the engine had proved successful, he wrote to Boulton on June 21, 1781, regarding his part in refinancing their debt, "When I executed the mortgage, my sensations were such as were not to be envied by any man who goes to death in a just cause, nor has time lessened the acuteness of my feelings." And, as his abandonment of the steam engine project when his friends could provide no more money indicates, Watt was not one to perform the entrepreneurial function of persuading bankers to advance funds.

Boulton's enthusiasm for new ventures never flagged. When one project no longer absorbed his attention and capital, he began searching for another. Watt, one the other hand, was anxious to retire from the arena as soon as his engine's success was assured. The situation in 1785 is typical. With his debts paid off for the first time in a decade, Boulton plunged into a copper-market-stabilization scheme.[26] In contrast, Watt wrote to Boulton on November 5 of that year, "On the whole, I find it now full time to cease attempting to invent new things, or to attempt anything which is attended with any risk of not succeeding, or of creating trouble in the execution. Let us go on executing the things we understand, and leave the rest to younger men, who have neither money nor character to lose." Similarly, when their partnership agreement expired in 1800, Watt retired, at the age of 64, from active business life, while Boulton, at 70, became engrossed in a coin-minting venture.

Finally, we see distinct differences between Boulton and Watt in terms of Schumpeter's set of motivational characteristics. As just one example, Boulton wanted to manufacture engines for all the world; Watt asserted that he would rather have a modest income with fewer risks and troubles.[27]

To sum up, Boulton and Roebuck appear to have met rather well the specifications for Schumpeter's entrepreneur-innovator, as well as providing needed capital. In contrast, it is unlikely that Watt would have persisted in the development of his engine without the business support and drive of Roebuck and Boulton. Watt himself admitted that "without [Boulton] the invention could never have been carried by me to the length it has been."[28]

This does not mean that the roles of Boulton and Roebuck should be deemed more necessary or important than that of Watt. Too many histories of the Watt-Boulton steam engine venture have shown a distinct "one hero" bias, emphasizing the contribution of one principal while pointedly deprecating the other's. But Watt's inventive genius, the capital of Roebuck and Boulton, and the entrepreneurial contribution of Boulton were all necessary, and none was sufficient in itself for full and timely exploitation of Watt's basic idea. A theory of technological change must recognize that contributions are essentially complementary, just as the theory of conventional production recognizes that land, labor, and capital are complementary.[29]

2.3 Technical Development of the Engine: Invention or Innovation?

Thus far we have viewed the post-1765 effort largely from an economic perspective. But what were the actual technical activities that those expenditures supported? In Usher's theory they are included under the critical-revision step, but do they deserve a position subordinate to the act of insight, as at least some of his writings imply? And where, if at all, do these activities fit into Schumpeter's concept of innovation? To answer these questions, we must examine the technical work Watt and his associates carried out between 1765 and 1780.

In very broad perspective the effort took the form of building, testing, modifying, and retesting models of increasing scale and sophistication. Although there are ambiguities in the evidence, it would appear that during the 1765–66 period Watt built three models: the original test model with a $1\frac{3}{4}$-inch brass cylinder but no steam jacket; a $1\frac{2}{5}$-inch sheet-iron cylinder model with a steam jacket; and a model with a 5- or 6-inch copper cylinder and a wooden steam jacket.[30] Several more models with 7- to 8-inch cylinder diameters were built in various configurations during the next two years and tested intermittently. Then, in April 1769, a more or less full-scale engine with an 18-inch cylinder of tin was fabricated. This step up to practical operating scale led to many difficulties. As Watt wrote of Roebuck's plan in 1772 to perfect the engine without his help by experimenting with a smaller and less expensive model, "he had turned his thoughts towards the engine not recollecting that I had been sufficiently successful with an engine of that size formerly, and that it was only in the 18-inch engine that the difficulties appeared. I have, however, dissuaded him from it, as, without flattering myself, I cannot imagine that he can find out in a few days all the difficulties, and the means of avoiding them, which have cost me so much labor." [31] This 18-inch engine was removed from Kinneil to Soho in 1773, where it was redesigned and rebuilt in 1774 and 1775 to serve as a successful prototype for the first commercially erected Watt-Boulton engines: a 50-inch water-pumping model for the Bloomfield Colliery and a 38-inch model for blowing John Wilkinson's blast furnaces, both set to work in March 1776.

The problems encountered with the various early test models were numerous, and Watt proposed and tried out an even greater number of solutions. Watt's comment in 1769 is typical. "I have been trying experiments on the reciprocating engine, and have made some alterations for the better and some for the worse, which latter must return to their former form." [32] Dickinson and Jenkins have observed, "When we reflect on the exhaustive character of these experiments, we can hardly wonder that in after days Watt spoke as if he had explored every possible combination of which the steam engine was capable." [33] Indeed, the development effort may have been complicated by Watt's desire to perfect every facet of the engine's operation—a quest opposed first by Roebuck and then by Boulton, who were anxious to press forward to commercial results with all possible dispatch. Watt himself admitted later in a third-person account of his work: "Had W. been content with the mechanism of steam-engines as they then stood, his machine might soon have been brought before the public; but his mind ran upon making engines *cheap* as well as *good* and he had a great hankering after inverted cylinders and other modifications of his invention, which his want of experience in the practice of mechanics in great, flattered him would prove more commodious than his matured experience has shown them to be. He tried, therefore, too many fruitless experiments on such variations." [34] Dickinson suggests that Watt's tremendous ability to conceive many alternative solutions to a problem may actually have delayed the engine development effort. "This very fertility of mind ... may almost be said to have delayed his progress. Of a number of alternatives he does not seem to have had the flair of knowing which was the most practicable, hence he expended his energies on many avenues that led to dead ends. In truth this is the attitude of mind of the scientist rather than that of the craftsman. Still, unless he had explored these avenues, he could not be certain that they led nowhere." [35]

One of the most troublesome aspects of Watt's engine was the piston-cylinder arrangement. For the engine to work efficiently, the piston had to fit tightly within the cylinder throughout its stroke so the vacuum would not be dissipated, and yet excessive friction also had to be avoided. Techniques of metalworking at the time were not adequate to secure a tight metal-to-metal fit, and so other means had to be devised. Newcomen had solved the problem for his atmospheric engine by affixing a flexible leather disk atop the piston and by keeping a quantity of water in the cylinder above the piston and disk as a seal. But this method was less suitable for Watt's engine, since Watt wanted to keep the cylinder as hot as possible, and he knew that water used as a seal would invade the cylinder and absorb heat from the working steam.[36] He experimented with one approach after another. He tried tin, copper, wood, and cast iron for his cylinders and pistons to see which materials could be worked to the closest tolerances and still retain sufficient structural strength and durability. (The tin cylinder employed in the 18-inch Kinneil engine was rejected, for example, because it would not retain its shape.) He considered square pistons, round pistons, and flexible pistons (which could be inflated with fluid to make a tight fit). He experimented with piston disks and rings of leather, pasteboard, cloth, cork, oakum, hemp, asbestos, a lead-tin alloy, and a copper-lead alloy. To help seal the piston, he tried mercury, oil, graphite, tallow, horse dung, vegetable oil, and a variety of other materials.

The problem was greatly alleviated by an achievement essentially unrelated to the work of Watt. In 1774 John Wilkinson (principal in one of the first two firms to employ the Watt-Boulton engine) patented a new type of boring mill which significantly increased the accuracy to which cylinders could be fabricated. The first bored cast-iron cylinder made by Wilkinson with his new technique arrived at Soho in April 1775, and it was used to resurrect the previously deficient 18-inch engine brought from Kinneil. From then until 1795 Wilkinson was the regularly recommended supplier for Watt-Boulton cylinders and pistons. Only three or four engines were built to Watt's design without Wilkinson cylinders during that twenty-year period.[37]

It is frequently stated that Wilkinson's invention was vital to the success of the Watt-Boulton steam engine.[38] This view must be qualified. Surely the engine could have been operated without Wilkinson's cylinders, as the erection of even the few non-Wilkinson engines implies. Furthermore there is some evidence that the earlier cylinder problems were not insuperable. Watt wrote to his father on December 11, 1774, several months before the first Wilkinson cylinder arrived at Soho, that the 18-inch engine was "now going, and answers much better than any other that has yet been made, and I expect that the invention will be very beneficial to me." Still earlier, after discussing some of the piston-packing adversities experienced in experiments with the 18-inch engine at Kinneil, Watt wrote that even if no solutions better than those already tried could be found, the engine would probably consume only half as much steam as the atmospheric engines then in common use.[39] It is also likely that the Newcomen solution could have been adopted, if Watt had been willing to settle for the additional efficiency provided by his separate condenser and not worry about a loss of heat through the evaporation of sealing water.[40] Thus it seems more reasonable to conclude that the Wilkinson invention was essential for the level of technical and economic success actually attained by the Watt-Boulton engine, but that at least moderate success could have been achieved without it.

Perhaps as problematic as the cylinder-piston question was the matter of the design of the condenser. In fact, during the trials of the 18-inch engine in 1769–70 at Kinneil, the condenser proved to be the main source of difficulty. In the course of ten years Watt tried a great number of approaches and designs. Up to 1775 he emphasized the surface-condenser approach, with cooling water circulated outside the chambers within which the steam condensed. But then he changed to Newcomen's water-injection approach to simplify the mechanism, to achieve greater condensing capacity within a given volume, and to prevent gradual deterioration of the condenser's efficiency by accumulation of mineral deposits on the vessel walls. During the period when Watt favored the surface-condensation approach, he considered plate designs, tube designs, worm designs, flooded designs, and unflooded designs and a variety of materials and fabrication methods. Many experiments were required to determine the proper capacity of a condenser for an engine of any given size. After the change to injection condensing in 1775, several different condenser and pump-system designs were tested.

This same pattern was repeated to a greater or lesser extent for each of the other components of the Watt-Boulton steam engine. Only a few examples can be added here. The valves and their working gear were redesigned completely several times, first along the lines of the Newcomen engine and later following different approaches. Iron and copper boiler bottoms were tried, and experiments were conducted to determine the necessary steam outputs for engines of various sizes. The early small models constructed by Watt had no beams and were inverted relative to the Newcomen design (i.e., the vacuum was formed above rather than below the piston), but for the 18-inch Kinneil engine Watt shifted to a conventional beam design. He then adhered in general practice to the Newcomen approach, although in 1776 an inverted engine was designed for John Wilkinson. To determine which designs and materials were best, beams in many different configurations were fabricated and subjected to destructive testing.

In general, extensive testing of every conceivable practical solution seems to have been a major characteristic of the technical activities pursued from 1765 to 1780, and the degree of insight associated with most of the individual solutions tended to be low. New designs and materials were proposed, not only to solve strictly mechanical and technical problems but also to simplify the fabrication of parts, to facilitate the erection and maintenance of engines, to prolong the life of engine components, to avoid expensive materials, to increase the engine's operating efficiency, and even to avoid having to buy components from vendors whose prices were too high.[41] This technical work involved not just the inventor Watt but also Boulton and a number of skilled craftsmen whose assignments included fabrication, erection, testing, and even suggesting new designs. In many ways the Boulton & Watt shops at Soho during the late eighteenth century clearly anticipate our industrial research and development laboratories of the twentieth century.[42]

Once the basic engine design had been more or less proved and emphasis shifted to the design and erection of engines for industrial use, technical activities of a noninventive nature continued. The basic design had to be modified for various specific applications—there were engines in many different sizes and configurations for use in pumping, blowing, and hammering, each requiring special attention to unique problems. For many years Watt did most of this work himself, at such an expenditure of time that he was unable to devote attention to more creative activities. A great deal of the time of Watt, Boulton, and their firm's most skilled workers was also spent away from Soho superintending the erection of new engines and troubleshooting temperamental engines already erected. Finally, many experiments were conducted to collect engineering data on potentialities of engines and strengths of materials, as well as to determine the savings of coal afforded by the Watt-Boulton engine over atmospheric engines for the purpose of setting royalties.

In sum, it appears that the great bulk of the technical activity applied to the steam engine after Watt's basic work in 1765 does not qualify as invention in the strictest Usherian sense. The problems tended to define themselves through experimental failures instead of requiring significant perception of an unsatisfactory pattern; the level of insight associated with proposed new solutions was typically low; and optimal solutions were selected from a wide variety of alternative approaches through empirical analysis. Such activities may of course be classified as critical revision under a four-step conceptualization of the inventive process. Still, accounting as they did for most of the substantial time and effort expended before Watt's fundamental ideas were translated into an economically advantageous machine, they occupied a position that can scarcely be subordinated to the inventive acts of insight.[43] Technical activities of this nature also hold no special position in the Schumpeterian concept of innovation, and yet their successful prosecution must be one of the entrepreneur's prime concerns. Perhaps the best solution is to apply to such activities the term "development" (from the broader modern term "research and development") and to recognize that development, like investment, is a necessary complement to invention and innovation in the process of technological change.[44]

2.4 Improvements

From 1775 through 1780 most of James Watt's energies were absorbed in designing steam engines for specific applications according to the general technical concepts tested successfully at Soho prior to that time, supervising the erection of those engines on the spot, and troubleshooting. By 1781, however, he found it possible and desirable to concentrate again on more original work. This effort yielded a number of significant improvements, including devices to convert the engine's reciprocating motion into rotary motion, the double-acting engine, expansive working, an automatic centrifugal governor, and a compound (two-cylinder) engine.

No attempt can be made here to describe these improvements. Many were logical extensions of Watt's original idea, requiring relatively little new insight but considerable trial and error. In other instances (especially in the invention of the centrifugal governor and of a parallel-motion mechanism for use with the double-acting engine) a high level of creative insight was revealed. The end result of the invention of the parallel-motion mechanism, however, could have been obtained with less ingenious alternative solutions. The centrifugal governor, an important stimulant to later technological progress in other fields, is even more difficult to assess, since the basic idea was not original with Watt. Although exceptions must be recognized, for the most part the activities during this improvement period appear more like those of the 1765–75 design-development period than like the 1764–65 period of analytical and creative work.

2.5 The Role of Patents in the Steam Engine's History

The available material provides some indication of how one economic policy—the granting of patent monopolies—affected the Watt-Boulton invention and development effort. At least since James I accepted the Statute of Monopolies in 1624, the underlying principle of patent systems has been to encourage technological progress by granting to inventors temporary monopolies of their inventions. The objective is often defined in popular discussion as encouraging invention, although, as the foregoing analysis has illustrated, invention strictly defined is a necessary but not a sufficient condition for technological progress.

The existence of a patent system seems to have had little or no influence on Watt's invention of the separate-condenser principle. His introduction to the problem came when he was hired to repair a Newcomen engine model. The experiments that led to Watt's historic insight—costing little more than his spare time—originated in that task and were sustained as a result of scientific curiosity.[45]

It is less clear whether, after the separate-condenser idea was conceived, Watt would have invested his time and his friends' money in reducing the invention to practice. He apparently gave no immediate consideration to obtaining a patent, although the possibility of eventual patent protection could have been in the back of his mind. Not until three years after his strategic insight did Watt, with the encouragement of Roebuck, apply for a patent. By that time Watt had (through borrowing) committed some £1,000 to the development of his invention, relying mainly on secrecy to protect his investment.

There is reason to believe that application for a patent was a condition of Roebuck's entry into partnership with Watt. Whether or not Roebuck's interest would have been sustained in the absence of patent protection is impossible to determine. We know, however, that due to financial difficulties Roebuck contributed little more to the development than the sum agreed upon in 1768.

Thus we must ask whether Boulton would have participated in the project without patent protection. The status of Watt's patent was clearly of concern to Boulton. When Watt arrived at Soho in May 1774 to begin work on the engine under Boulton's patronage, less than ten years remained of the patent's term. Boulton recognized that the engine venture would be costly; a 1775 estimate of £13,000 has been mentioned earlier. There was clearly a risk that the investment would not be recovered before the patent expired.[46] In any event a decision to seek extension of the patent must have been made by December 1774, for on January 13, 1775, Watt communicated to Boulton a lawyer's advice "that we might surrender up the present patent, and that he did not doubt a new one would be granted." A petition to Parliament was submitted in February 1775, and after some heated debate, the petition was enacted into law and received final approval in May.

These actions on the part of Boulton and Watt do not prove that, without the extension, Boulton's support would have been withdrawn. Boulton's investment before extension became certain was considerable. By May 1775 the 18-inch Kinnell engine had been completely rebuilt, the first Wilkinson cylinder was on hand, and cumulative development expenditures of £3,000 (including Roebuck's share of more than £1,200) had been recorded. Nevertheless, although the integrity of self-serving declarations must be held suspect, Watt and Boulton (who was a gifted lobbyist, among other things) must have argued convincingly to members of Parliament that their work would be impeded unless the extension were secured, for the enabling bill reads in part as follows:

AND WHEREAS, in order to manufacture these engines with the necessary accuracy, and so that they may be sold at moderate prices, a considerable sum of money must be previously expended in erecting mills, and other apparatus; and as several years, and repeated proofs, will be required before any considerable part of the publick can be fully convinced of the utility of the invention, and of their interest to adopt the same, the whole term granted by the said Letters Patent may probably elapse before the said JAMES WATT can receive an adequate advantage to his labor and invention:

AND WHEREAS, by furnishing mechanical powers at much less expense, and in more convenient forms, than has hitherto been done, his engines may be of great utility in facilitating the operations in many great works and manufactures of this kingdom; yet it will not be in the power of the said JAMES WATT to carry his invention into that complete execution which he wishes, and so as to render the same of the highest utility to the publick of which it is capable, unless the term granted by the said Letters Patent be prolonged.[47]

Of the situation in 1775, Watt wrote much later, "Prior to the Act of Parliament we had sold no engines; though we had made some, they were merely to satisfy ourselves,—and, had the Act not passed, the invention had fallen to the ground;—so much did we foresee the moral difficulties before us, and the great necessary expenditure."[48] Again, this appraisal may have been tempered by hindsight. Still the patent extension's importance to Boulton is also indicated by the fact that his partnership with Watt did not begin formally until after the extension had been enacted, and its termination date was set as the extended patent's expiration date. Thus there are reasonable grounds for inferring that Boulton's decision to invest in the project was influenced by the certainty of at least some patent protection, if not by the possibility of extended protection. In this case the grant of a patent monopoly was a probable incentive for investment in technological innovation, although not an incentive for invention.

Had there been no patent protection at all, and had Boulton nonetheless invested in the steam engine venture, Boulton and Watt certainly would have been forced to follow a business policy quite different from that which they actually followed. Most of the firm's profits were derived from royalties on the use of engines rather than from the sale of manufactured engine components, and without patent protection the firm plainly could not have collected royalties. The alternative would have been to emphasize manufacturing and service activities as the principal source of profits, which in fact was the policy adopted when the expiration date of the patent for the separate condenser drew near in the late 1790s. But establishment of the requisite manufacturing facilities probably would have called for more capital than Boulton was in a position to supply at the time. And the manufacturing which *was* done by Boulton & Watt during the firm's early years was generally unprofitable—due in part to an emphasis on high quality which was motivated in turn by the desire for maximum engine performance and hence (since royalties were based upon operating cost savings) high royalties.[49] The necessity of charging high prices to cover costs might also have inhibited any substantial expansion of the firm's sales of manufactured goods.[50] Whether in the absence of patent protection a different attitude toward quality would have been adopted and whether emphasis on manufacturing would have led the original partners to implement significant efficiency-increasing production measures, as their sons did during the late 1790s, can only be left to speculation.[51]

It is possible to conclude more definitely that the patent litigation activities of Boulton & Watt during the 1790s did not directly incite further technological progress. The 1769 patent was successfully defended against charges of invalidity, persons exploiting inventions that infringed the separate-condenser principle were prosecuted and enjoined, and users of the Boulton & Watt engine who were in arrears on their royalties were compelled to pay up. The effect of these actions for Boulton & Watt was mainly one of income redistribution: back royalties collected in Cornwall alone after the patent's validity was affirmed amounted to about £30,000.[52] No prospective new inventions or developments were at stake in these patent actions. Still two indirect effects on the rate of technological progress may be identified. First, Boulton & Watt's refusal to issue licenses allowing other engine makers to employ the separate-condenser principle clearly retarded the development and introduction of improvements.[53] On the other hand, it is possible that the handsome profits realized by Boulton and Watt provided a striking success story that encouraged others to accept the risks and burdens of invention, development, and innovation.[54] Naturally, there is no way of demonstrating the existence or strength of such an indirect effect.

2.6 Conclusion

It would be presumptuous to suggest modifications in the theories of Usher and Schumpeter on the basis of a single case study. The dangers in generalizing from one example are well known, and the models of both authors are susceptible to a diversity of interpretations. Still the evidence examined here at least suggests that Usherian invention and Schumpeterian innovation are logically distinguishable and that both invention and innovation, along with investment, are necessary and complementary functions in the advance of technology.[55]

The position of the function "development," as defined in this paper, is more ambiguous. The successful accomplishment of development tasks is a concern of the Schumpeterian innovator, and the activities themselves are an important claimant upon the investor's capital. Development can also be subsumed under Usher's "critical revision." Yet the amount of time and effort devoted to development as opposed to more insightful activities by Watt implies the need for a less subordinate treatment. Nor was the Watt-Boulton case unique in this respect. Ten years of experimental work occurred before Thomas Newcomen had a satisfactory version of the engine that dominated the first half of the eighteenth century.[56] Six years of development preceded successful operation of Jonathan Hornblower's compound expansive engine, a competitor to the Boulton & Watt engine later blocked by Watt's patent.[57] And in extending Watt's basic patent, Parliament in 1775 called attention to "the many difficulties which *always* arise in the execution of such large and complex machines, . . . and the long time requisite to make the necessary trials."[58] In view of this experience one might wish to assign development a functional status equal to that of invention, innovation, and investment.

Although each of the functions appears to be a necessary condition for technological advance, it is possible that innovation, investment, and development are more sensitive to economic variables than invention is. Inventive acts of insight may follow, as in the steam-engine experience, from scientific curiosity and a fortuitous combination of chance factors without any direct stimulus from profit expectations or such public policies as the granting of patent monopolies. In the case at hand, execution of the innovative, investment, and developmental functions depended much more directly than Usherian invention on these economic factors. Such a relationship, if valid more generally, may have significant implications for public policy. As Judge Jerome Frank observed in 1942, "The controversy between the defenders and assailants of our patent system may be about a false issue—the stimulus to invention. The real issue may be the stimulus to investment. On that assumption a statutory revision of our patent system should not be too drastic. We should not throw out the baby with the bathwater."[59] Certainly the question of what patent monopolies in fact stimulate deserves further attention by students of technological history.

Notes

1. A. P. Usher, *A History of Mechanical Inventions* (rev. ed.; Cambridge, Mass., 1954), pp. 60–65.

2. *The Theory of Economic Development*, trans. Redvers Opie (Cambridge, Mass., 1934), pp. 74–94. See also his *Business Cycles* (New York, 1939), especially pp. 84–98.

3. *Theory of Economic Development*, pp. 88–89.

4. In connection with these experiments it would appear that Watt independently rediscovered the theory of latent heat originally enunciated in 1761 by his friend Joseph Black, although some controversy exists on this point. See Milton Kerker, Science and the Steam Engine, *Technology and Culture* 2 (Fall 1961): 381–390.

5. Letter, Watt to the Chief Justice of Common Pleas, 1795, cited in T. S. Ashton, *Iron and Steel in the Industrial Revolution* (2d ed.; Manchester, 1951), p. 61. There is no surviving contemporary record by Watt of his earliest experiments.

6. From an account apparently written by Watt in 1814, cited in J. P. Muirhead, *The Origin and Progress of the Mechanical Inventions of James Watt* (London, 1854), vol. 1, lxxiii–lxxiv. Unless otherwise indicated, all of the Watt correspondence cited here is reproduced chronologically in Muirhead, vols. 1 and 2.

7. Analysis of the available evidence suggests that there were three early models, not two— the model with a $1\frac{3}{4}$-inch brass cylinder but no steam jacket described in the text; one with a $1\frac{2}{3}$-inch iron cylinder and a steam jacket; and the large model (probably with a five- or six-inch copper cylinder) referred to here by Watt. In *James Watt and the Steam Engine* (Oxford, 1927), pp. 92–96, H. W. Dickinson and Rhys Jenkins propose that the $1\frac{3}{4}$-inch model and the $1\frac{2}{3}$ inch model were one and the same. However, there is good reason to doubt such an inference. What is purported to be the $1\frac{2}{3}$-inch model is preserved in the Science Museum at South Kensington, London. Accounts by both Watt and Dr. John Robison cited in Muirhead (*The Origin and Progress of the Mechanical Inventions of James Watt*) state quite explicitly that the cylinder of the $1\frac{3}{4}$-inch model was hastily improvised from a physician's syringe and had no steam jacket. It seems plausible that Watt performed a quick, crude test of his theory with the $1\frac{3}{4}$-inch syringe model and then built the more elaborate $1\frac{2}{3}$-inch model to determine what effect the combination of a separate condenser and steam-jacketing would have on steam consumption.

8. *History of Mechanical Inventions*, pp. 71–72.

9. Watt to Dr. William Small, August 30, 1772.

10. Cited in Paul Mantoux, *The Industrial Revolution in the Eighteenth Century*, trans. Marjorie Vernon (rev. ed.; New York, 1933), p. 332.

11. Ibid. p. 335, cited from the *Journal of the House of Commons*, XXV, 142. Mantoux reports an estimate by S. Timmins that £47,000 were actually expended for construction, equipment, and other costs, although it is not known how the estimate was derived from incomplete company records. In an article much more skeptical of Boulton's contribution, J. E. Cule asserts that "the total cost of launching the enterprise was £3,370" (Finance and Industry in the Eighteenth Century: The Firm of Boulton and Watt, *Economic History*, *Supplement to Economic Journal* 4 [February 1940]: 320). He does not state what this estimate includes, but it apparently excludes Roebuck's contribution (which was taken over by Boulton in settlement of debts) and the losses borne by the firm in trouble-shooting initial installations and in producing engine components.

The existence of such widely varying estimates of the firm's actual original investment suggests the need for further research in the primary sources. More accurate information would provide a much clearer picture of the degree of risk actually assumed by Boulton.

12. H. W. Dickinson, *Matthew Boulton* (Cambridge, 1936), pp. 36, 109–110. From 1762 to 1780, Boulton & Fothergill incurred net losses amounting to £11,000 on a total capital of £20,000.

13. There is also evidence that Newcomen, as the victim of an unfortunate patent-rights situation, did not profit significantly from his invention.

14. Watt to Dr. Small, July 25, 1773.

15. As events turned out, Boulton & Watt did relatively little manufacturing of engines up to roughly 1795. Apparently because of the scarcity of capital and skilled labor and because the energies of Watt and Boulton were fully absorbed in design work, experiments, supervision of the erection of engines, and promotion of their venture, manufacturing activities were confined largely to key components such as nozzles and valves. Nearly all of the firm's early profits were derived from royalties paid by engine-users.

16. *Theory of Economic Development*, p. 66.

17. Ibid., pp. 75, 78.

18. Ibid., p. 89.

19. Ibid., pp. 92, 78.

20. Ibid., p. 93.

21. Cule, *Finance and Industry in the Eighteenth Century*, pp. 320–324.

22. Ibid.

23. See Schumpeter, *Theory of Economic Development*, especially p. 78.

24. See Erich Roll, *An Early Experiment in Industrial Organization* (London, 1930), especially pp. 10–11.

25. Dickinson and Jenkins, *James Watt and the Steam Engine*, p. 52. It should be noted that Cule, Finance and Industry in the Eighteenth Century, raises certain points that might appear to deny both the fact and the general interpretation of the firm's borrowing. He argues first that no money was borrowed to finance the Boulton and Watt venture; that in 1772 Boulton sold his Parkington estate to provide all the funds necessary for the steam-engine enterprise. This analysis of Boulton's intent is dubious, since in 1772 Boulton's negotiations to acquire a part of Roebuck's steam-engine interest were stalemated indefinitely. A more likely reason for the sale was Boulton & Fothergill's urgent need for cash. The partnership, in fact, immediately absorbed £6,000 of the proceeds.

It also seems most difficult to isolate, as Cule has, Boulton's financial transactions as a partner in Boulton & Watt from those as partner in Boulton & Fothergill. He required a certain amount of cash to meet the minimum demands of the two firms together, and this joint demand necessitated both the sale of his personal assets and borrowing, including later refinancing secured additionally by Watt's interest in certain engine royalties. Had Boulton not borrowed as partner in the hardware firm, or had the firm collapsed, the steam-engine firm would have been deprived of capital essential to its initial or continued existence.

Cule also implies that Boulton was "unbusinesslike" for borrowing £7,000 at a 10 percent interest rate, while Watt was a shrewder business man for urging reduction of the loan through cash payments on the principal. The opposite conclusion might as easily be drawn from the evidence. Perhaps the 10 percent rate was exorbitant, but it was the best Boulton could do in tight circumstances. The conventional economic theory of profit maximization indicates that funds should be borrowed in an imperfect capital market as long as the additional interest cost is less than the return from investments which would be foregone unless the funds are borrowed. Up to about 1785 the operations of Boulton & Watt were severely constrained by capital scarcity. This condition, plus the high *average* returns to the firm's investment, leads me to suspect that, unless there were substantial discontinuities in investment opportunities, the return on marginal investment would have exceeded the 10 percent cost of capital. By similar reasoning, one might conclude that short-term borrowing through discounting bills of exchange (successfully opposed by Watt, to Cule's evident satisfaction) would have been profitable.

26. This was not completely unrelated to the steam-engine business, since Boulton recognized that the level of royalties received from engines used in Cornish copper mines depended upon the copper price level.

27. See, e.g., his letters to Boulton of October 31, 1780, and to Small in August 1772.

28. Quoted in H. W. Dickinson, *James Watt: Craftsman and Engineer* (Cambridge, 1936), p. 200. Dickinson adds his own opinion that without Boulton, Watt "would never have brought his engine into general use, nor derived any reward for his invention, nor followed it up by those equally brilliant inventions connected with the rotative engine."

29. One might still wish to stress Watt's contribution because of its uniqueness, whereas generalized capital and entrepreneurship were present in modest abundance in eighteenth-century England. Economic theory holds that complementary factors are valued on the basis of supply (degree of scarcity) and demand (contribution to society's express wants). In the steam engine case, while Watt's inventive genius was clearly scarce, capital and entrepreneurship for the specific venture were perhaps equally scarce due to market imperfections.

30. See n. 7.

31. Watt to Dr. Small, November 7, 1772.

32. Watt to Dr. Small, January 28, 1769.

33. Dickinson and Jenkins, *James Watt and the Steam Engine*, p. 102.

34. Watt, "A Simple Story" (1796), cited in Muirhead, *The Origin and Progress*, p. lxxxix.

35. *James Watt*, p. 40. For an analysis of analogous problems in twentieth-century technical developments, see M. J. Peck and F. M. Scherer, *The Weapons Acquisition Process: An Economic Analysis* (Boston, 1962), pp. 263–264, 488–492, and 495–501. See also my comment in National Bureau of Economic Research, *The Rate and Direction of Inventive Activity* (Princeton, N.J., 1962), pp. 501–502.

36. To keep the cylinder hot, Watt also decided to break with the Newcomen approach of using the atmosphere to push the piston into the vacuum formed by steam condensation. He used steam instead of air for this purpose by enclosing the cylinder on both sides of the piston and employing a more complex valving system. This approach later provided the basis for a double-acting engine with steam being condensed on both sides of the piston, forming alternating vacuums to power the piston both upward and downward.

37. See Roll, *An Early Experiment*, pp. 25–35, 55–57, and 157–160, and Ashton, *Iron and Steel*, pp. 62 ff., for accounts of Wilkinson's business relationships with Boulton & Watt, which deteriorated during the 1790s to the point where Boulton & Watt set up their own ironworking shop using Wilkinson's boring-mill technique.

38. See Dickinson and Jenkins, *James Watt and the Steam Engine*, p. 43; Roll, *An Early Experiment*, p. 25; and Ashton, *Iron and Steel*, p. 63.

39. Watt to Dr. Small, September 20, 1769.

40. This view is held by Dickinson and Jenkins, *James Watt and the Steam Engine*, p. 108.

41. To illustrate the last objective, a major change from using an integral outer cylinder (steam jacket) was decided on to permit engine-users to buy the outer cylinder from manufacturers other than Wilkinson, about whose prices they had complained (Dickinson and Jenkins, *James Watt and the Steam Engine*, p. 193; see also Roll, *An Early Experiment*, pp. 34–35).

42. Dickinson and Jenkins (*James Watt and the Steam Engine*, p. 1) remark about Watt: "Indeed the business of mechanical engineering may be said to have been set on foot by him."

43. It would be incorrect to state unequivocally that Usher subordinates critical revision to acts of insight. In his basic work the tendency to do so is pronounced, but in a later elaboration he distinguishes inventive acts of insight from the broader "process of invention," and he warns against overemphasizing high-level acts of insight while underemphasizing elements

of novelty arising from acts of skill (A. P. Usher, Technical Change and Capital Formation, in the National Bureau of Economic Research conference report, *Capital Formation and Economic Growth*, Princeton, N.J., 1955, pp. 523–550 and esp. pp. 523 and 527). His description of the critical revision phase—"a very intimate interweaving of minor acts of insight and acts of skill"—fits the steam engine case rather well (p. 528). My only objection to this revised schema is the somewhat confusing double meaning attached to "invention," one definition focusing on acts of insight and the other (process) definition embracing most or all aspects of pioneering technological advance.

44. In fact, in the article cited in note 43 Usher defines the fourth step of his inventive process as "critical revision and development" rather than critical revision alone, as in his book.

45. For his work on the model Watt was paid £5 11s. in June 1766 (Dickinson and Jenkins, *James Watt and the Steam Engine*, p. 22). Interestingly, if Watt had been hired by a government agency such as the U.S. National Aeronautics and Space Administration or the Atomic Energy Commission in 1964, he probably would have been unable to secure a patent on his invention, since any patent obtained in connection with contracts from those agencies must normally be assigned to the government.

In assessing the importance of the patent system to Watt's invention, one must not be misled by the vigorous statements Watt made on behalf of stronger patent laws during the 1780s (see Roll, *An Early Experiment*, pp. 145–147). His concept of "invention" appears to have included developmental activities, and in advocating patent protection for the "first introducers" in England of inventions made abroad, he seems to have had in mind the necessity of encouraging the Schumpeterian innovative role. It is hardly necessary to note also that Watt was not without the kind of vested interest that has made all debates on the patent system so acrimonious.

46. Most authors indicate that the investment would not have been recouped if the patent expired on schedule in 1783 and if no further revenues were obtained from then on. Cule's paper, however, can be interpreted as saying that cumulative revenues exceeded cumulative costs at an earlier date.

47. 15 George III, c. 61 (1775).

48. Watt to Mr. T. Parker, June 2, 1797.

49. See Roll, *An Early Experiment*, pp. 121–122.

50. Ibid., pp. 56–57.

51. Ibid., pp. 156–157, 275.

52. Dickinson and Jenkins, *James Watt and the Steam Engine*, p. 336. This is what was actually obtained through threats and negotiation. In 1799 Boulton & Watt claimed that the back royalties owed them in Cornwall amounted to more than £162,000 (Dickinson, *Matthew Boulton*, p. 176).

53. See Dickinson and Jenkins, *James Watt and the Steam Engine*, pp. 42 and 69–70; Roll, *An Early Experiment*, p. 143.

54. Watt, who started in business by borrowing, left an estate of £60,000 at his death in 1819 (Dickinson and Jenkins, *James Watt and the Steam Engine*, p. 79). Boulton's estate in 1809 was £150,000 (Dickinson, *Matthew Boulton*, p. 201). See Schumpeter, *Capitalism, Socialism, and Democracy* (3d ed.; New York, 1950), pp. 73–74.

55. For a contrary conclusion see Vernon W. Ruttan, Usher and Schumpeter on Invention, Innovation, and Technological Change, *Quarterly Journal of Economics* 73 (November 1959): 596–606. Usher also in a very few sentences rejects the Schumpeterian distinction between invention and innovation by what seems to me to be an extension of his own schema (*Capital Formation and Economic Growth*, pp. 527, 534).

56. H. W. Dickinson, The Steam Engine to 1830, in *A History of Technology*, vol. 4, eds. Charles Singer, E. J. Holmyard, A. R. Hall, and Trevor I. Williams (London, 1958), p. 175.

57. Dickinson and Jenkins, *James Watt and the Steam Engine*, pp. 57, 304.

58. 15 George III, c. 61 (1775) (italics added).

59. *Picard* v. *United Aircraft Corporation*, 128 F. 2d 632, 643 (1942). See also F. M. Scherer, S. E. Herzstein Jr., A. W. Dreyfoos, W. G. Whitney, O. J. Bachmann, C. P. Pesek, C. J. Scott, T. G. Kelly, and J. J. Galvin, *Patents and the Corporation* (2d ed.; Boston, 1959), esp. chs. 5 and 14.

3 Interindustry Technology Flows in the United States

3.1 Introduction

Economists of as diverse persuasion as Adam Smith, Karl Marx, and Joseph Schumpeter have argued that material standards of living depend critically on the level of technology. More recently, industrial research and development (R & D) has been identified as a potentially important source of technological change and hence growth in productivity (i.e., output per worker). However, there is surprisingly little solid quantitative evidence about the links between R & D and productivity, whose retarded growth in recent years has become a matter of concern. This article reports some results of an effort to narrow the knowledge gap.

At the heart of the problem is the fact that industrial R & D is directed toward creating and improving new products as well as new production processess. A new process in the sense used here is a technical improvement in one's own production methods, whereas a new product is an improvement sold to others, either to other business enterprises or to consumers. Resources devoted to process R & D normally lead directly to productivity improvements within the enterprise or industry performing the R & D. More output can be produced with a given quantity of labor, capital, and other material input. New products, however, are by definition sold to others. If the new product is a consumer good, it presumably enhances the quality of life directly. If it is a producer good or intermediate sold externally, it serves to improve output-input relationships or the quality of output in the buying industries. With a new turbojet engine product, for example, the R & D is performed in the aircraft engine industry, but the productivity effect often shows up in lower energy consumption or faster, quieter, and more reliable operation of equipment used by the quite distinct airlines industry.

Therein lies the rub. From surveys sponsored by the U.S. National Science Foundation and others, we have extensive statistics concerning expenditures on research and development classified by industries performing the R & D. But there is a dearth of systematic quantitative information on the ultimate beneficiaries of industrial R & D outlays, once they become embodied in new or improved products flowing across industry boundaries. Given this statistical asymmetry, economists inves-

Source: *Research Policy* 11 (August 1982): 227–245. ©1982 North-Holland Publishing Company.

Table 3.1
Schmookler's invention flows matrix (hypothetical)

Industry making the invention	Industry using the invention				Total inventions made
	Industry I	Industry II	Industry III	Consumers	
Industry I	3	7	0	5	15
Industry II	2	11	18	9	40
Industry III	5	3	1	1	10
Total inventions used	10	21	19	15	65

tigating the links between R & D and productivity growth have (with only limited exceptions) been forced to assume that the productivity-enhancing effect occurs solely within the R & D-performing industry [1]. This is more wrong than right, since three-fourths of all industrial R & D is devoted to new or improved products, as distinguished from processes.

A conceptually correct approach to the problem was first proposed by Jacob Schmookler in 1966 [2]. Extending the input-output analysis ideas of Wassily Leontief, Schmookler argued that the structure of industrial technology flows was best characterized in terms of a two-way matrix (table 3.1), with industries performing R & D and originating inventions comprising the rows and industries (including end consumers) using those inventions comprising the columns. Each numerical element in the matrix represents the flow of technology from a particular originating industry to a particular using industry. Diagonal elements indicate process technology. The sum across a row shows the total amount of technology originating in an industry. Such origin totals (in R & D dollar terms) are available from annual National Science Foundation surveys. The sum down a column gives the total amount of technology used by an industry. In pathbreaking research with invention patents, Schmookler was able to estimate the column sums (but not the individual cell values) for the flow of capital goods technology to a small sample of using industries. Further progress was interrupted by his untimely death in 1967.

Schmookler's research emphasized counts of patents. These have important limitations as cross-sectional measures of industrial efforts to advance technology, in part because the "propensity to patent" varies from one industry to another. The research that will be reported here revealed among other things that the average number of U.S. patents obtained per million dollars of company-financed 1974 research and development ranged from a low of 0.47 in motor vehicles to 3.98 in industrial electrical equipment, with an average across all industries of 1.70 [3].

3.2 Constructing a Technology Flows Matrix for the U.S. Economy

The recent availability of an unusually rich U.S. R & D data source makes it possible to overcome this problem and hence view invention patents as carriers of underlying R & D expenditures rather than as units of invention in their own right. That source is the Federal Trade Commission's line of business survey for 1974, which among other things collected data on the R & D outlays of 443 large U.S. industrial corporations disaggregated into some 4,274 separate lines of business pursued by the companies [4]. A company like, say, General Electric was asked under the survey instructions to break its sales and R & D expenditures into such categories as turbojet engines, electric motors, light bulbs, small appliances (e.g., hair dryers), and synthetic resins rather than report them, as is done for National Science Foundation surveys, in one lump assigned to GE's "primary" industry (i.e., industrial electrical equipment). The line of Business survey data allowed one for the first time to achieve a precise match between industrial invention patents and the R & D expenditures supporting activities that gave rise to the inventions.

With this possibility in view, a team of engineering and chemistry students at Northwestern University was put to work examining the printed specifications of the 15,112 U.S. invention patents obtained between June 1976 and March 1977 by the 443 corporations reporting under the FTC's 1974 line of business survey. Each individual patent was coded according to industry of origin, industry(ies) in which use of the invention was anticipated, and various other details [5]. The codings by industry of use were based in a rather straightforward way on applicants' descriptions of how their inventions were expected to satisfy the "utility" criterion for patentability. Determining industries of origin was somewhat more difficult, since it was necessary to track as closely as possible the industry breakdowns used by companies in reporting their R & D expenditures by line of business. To facilitate the task, the coding team used an extensive accumulation of information on company organization, including data on the products developed or produced at the various geographic locations to which inventors' addresses could be traced. Once the codings were completed and checked, each patent was linked to its originating line of business report. All matching problems were checked against additional information in the FTC files, and when appropriate, corrections were made. At the conclusion of the matching procedure, each patent was "tagged" with the average R & D outlay per patent in its appropriate line of business. Thus, the R & D dollars, as well as raw patents, could be flowed out to industries in which the patented inventions' use was anticipated.

Products versus Processes

Consistent with prior surveys, the classification effort revealed that 26.2 percent of the inventions were processes for use within the originating industry. The complete breakdown by use category (including industrial products that also had consumer applications) was as follows:

Internal processes	26.2%
Consumer goods only	7.4%
Industrial materials products	21.6%
With consumer uses too	8.7%
Capital goods products	44.8%
With consumer uses too	7.8%

Sample Coverage

The 443 corporations whose patents were analyzed received 61 percent of all U.S. patents issued to domestic industrial corporations during the sample period. Their 1974 company-financed R & D outlays of $10.6 billion amounted to 72 percent of the comparable all-industry total reported from a National Science Foundation survey [6]. The R & D dollars linked to each patent were inflated by a factor reflecting the sample's fractional coverage of total population sales for each of 263 industry categories. The mean sales coverage ratio was 0.61, the same as the sample's coverage of industrial corporation patents. However, the inflated sample results do not characterize total industrial technology flow relationships exactly for at least five reasons. First, inventions patented by the characteristically smaller enterprises excluded from the sample might not have use patterns identical to those of sample members. Second, some results of industrial research and development are not patentable, and their interindustry flows will be overlooked by our methodology. Third, inventions originating in government and university laboratories are not included. The omission of government work (accounting for 2.6 percent of all U.S. patents in 1976) is particularly important for military, space, agricultural, medical, and (only recently) energy applications. University scientists generate few patented inventions, but their basic research enhances the fecundity of industrial laboratories, whose inventive output is our main focus. Fourth, the inventions of "independent inventors" are not covered by the sample. In 1976 individuals with no corporate assignment relationship received 20 percent of all U.S. invention patents. A special small sample revealed that 32 percent of domestic independent inventor patents had consumer goods applications alone (compared to 7 percent for our industrial patent sample). And fifth, the inventions of foreign nationals are also excluded. Foreign corporations accounted for 26 percent of all U.S. patents issued in 1976 and were disproportionately significant in certain industries such as textiles, shoe making, steel, and corn products refining. The difficulty of linking small-firm, university, government, independent, and foreign inventors' inventions to specific origin industries and the impossibility of obtaining corresponding R & D data precluded more exhaustive coverage.

Despite these limitations, the sample systematically covers the preponderance of American industry, which is peculiarly well-suited to such an analysis because of its unusually high degree of technological autarky. Thus the data are believed to measure tolerably well the flow of technology into the main stream of the U.S. industrial economy. In this respect it is interesting to note that there are substantial similarities in origin *versus* use and process *versus* product invention patterns between our sample and one analyzed by Pavitt and others covering 2,154 significant technological innovations introduced by British industry between 1945 and 1980 [7].

Specific-Use, General-Use, and Public Goods Inventions

Under our coding procedures a patent could be assigned to as many as three industries of use. Not all inventions are so narrowly constrained in their applications, however. Some, such as new paints, gasoline additives, computers, electrical switchgear, and copying machines, are used to a greater or lesser degree by many or even all industries. Therefore a dichotomy was drawn (with some further complications ignored here) between "specific-" and "general-" use inventions. For the 8,852 specific-use inventions, utilization was expected to occur primarily in explicitly identifiable industries, and the R & D dollars linked to those patents were allocated only to the coded industries [8]. R & D underlying the 5,166 general-use inventions, on the other hand, was flowed out in proportion to the origin industry's 1972 sales to as many as 285 potential user industries, as determined from a carrier matrix derived with modifications from the 1972 input-output tables for the U.S. economy [9].

Numerous other methodological problems had to be solved in estimating the technology flow matrices [5]. One is important enough to merit attention here. It concerns the question of whether inventions are "public" or "private" goods in the sense used by economists. A public good is one whose use by one group (e.g., an industry) does not diminish its availability for use by other groups. Although there are arguments to the contrary, the consensus among economists would probably be that inventions are better characterized as public goods rather than private goods. Nevertheless, technology flow matrices were prepared under both assumptions. Under the public goods assumption, if an invention entailing R & D costs of $1 million was sold in equal amounts to each of three industries, each using industry was presumed to have benefitted from $1 million of embodied R & D. Or with unequal sales, the largest using industry received $1 million of embodied R & D input and smaller industries received benefits scaled down by the ratio of their purchases to the largest user's purchases. A disadvantage of the public goods approach is that using industry R & D embodiments sum to a total greater than origin industry outlays. Because of this problem, I present here only matrices constructed under the alternative "private goods" assumption. That is, if a $1 million invention is used by three industries with equal purchase volumes from the originating industry, each using industry is credited with $333,333 of R & D usage. An exception to this convention was made for consumer goods inventions, which were treated as public goods not diminishing the flow of R & D dollars to industrial using sectors.

3.3 The Technology Flows Matrix

Table 3.2 presents the resulting estimates aggregated to the level of 41 origin sectors (the rows) and 53 using sectors (the columns). All entries are in millions of dollars. Blank cells denote R & D flows of less than $50,000. Reading across the row for industry 18, we find that rubber and plastic products makers performed $419.8 million in R & D, of which $13.7 million was embodied in products (e.g., tractor tires) purchased by the agriculture sector, $203.0 million (from column 18) was used internally within rubber and plastic products (e.g., as process technology), and (skipping to the last column) $111.9 million was embodied in consumer products ranging from passenger car tires to plastic food storage wrap. The diagonal elements of the matrix represent the use of process technology. Entries marked "d" had to be suppressed to comply with the requirement that no underlying R & D data (from the Federal Trade Commission survey) be disclosed for individual companies. Most such deletions involved small amounts of R & D. Over the entire matrix, only 11 entailed R & D flows exceeding $10 million. Reading down column 18, we see that the rubber and plastic products sector purchased products embodying an estimated $21.6 million of R & D from the textile industry (e.g., for tire cord); $169.1 million, mostly for synthetic rubber, from origin sector 13; $9.7 million from the "other machinery" sector; and so on, with total R & D usage (in the last row) summing to $496.5 million.

Interindustry Balances

In rubber and plastics the R & D origin and use totals are relatively evenly balanced. This is not true for many other sectors. Printing and publishing businesses used processes and products (including paper, inks, and electronic typesetters) embodying $147.7 million of R & D but performed only $67 million, or 46 percent of used R & D. Other industries with low origin to use ratios were lumber and wood products (0.55), ferrous metals (0.62), textiles (0.71), and apparel and leather (0.75). At the other extreme was the farm machinery industry, originating 10.4 times as much R & D as it used. Other major "exporters" of technology were computers and other office equipment, with an 8.7 origin/use ratio, construction and mining machinery (8.0), and instruments (7.05).

Inspection of table 3.2 reveals that some industries, such as food and tobacco, apparel, paper products, pharmaceuticals, household appliances, and motor vehicles, devoted the bulk of their product (i.e., off-diagonal) R & D to consumer goods. For all industries together, consumer goods accounted for only $4.1 billion of R & D flows (out of a non-double-counted total of $14.7 billion) when products that were both consumer and producer goods are included, as in table 3.2, or approximately $1.1 billion when the analysis is limited to products that were solely consumer goods. Some industries such as agricultural chemicals, farm machinery, aircraft, missiles, and other transportation equipment specialize in supplying advanced technology to a very few using sectors (including defense and space operations). Still others such as organic and other chemicals, rubber and plastic products, fabricated metal products (spanning narrowly defined product lines ranging from bottle caps to nuclear reactors), computers, and instruments are active in providing new technology to a broad array of using industries. These tend to preside over rich

Table 3.2
Technology flows matrix for company-financed 1974 R & D outlays

	Origin R & D	Agri- culture 1	Min- ing 2	Food prod- ucts 3	To- bacco prod- ucts 4	Tex- tile prod- ucts 5	Ap- parel prod- ucts 6	Lum- ber and wood 7	Fur- niture 8	Paper prod- ucts 9	Pub- lish- ing 10	Inor- ganic chem- icals 11	Or- ganic chem- icals 12
1 Agriculture and forestry	128.1	d											
2 Mining, exc. petroleum	60.3		45.2										
3, 4 Food and tobacco products	444.9	7.9		257.8	20.4	0.2			0.8	d	d		0.1
5 Textile mill products	179.3	0.8		0.2		128.4	8.1	0.3		0.5	0.2		
6, 19 Apparel and leather products	55.5	d		d	d	d	16.5	d	d	d	d		d
7 Lumber and wood products	72.6	0.4		0.2		0.2	0.1	64.2	0.6	0.1	0.2		
8 Furniture	51.1	0.1	0.1	0.3		0.1	0.1	0.3	7.8	0.2	0.2		
9 Paper mill products	202.3	6.0	0.1	25.8	0.1	1.2	0.3	0.4	0.4	86.4	3.1	0.1	0.1
10 Printing and publishing	67.4	0.1		0.4		0.1				0.1	32.7		
11 Industrial inorganic chemicals	159.2	1.2	0.1	d	0.8	1.7	0.1	0.1		4.6	0.3	90.8	3.3
12 Industrial organic chemicals	297.2	3.0	0.2	2.7	d	11.8	0.4	1.3	0.1	5.9	d	1.1	163.3
13 Synthetic resins, fibers, rubber	601.6	1.6	0.5	2.8	d	32.0	11.8	1.1	0.8	13.9	0.5	d	0.8
14 Pharmaceuticals	557.3	32.0		0.2						d			
15 Agricultural chemicals	186.7	142.8		d						d			0.1
16 Paints, toiletries, explosives, and other chemical products	485.7	3.9	4.2	11.1	0.2	26.3	0.2	7.8	4.5	20.5	13.4	0.7	1.4
17 Petroleum extraction and refining	380.3	4.0	0.7	1.1	0.1	0.3	0.4	0.9	0.1	1.0	0.3	0.2	0.3
18 Rubber and plastic products	419.8	13.7	2.8	18.1	0.7	3.0	1.1	d	3.5	5.0	2.2	0.7	0.8
20 Stone, clay, and glass products	265.0	0.9	0.1	d	0.1	d	0.1	2.4	1.0	d	0.3	0.1	0.2
21 Ferrous metals	189.3	d	0.1	0.1				0.1	0.4				d
22 Nonferrous metals	156.9	d	0.1	d		0.1	0.1	0.3	0.2	0.1	0.4	0.2	0.4
23 Fabricated metal products	552.7	5.3	3.0	28.0	0.2	0.7	0.7	4.5	2.7	7.4	0.9	1.0	2.7
24 Engines and turbines	282.2	10.4	3.2	2.2	0.3	0.6	0.6	1.1	0.3	2.5	0.9	0.4	1.0

25	Farm machinery	199.3	165.4											
26	Construction, mining, and materials handling equipment	351.2	2.0	65.9	4.6	0.3	1.2	0.3	7.3	0.3	1.3	0.6	0.3	0.8
27	Metalworking machinery	121.5	5.4	0.2	0.4		0.1		2.8	0.5	d	9.1		
28	Other machinery	691.0	17.6	8.0	56.9	1.5	18.9	1.9	7.8	1.1	20.9	40.1	5.0	10.1
29	Computers and office equipment	1153.0	2.9	2.4	15.9	0.6	9.4	3.4	1.6	1.7	10.1	13.4	1.8	5.0
30	Industrial electrical equipment	205.9	0.3	1.6	1.3		1.1	0.2	0.5	0.3	2.5	0.3	0.7	1.6
31	Household appliances	102.7	0.1		0.1		0.4	2.2	0.6					
32	Lamps, batteries, ignition, X-ray, and other electrical equipment	233.3	8.1	0.6	2.5	0.1	0.5	0.3	1.3	0.4	0.7	0.7	0.2	0.4
33	Radio and communication equipment	1227.7	5.1	1.6	5.3	0.7	1.5	1.5	1.5	0.7	1.7	2.4	0.5	0.9
34	Electronic components	594.9	0.5	0.2	0.7		0.6	0.2	0.2	0.1	0.4	0.7	0.1	0.3
35	Motor vehicles and equipment	1518.0	78.0	10.6	25.4	1.1	5.0	3.6	17.1	3.9	5.4	10.0	0.9	2.2
36	Aircraft	659.4	0.3		0.2				0.1		0.2	0.1		0.1
37	Missiles, spacecraft, and ordnance	122.7			d									d
38	Other transportation equipment	140.1		d										d
39	Measuring and medical instruments, photo equipment, and timepieces	1036.4	6.3	2.1	8.1	0.8	3.3	1.5	2.0	0.9	7.2	20.7	2.4	5.3
40	Miscellaneous manufactures	211.6	d	0.1	0.6	0.1	0.9	1.3	0.6	0.3	0.2	0.5	0.1	0.1
41, 42	Trade and finance and real estate	39.7												
43	Transportation and public utilities	47.2												
44, 45	Construction and services, including R & D services	266.0	0.7	d	0.7	0.1	0.2	0.2	0.2	0.1	0.3	0.3	d	5.5
	Total R & D dollars used		361.8	157.3	493.4	29.8	250.8	57.2	131.1	33.7	206.0	147.7	108.8	207.6

Table 3.2 (continued)

		Origin R&D	Synthetic resins etc. 13	Pharmaceuticals 14	Agri. chemicals 15	Other chem. products 16	Petroleum 17	Rubber and plastics 18	Leather products 19	Stone, clay, and glass 20	Ferrous metals 21	Non-ferrous metals 22	Fab. metal products 23	Engines and turbines 24
1	Agriculture and forestry	128.1												
2	Mining, exc. petroleum	60.3	d			d		d						
3, 4	Food and tobacco products	444.9	0.1	d	0.1	d	0.1	0.1	d	0.1	0.1		d	
5	Textile mill products	179.3					0.1	21.6	d	0.1		0.1	d	d
6, 19	Apparel and leather products	55.5				d		d	0.9	d	d	d	d	
7	Lumber and wood products	72.6				0.1	0.1	0.1		0.3	0.2	0.2	0.3	
8	Furniture	51.1				0.1	0.1	0.1		0.1	0.2	0.1	0.2	
9	Paper mill products	202.3	1.0	0.7		1.0	1.5	1.2	0.2	0.9	0.1	0.1	0.6	
10	Printing and publishing	67.4	0.1	0.1		0.1	0.1	0.1		0.1	0.1		0.1	
11	Industrial inorganic chemicals	159.2	1.8	0.2	0.3	6.1	9.3	0.4		0.9	2.5		1.6	d
12	Industrial organic chemicals	297.2	24.1	1.2	2.3	19.0	7.1	13.8		2.7	1.6	2.2	0.8	
13	Synthetic resins, fibers, rubber	601.6	70.8	d		23.9	2.3	169.1	d	6.4	0.9	10.0	2.7	
14	Pharmaceuticals	557.3	d	71.0		d			1.7					
15	Agricultural chemicals	186.7		d	34.2	d		d						
16	Paints, toiletries, explosives, and other chemical products	485.7	9.6	1.0	0.1	85.4	13.8	16.2	2.5	5.4	3.5	3.8	31.8	0.1
17	Petroleum extraction and refining	380.3	0.3	0.1		0.8	312.7	0.7	0.1	0.6	0.6	0.4	1.5	0.1
18	Rubber and plastic products	419.8	1.3	1.3	0.1	4.3	3.8	203.0	1.9	2.5	1.0	5.1	4.6	0.2
20	Stone, clay, and glass products	265.0	0.1	d		1.3	d	d		155.3	11.3	0.3	2.7	1.1
21	Ferrous metals	189.3	d	d			d	0.1	0.1	0.1	164.2	0.3	9.7	d
22	Nonferrous metals	156.9		0.1		0.2	d	0.1	0.3	0.3	2.8	102.9	7.0	0.8
23	Fabricated metal products	552.7	1.5	0.7	1.4	d	7.4	1.1	0.1	1.3	12.3	2.3	127.7	3.0
24	Engines and turbines	282.2	0.5	0.2	0.3	0.5	6.5	0.6	0.1	1.1	2.0	1.1	1.9	38.9

	Industry													
25	Farm machinery	199.3											0.1	1.0
26	Construction, mining, and materials handling equipment	351.2	0.7	0.2		0.3	17.7	0.4	0.2	5.8	3.4	1.3	1.9	1.0
27	Metalworking machinery	121.5	0.1		d		0.1	1.4	d	0.9	14.5	7.5	15.1	1.0
28	Other machinery	691.0	5.4	2.1	1.6	3.4	16.2	9.7	d	13.6	35.4	9.1	16.0	1.1
29	Computers and office equipment	1153.0	4.8	6.2	1.3	8.6	20.6	8.1	1.6	8.5	19.0	5.3	10.2	5.5
30	Industrial electrical equipment	205.9	0.6		0.5	0.3	4.0	0.5		d	8.2	4.9	5.1	0.7
31	Household appliances	102.7					0.1						0.1	
32	Lamps, batteries, ignition, X-ray, and other electrical equipment	233.3	0.3	0.2	0.1	0.3	1.2	2.0	0.1	0.8	4.6	0.5	1.3	0.4
33	Radio and communication equipment	1227.7	0.6	0.6	0.2	1.0	7.6	1.6	0.3	1.9	2.4	1.0	3.4	0.5
34	Electronic components	594.9	0.2	0.2	0.1	0.3	0.9	0.4	0.1	0.6	0.7	0.2	0.6	0.2
35	Motor vehicles and equipment	1518.0	0.9	1.7	0.6	2.3	16.7	2.6	1.2	11.4	4.2	2.5	14.2	0.8
36	Aircraft	659.4					0.5	0.1		0.1	0.1	0.1	0.2	
37	Missiles, spacecraft, and ordnance	122.7	d		d		d							
38	Other transportation equipment	140.1			d		d			0.1				
39	Measuring and medical instruments, photo equipment, and timepieces	1036.4	2.8	4.2	1.3	4.3	13.5	4.0	0.4	5.1	6.6	3.1	5.7	0.7
40	Miscellaneous manufactures	211.6	0.1	0.1		0.2	1.4	0.3	0.1	0.2	0.4	0.1	0.7	
41, 42	Trade and finance and real estate	39.7												
43	Transportation and public utilities	47.2												
44, 45	Construction and services, including R & D services	266.0	d	0.1	d		24.4	0.3		0.3	5.0	0.7	0.4	
	Total R & D dollars used	d	332.1	95.3	45.7	180.3	496.5	470.0	16.6	232.0	307.8	166.1	270.3	56.9

Table 3.2 (continued)

	Origin R&D	Farm machinery 25	Construction equip. 26	Metalworking machinery 27	Other machinery 28	Office equipment 29	Indust. electrical 30	Appliances 31	Other electrical 32	Communications equip. 33	Electronic components 34	Motor vehicles 35	Aircraft 36
1 Agriculture and forestry	128.1												
2 Mining, exc. petroleum	60.3												
3,4 Food and tobacco products	444.9											d	
5 Textile mill products	179.3				0.2			0.1	0.1			0.6	
6,19 Apparel and leather products	55.5		d	0.1	d				d	d		d	
7 Lumber and wood products	72.6				0.1					0.1		0.1	
8 Furniture	51.1		0.1		0.2	0.1		0.1	0.1	0.5	0.1	0.5	0.1
9 Paper mill products	202.3				0.3	0.1		0.2	d	0.2	0.1	0.3	0.1
10 Printing and publishing	67.4				0.1		0.1			0.1		0.1	0.1
11 Industrial inorganic chemicals	159.2	0.1	0.1		0.2	d			d	0.2	1.1	2.7	0.3
12 Industrial organic chemicals	297.2				0.4	d		0.1	0.6	d	2.0	0.3	0.1
13 Synthetic resins, fibers, rubber	601.6				0.5	0.1	0.8	1.9	1.9	1.1	1.8	12.0	1.2
14 Pharmaceuticals	557.3												
15 Agricultural chemicals	186.7												
16 Paints, toiletries, explosives, and other chemical products	485.7	0.6	0.8	0.3	2.0	2.4	2.0	5.7	0.9	d	4.7	19.3	1.3
17 Petroleum extraction and refining	380.3	d	0.1	0.2	0.7	0.1	0.2		0.1	0.1	0.1	0.5	0.3
18 Rubber and plastic products	419.8	0.4	0.9	0.3	1.6	1.1	1.0	1.5	2.6	1.0	1.2	7.3	0.8
20 Stone, clay, and glass products	265.0	0.1	0.4	0.7	d	0.1	d	0.3	0.7	1.0	d	5.6	2.1
21 Ferrous metals	189.3	0.3	0.6	0.3	1.2	d	1.7	0.4	0.3	0.3	0.1	2.8	0.1
22 Nonferrous metals	156.9	0.2	0.3	d	1.3	0.2	1.3	0.3	2.3	0.6	1.2	1.4	1.3
23 Fabricated metal products	552.7	1.0	2.0	1.5	7.2	0.8	1.6	1.4	1.6	1.8	0.9	11.0	16.3
24 Engines and turbines	282.2	0.3	1.7	0.3	3.9	0.2	0.9	0.2	0.3	0.5	0.3	1.8	0.9
25 Farm machinery	199.3	d										0.1	

#	Industry													
26	Construction, mining, and materials handling equipment	351.2	0.5	16.0	0.4	2.0	0.7	0.4	0.4	0.5	1.0	0.9	5.7	0.2
27	Metalworking machinery	121.5	1.3	2.2	d	7.4	0.8	1.8	0.7	2.0	1.3	1.1	12.2	3.2
28	Other machinery	691.0	0.8	1.6	2.7	64.9	1.5	1.3	8.0	2.5	1.8	3.3	16.2	1.5
29	Computers and office equipment	1153.0	3.5	7.3	2.9	12.9	110.5	4.2	1.4	3.3	16.5	6.6	17.1	20.5
30	Industrial electrical equipment	205.9	0.6	2.9	2.2	15.6	2.6	34.4	3.8	1.7	0.7	0.8	1.4	0.4
31	Household appliances	102.7							6.8	d	0.1		0.1	
32	Lamps, batteries, ignition, X-ray, and other electrical equipment	233.3	1.6	1.4	0.3	1.3	0.6	0.2	0.4	27.8	0.6	0.3	12.2	0.4
33	Radio and communication equipment	1227.7	0.4	0.9	0.7	2.2	1.2	1.1	0.5	1.2	106.3	2.0	6.2	17.6
34	Electronic components	594.9	0.1	0.3	0.1	0.8	3.9	0.6	0.4	0.6	6.5	386.4	3.1	4.6
35	Motor vehicles and equipment	1518.0	2.4	2.9	1.2	5.1	1.5	1.0	0.8	1.1	2.0	1.5	158.8	0.8
36	Aircraft	659.4				0.1							0.4	160.5
37	Missiles, spacecraft, and ordnance	122.7												d
38	Other transportation equipment	140.1											d	
39	Measuring and medical instruments, photo equipment, and timepieces	1036.4	0.5	1.0	0.9	5.5	2.3	3.0	5.9	2.1	12.4	11.4	6.8	9.7
40	Miscellaneous manufactures	211.6	0.1	0.1	0.1	0.3	0.1		0.1	0.1	0.1	0.1	0.5	0.1
41,42	Trade and finance and real estate	39.7												
43	Transportation and public utilities	47.2												
44,45	Construction and services, including R & D services	266.0	0.1	0.1	0.1	0.3	0.1			d	d	d	0.5	0.1
	Total R & D dollars used		19.2	43.8	22.4	141.1	131.9	59.0	41.7	72.2	185.6	446.4	308.1	245.0

Table 3.2 (continued)

	Origin R&D	Missiles and ordnance 37	Other transportation equipment 38	Instruments 39	Misc. manufactures 40	Trade 41	Finance, insurance, and real estate 42	Ground transportation 43A	Air transportation 43B	Water transportation 43C	Telecommunications 43D	Electric, gas, and sanitary utilities 43E	Construction 44
1	**Agriculture and forestry**	128.1											
2	Mining, exc. petroleum	60.3										d	
3,4	Food and tobacco products	444.9				0.3	16.0	0.4	d	0.3		d	d	0.3
5	Textile mill products	179.3		d			0.8	1.0	0.2	0.3	0.1	0.1	0.1	0.8
6,19	Apparel and leather products	55.5			d	d	d	d	d	d		d	d	
7	Lumber and wood products	72.6	0.1	0.2		0.3	0.6	0.4	0.2			0.1	0.4	0.3
8	Furniture	51.1		0.2		0.1	7.0	2.0	0.3	d		0.2	0.2	0.6
9	Paper mill products	202.3			0.9	0.6	14.7	1.0	0.5	0.3		0.2	0.3	1.4
10	Printing and publishing	67.4			0.1		2.5	1.1	0.2	0.1		0.2	0.2	0.4
11	Industrial inorganic chemicals	159.2	0.1	0.4	d	0.1	1.7	0.9	0.3	0.1		0.2	d	1.0
12	Industrial organic chemicals	297.2		0.1	d	0.3	1.6	0.7	0.3	0.1	d	0.2	0.8	0.6
13	Synthetic resins, fibers, rubber	601.6	0.2	0.7	3.7	4.8	1.2	1.0	0.5	0.2	0.1	0.3	0.4	1.1
14	Pharmaceuticals	557.3												
15	Agricultural chemicals	186.7					0.2	0.1	0.2				0.1	0.1
16	Paints, toiletries, explosives, and other chemical products	485.7	0.3	3.6	1.3	3.4	9.5	2.7	2.5	0.3	0.5	2.1	7.5	16.3
17	Petroleum extraction and refining	380.3	0.1	0.1	0.2	0.3	13.3	2.9	5.1	2.9	1.0	0.3	5.7	6.1
18	Rubber and plastic products	419.8	0.3	0.7	1.9	2.9	22.2	9.5	12.4	0.9	d	1.3	5.8	9.7
20	Stone, clay, and glass products	265.0	0.2	0.3	d	0.7	8.3	2.0	0.9	0.3	d	1.6	5.3	9.0
21	Ferrous metals	189.3	0.2	0.5	0.2	0.3	d		d		d		d	1.6
22	Nonferrous metals	156.9	0.5	0.3	0.5	0.4	0.8	0.5	0.7			d	1.8	0.4
23	Fabricated metal products	552.7	0.7	2.9	1.7	1.0	11.7	9.4	8.1	3.3	0.4	5.1	151.2	17.1

24	Engines and turbines	282.2	0.3	8.5	0.6	0.3	12.0	8.9	7.8	1.0	6.4	1.7	75.8	10.2
25	Farm machinery	199.3		0.1		0.3	d	5.9	3.9	2.3	0.2		0.1	2.4
26	Construction, mining, and materials handling equipment	351.2	0.1	2.4	3.9	1.1	10.2	1.6	3.9	3.5	2.3	2.3	1.2	154.4
27	Metalworking machinery	121.5	0.8	0.7	2.4	2.1	2.3	0.1	0.3	4.3	1.2	43.7	d	6.6
28	Other machinery	691.0	0.9	2.7	16.8	3.7	64.0	11.5	8.4	3.5	1.2	25.8	33.0	20.5
29	Computers and office equipment	1153.0	3.8	3.5		97.5	176.4		20.9	4.3	1.5	0.5	26.1	2.3
30	Industrial electrical equipment	205.9	0.2	2.4	1.6	0.8	2.1	1.8	2.5	0.3	0.4	0.5	52.0	1.8
31	Household appliances	102.7		0.2			4.1	2.8	0.2			0.1	0.1	0.2
32	Lamps, batteries, ignition, X-ray, and other electrical equipment	233.3	0.1	1.1	2.4	0.5	13.0	6.1	11.4	19.7	0.6	8.8	11.5	5.7
33	Radio and communication equipment	1227.7	3.6	2.2	1.7	0.9	31.8	20.9	11.7	75.6	12.2	417.7	11.0	16.1
34	Electronic components	594.9	1.5	0.5	2.2	0.8	4.7	5.7	2.2	3.9	0.2	43.7	2.3	1.7
35	Motor vehicles and equipment	1518.0	0.8	1.1	7.0	3.8	288.8	99.0	185.3	5.9	2.5	9.5	43.9	125.1
36	Aircraft	659.4	0.9	0.2		0.7	0.4	0.5	360.4		0.1		4.1	0.5
37	Missiles, spacecraft, and ordnance	122.7	22.0						0.3		6.4	d	d	d
38	Other transportation equipment	140.1		d		d	d	59.9	d	6.4		d	d	d
39	Measuring and medical instruments, photo equipment, and timepieces	1036.4	2.5	2.1	88.8	1.2	33.1	26.8	14.7	35.4	2.7	9.3	35.0	13.9
40	Miscellaneous manufactures	211.6		1.2	0.4	77.5	3.9	2.3	0.7	d	d	d	0.6	1.6
41,42	Trade and finance and real estate	39.7				(	d	)	d		d	d	d	
43	Transportation and public utilities	47.2							d		d	d	d	
44,45	Construction and services, including R & D services	266.0	0.2	0.2	0.2	0.2	4.3	2.5	0.9	d	0.6	0.6	4.7	2.2
	Total R & D dollars used		40.8	44.8	147.0	108.8	727.9	409.7	364.9	524.1	84.1	542.8	493.9	432.9

Table 3.2 (continued)

	Origin R&D	Medical services 45A	All other services 45B	General government 46	Defense and space 47	Final consumption 48	Row code
1 Agriculture and forestry	128.1	d			d	d	1
2 Mining, exc. petroleum	60.3					0.0	2
3, 4 Food and tobacco products	444.9	0.9	2.5	0.4	d	143.1	3, 4
5 Textile mill products	179.3	0.7	d	0.4	0.2	18.2	5
6, 19 Apparel and leather products	55.5	d	d	d	d	37.7	6, 19
7 Lumber and wood products	72.6	0.2	1.5	0.4	0.2	2.8	7
8 Furniture	51.1	d	7.1	1.3	1.1	22.4	8
9 Paper mill products	202.3	2.4	4.0	1.6	0.4	73.3	9
10 Printing and publishing	67.4	0.2	d	0.8	1.3	13.9	10
11 Industrial inorganic chemicals	159.2	0.8	1.6	1.7	1.9	8.8	11
12 Industrial organic chemicals	297.2	2.9	2.3	1.5	9.9	14.1	12
13 Synthetic resins, fibers, rubber	601.6	2.0	4.6	1.5	2.9	10.0	13
14 Pharmaceuticals	557.3	321.4	d	0.8	0.1	462.0	14
15 Agricultural chemicals	186.7	d	1.0	0.5	0.1	80.2	15
16 Paints, toiletries, explosives, and other chemical products	485.7	4.7	23.7	9.1	3.9	161.9	16
17 Petroleum extraction and refining	380.3	1.0	5.5	3.1	3.2	53.2	17
18 Rubber and plastic products	419.8	4.8	18.1	7.2	3.9	111.9	18
20 Stone, clay, and glass products	265.0	1.7	3.7	4.6	2.1	36.8	20
21 Ferrous metals	189.3		d		0.1	0.0	21
22 Nonferrous metals	156.9	1.2	0.7	0.5	3.0	9.6	22
23 Fabricated metal products	552.7	3.2	19.8	8.4	29.7	106.6	23
24 Engines and turbines	282.2	2.4	21.1	15.6	15.3	59.6	24
25 Farm machinery	199.3	0.3	4.6	0.5	0.1	33.1	25

No.	Industry							No.
26	Construction, mining, and materials handling equipment	351.2	4.7	3.5	8.1	10.5	4.0	26
27	Metalworking machinery	121.5	7.8	6.6	1.6	0.9	12.2	27
28	Other machinery	591.0	19.8	64.3	12.1	26.8	111.6	28
29	Computers and office equipment	1153.0	13.6	224.2	75.6	75.2	45.0	29
30	Industrial electrical equipment	205.9	0.2	7.9	5.2	4.7	25.4	30
31	Household appliances	102.7	26.0	10.1	0.4	d	94.1	31
32	Lamps, batteries, ignition, X-ray, and other electrical equipment	233.3	8.8	13.5	7.2	20.9	120.0	32
33	Radio and communication equipment	1227.7	2.6	38.1	39.4	220.6	223.2	33
34	Electronic components	594.9	16.9	28.2	11.7	50.0	46.2	34
35	Motor vehicles and equipment	1518.0	0.2	204.7	79.8	27.7	1345.9	35
36	Aircraft	639.4		0.4	6.5	120.1	d	36
37	Missiles, spacecraft, and ordnance	22.7	d	d	d	93.2	d	37
38	Other transportation equipment	20.1	d	d	d	d	51.7	38
39	Measuring and medical instruments, photo equipment, and timepieces	1056.4	207.0	142.0	35.6	60.2	342.5	39
40	Miscellaneous manufactures	211.6	1.7	29.0	4.3	1.8	86.9	40
41, 42	Trade and finance and real estate	39.7					0.0	41, 42
43	Transportation and public utilities	47.2					0.0	43
44, 45	Construction and services, including R & D services	266.0	d	72.6	d	d	14.0	44, 45
	Total R & D dollars used	684.6	684.6	1000.3	378.1	842.2	4111.4	

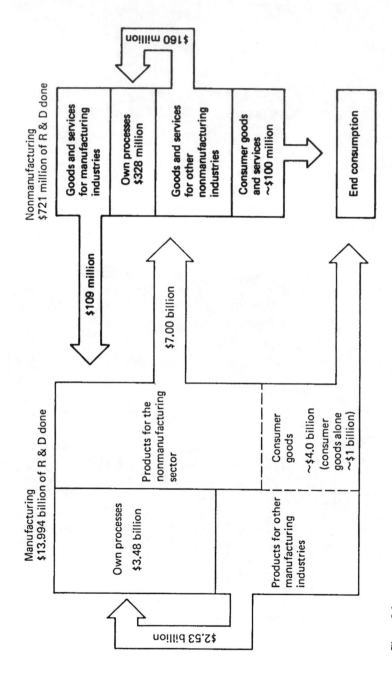

Figure 3.1
Technology flows from and within the manufacturing sector

science bases that can be tapped, often on a custom-tailored basis, to a host of specific industrial demands.

Manufacturing versus Other Sectors

It has long been known that the vast bulk (i.e., more than 95 percent) of all company-financed industrial R & D is carried out in the manufacturing sector, which in 1974 originated 23.7 percent of U.S. gross national product. Figure 3.1 exploits the additive property of technology flow estimates made under a "private goods" assumption to show the gross flow relationships between and within manufacturing and nonmanufacturing. (The nonmanufacturing sector includes government as a user of R & D, but neither R & D done in government laboratories nor R & D performed by industry or universities and financed by the government is counted in the present analysis. It should be noted too that the estimates of R & D flows originating within nonmanufacturing are subject to much larger sampling errors than those for manufacturing.) From the figure it becomes clear how dependent the nonmanufacturing economy is upon manufacturing for new technology. Manufacturing enterprises "exported" to nonmanufacturing half of the $14 billion in R & D they originated. The amount of industrial (i.e., nongovernmental) R & D originated, financed, *and* used within nonmanufacturing was only 7 percent of the amount imported from manufacturing. Within manufacturing, the balance of flows is quite different. Of the $6.1 billion of R & D used, 57 percent consisted of process R & D—that is, R & D performed in the specific narrowly defined industry of use. Even more striking are the results of an analysis focusing only on capital goods inventions with specific uses in at most three narrowly defined manufacturing industries. Three-fourths of all such using industry-specific inventions originated within the using industry. Evidently, if one has comparative advantage at doing industrial R & D, as most larger manufacturing enterprises have, there is a tendency toward considerable self-sufficiency in developing one's own specialized production technology. When that comparative advantage is absent, as in most nonmanufacturing industries, one tends to rely heavily upon others for the technology one uses.

Government-Financed R & D

The R & D flows analyzed thus far have been those financed by the originating business enterprises. Industrial corporations also perform a substantial amount of R & D under contract, usually with the federal government reimbursing costs. Our analysis of the technology flows associated with this R & D is less complete and precise because of limitations in the facilitating patent data. The companies in our sample conducted $333 million of contract R & D in narrowly defined industries in which no government contract-related patents were recorded. This had two probable explanations: a low propensity to patent contract-related inventions (on which the patent holder's right to exclude is constrained by government license provisions) and incomplete company compliance with the requirement that patents obtained under federal contracts include notice of the contract connection. Through resort to contracting agency records, it was possible to identify a total of 325 sample company inventions originating under government contracts, but it is believed that another 75 patents eluded the search. The contract-related patents were linked to estimate the average amount of contract R & D per patent in their industry of origin, and these R & D dollars were flowed out to using sectors on the basis of the inventions' coded anticipated uses.

Table 3.3 summarizes the results. Sample companies obtained patents linked, after inflation by sampling ratios that probably underestimate the concentration of federal contract work, to contract R & D outlays of $6.77 billion. All but 16 percent of this total originated in five industry groups for which there were sufficiently many companies active to report spending details without violating confidentiality rules. Not surprisingly, the most prolific performers of federally financed R & D were the missiles and ordnance, communication equipment (i.e., radar and guidance system), and aircraft industries. Most of the technology developed thereby, at least as discerned through our analysis of patent specifications, was specific to defense and space applications (e.g., jet engine ducting applicable only to fighter-type aircraft, radars that operated at military-blocked frequencies or with special jam-proof features, semiconductors able to function in unusually severe environments). The airline industry was the largest beneficiary of specifically identifiable spillovers, especially from the development of lighter, more reliable turbojet engines. Consumer product uses embodying $158 million of federal contract R & D were also identified, in every instance from inventions that also had industrial uses. Federally supported R & D in "all other" industries yielded inventions with a higher proportion of industrial uses outside defense and space than R & D in the traditional aerospace industries. If the results of this incomplete federal

Table 3.3
Truncated federally supported industrial R & D flows matrix

Industry of origin	Federal R & D originated	Internal process R & D	43B air transport	47 defense and space	All other industrial uses
24 Engines and turbines	34	n[a]	n	11	23
29 Office equipment	336	n	n	214	122
33 Radio and communication equipment	1631	133	16	53	
34 Electronic components	202	100	n	99	3
36 Aircraft, including engines	1342	213	190	927	12
37 Guided missiles, spacecraft and ordnance	2162	448	0	1639	74
All other industries	1063	42	9	503	509
Total R & D originated	6770				
Total R & D used		936	214	4822	796

[a] n: not separately reported, but included in "all other industrial uses."

contract R & D analysis are combined with those for privately financed
R & D, we find that, of total 1974 U.S. R & D outlays amounting to
$21.5 billion ($14.7 billion company-financed and $6.8 billion federal),
$5.66 billion, or 26.4 percent, were associated with product inventions
flowing to the defense and space fields.

R & D and Productivity Growth

A principal motive for tracing R & D outlays from industries of origin
to industries of use is to understand better how R & D affects productivity
growth. The influence of R & D on productivity growth operates with a
lag. Our R & D data are for 1974, and so one should look to the late
1970s for the first signs of an effect. Data limitations and the need to
control for business cycle influences directed the main analysis toward
changes in output per worker hour over the business cycle peak-to-peak
period 1973 to 1978. Three sets of productivity data for this period, with
quite different measurement approaches and industry coverage, were
analyzed. We focus here on the results for the most comprehensive sample,
with 87 industry group observations covering virtually all of the manufacturing sector plus agriculture, crude oil and gas, railroads, air transport,
communications, and the combined electric-gas-sanitary services sector.
To obtain the productivity indexes for this sample, the current-dollar
value of an industry's sales was divided by an average price index for the
industry, usually derived from the U.S. Producer Price Index series. This
estimate of "real output" was then divided by industry hours of work
(including salaried personnel) to obtain an index of output per worker
hour. Needless to say, productivity growth comparisons based upon such
indexes can be no more reliable than the comprehensiveness of the output
value deflators (price indexes) used and the deflators' effectiveness in
tracking product quality changes.

The principal methodology was ordinary least-squares regression analysis, where ΔLP is the annual percentage change in an industry's real
output per worker hour from 1973 to 1978, ΔK is the annual percentage
change in the industry's gross constant-dollar plant and equipment/labor
ratio over the same period, PRODRD is 1974 company-financed product
R & D classified by industry of origin and divided through by 1974 origin
industry sales, and USERD is R & D (product plus process) flowed
through to industry of use and divided by using industry sales. The
USERD variable is defined under the "private good" assumption; vari-

ables constructed under a "public good" assumption had less explanatory power.

With all 87 industries included and with t-ratios given in subscripted parentheses, the fitted regression equation is

$$\Delta LP = -0.14 + 0.347 \, \Delta K + 0.289 \, PRODRD$$
$$ (3.30) (2.01)$$

$$ + 0.742 \, USERD; \hspace{4cm} (1)$$
$$ (1.89)$$

$$R^2 = 0.193.$$

Both R & D variables have positive, statistically significant coefficients, as does the capital/labor change variable.

The strength of the PRODRD variable, with a t-ratio marginally higher than the USERD variable, is surprising, since the logic underlying the technology flows matrix suggests that most productivity benefits would be realized by R & D-using, not product R & D-originating, industries. A strong product R & D-originating effect is plausible only to the extent that product innovators exercise strong monopoly power in their pricing or when there are systematic errors in measuring productivity. To test for the latter, the sample was divided (before any analyses were run) into two subsets: one for which the real output indexes used in computing productivity growth were based upon reasonably comprehensive output value deflators, and another for which the price deflator coverage was sufficiently sparse that there was reason to doubt the reliability of the computed real output and hence productivity indexes. For the 51 industry groups with "well measured" output indexes, the regression equation was as follows:

$$\Delta LP = -0.16 + 0.400 \, \Delta K - 0.182 \, PRODRD$$
$$ (2.90) (0.54)$$

$$ + 1.039 \, USERD; \hspace{4cm} (2)$$
$$ (2.53)$$

$$R^2 = 0.241.$$

Here, as expected, used R & D plays a powerful role, whereas PRODRD is statistically insignificant (with an implausible negative coefficient sign). For the 36 industry groups with "poorly measured" output indexes, the

regression equation is

$$\Delta LP = 0.08 + 0.310 \ \Delta K + 0.431 \ \text{PRODRD}$$
$$\qquad\qquad (1.82) \qquad (2.10)$$

$$+ \ 0.096 \ \text{USERD}; \qquad\qquad\qquad\qquad\qquad (3)$$
$$(0.10)$$

$$R^2 = 0.197.$$

An opposite pattern **emerges**; **used** R & D is insignificant, whereas PRODRD is significant. That the results with the poorly measured data are attributable to measurement error is suggested by the fact that when similar regressions are computed for a completely different sample using unusually high-quality productivity indexes based on physical (not value-deflated) output data, their coefficient significance pattern is the same as that of equation (2) rather than equation (3).

The R & D coefficient values in these equations can be interpreted, subject to certain caveats, as steady-state rates of return on investment in research and development. Except in equation (3), the USERD values indicate quite substantial social returns, on the order of 75 to 100 percent, for the processes and products flowing from R & D. Moreover the coefficient magnitudes are such that, if used R & D were increased by two standard deviations, annual productivity growth would rise by 1.1 to 1.5 percentage points. Thus important economic impacts are implied. Interpretation of the PRODRD coefficients is complicated by the possibility of serious measurement errors in the raw productivity data. For what they are worth, the coefficient estimates suggest private returns to product R & D (captured by the originator) in the range of 0 to 43 percent.

Additional analyses discussed more fully in [10] add further insights. Perhaps most important, in contrast to the results obtained by both myself and other scholars using highly aggregated data, there was no evidence with disaggregated industry data of a decline during the 1970s in the ability of R & D to drive productivity growth. There were also less conclusive indications that capital goods R & D has a more potent impact on productivity growth than materials R & D, and that at least some of the capital goods effect is best characterized as "embodied" in new capital investment. That is, the new technology and the capital equipment embodying it are joint and inseparable inputs into industrial production processes. Finally, dollar-denominated R & D usage variables had more explanatory power than raw patent counts, revealing the importance of weighting patents by their underlying R & D expenditures if one is to use patent data as an index of innovative output.

3.5 Conclusion

The new data presented in this article provide an unusually rich picture of the complex interdependences among industries in the process of technological change. Thus the statistics are of considerable interest in their own right. But more important, such data are vital to achieving a proper understanding of the links between technological innovation and economic progress, given the high fraction of industry R & D that is product oriented and the evidence that productivity growth, when well measured, comes from *used* R & D rather than product R & D at its point of origin.

Recognition of the importance of these linkages is widespread, and in response to the perceived need, there has been classic simultaneous invention. One approach is the work on significant British innovations by Pavitt and others at the University of Sussex [7]. Also, quite independent of my research with patents, the Canadian Patent Office has made impressive strides toward classifying by industries of origin and use a sample of Canadian patents from the 1973 to 1977 period and *all* such patents since 1978 [11]. The availability of such data should permit substantial progress toward understanding how new technology affects productivity growth in an "open" economy heavily dependent on foreign inventions. For the United States further progress requires an extension of my data, which were unable to cover all sources and uses of new technology and which provide a snapshot for only a single year. The obvious direction for improvement lies in classifying by origin industry (linked to FTC R & D data) and using industries all patented inventions, domestic and foreign, for additional years. This could be done either by specially trained Patent Office examiners, as in Canada, or by having inventors and their attorneys—the individuals in the best position to know—provide appropriate origin and use information. One hesitates to recommend still another government data collection program in a world of budgetary cutbacks and paperwork rebellions. Yet such a step, which would increase the costs of patent processing only trivially, would provide significant new leverage on the productivity growth question.

Notes

The research underlying this paper was conducted under National Science Foundation Grant PRA-7826526. Use is made of data collected under the Federal Trade Commission's line of business program. A review has been conducted to ensure that the figures in this paper do not disclose individual company line of business data.

References

1. The exceptions are Nestor E. Terleckyj, *Effects of R & D on the Productivity Growth of Industries: An Exploratory Study* (National Planning Association, 1974); and two other analyses using the Terleckyj indexes, Edwin Mansfield, Basic Research and Productivity Increase in Manufacturing, *American Economic Review* 70 (December 1980): 867, and John W. Kendrick and Elliot S. Grossman, *Productivity in the United States: Trends and Cycles* (Johns Hopkins University Press, Baltimore Md., 1980), pp. 100–111. See also Edwin Mansfield et al., Social and Private Rates of Return from Industrial Innovations, *Quarterly Journal of Economics* 91 (May.1977): 221.

2. Jacob Schmookler, *Invention and Economic Growth* (Harvard University Press, Cambridge, Ma., 1966), ch. 8.

3. F. M. Scherer, Research and Development Expenditures and Patenting, American Patent Law Association *Quarterly Journal* 10, nos. 1 and 2 (1982): 60.

4. U.S. Federal Trade Commission, *Statistical Report: Annual Line of Business Report; 1974* (Washington, D.C., September 1981).

5. For further methodological details, see F. M. Scherer, Using Linked Patent and R & D Data to Measure Inter-Industry Technology Flows, paper presented at the National Bureau of Economic Research conference on R & D, Patents, and Productivity, October 1981.

6. U.S. National Science Board, *Science Indicators: 1978* (Washington, D.C., 1979), p. 201.

7. Keith Pavitt, Some Characteristics of Innovative Activities in British Industry, manuscript, Science Policy Research Unit, University of Sussex, 7 January 1982, pp. 11–12.

8. It is for such specific-use inventions that one is likely to find the kind of originator-user locus indeterminacies and coordination emphasized by von Hippel. That is, an invention might be made as an internal process by the ultimate user, as a product by a specialized supplier to that user, or through a coordinated effort by both parties. See Eric von Hippel, The Dominant Role of Users in the Scientific Instrument Process, *Research Policy* 5 (July 1976): 212, and Appropriability of Innovation Benefit as a Predictor of the Functional Locus of Innovation, working paper, Sloan School of Management, Massachusetts Institute of Technology, June 1979. Although no systematic evidence is available from our study, it was clear from patent specifications that some "product" inventions resulted from a cooperative effort with users.

9. U.S. Department of Commerce, Bureau of Economic Analysis, *The Detailed Input-Output Structure of the U.S. Economy: 1972*, vol. 1 (Washington, D.C., 1979), and P. E. Coughlin et al., New Structures and Equipment by Using Industries, 1972, *Survey of Current Business* (July 1980): 45–54.

10. F. M. Scherer, Inter-Industry Technology Flows and Productivity Growth, *Review of Economics and Statistics* 64 (November 1982): 627.

11. E. D. Ellis, Canadian Patent Data Base: The Philosophy, Construction and Uses of the Canadian Patent Data Base PATDAT, *World Patent Information* 3 (1981): 13–18.

II THE THEORY OF MARKET STRUCTURE AND INNOVATION

At the forefront of my thoughts as I exited graduate school, having studied industrial organization with Jesse Markham, one of Schumpeter's most enthusiastic students, were the Schumpeterian conjectures concerning market conditions conducive to technological innovation. The argument that the *expectation* of a monopoly position stimulated R & D investment underlay my early work on the patent system. That notion was of course not new to Schumpeter. Much more novel was his suggestion that an *existing* monopoly position was an ideal platform for undertaking innovations. Early participants in the ensuing debate—such as J. K. Galbraith (1952, ch. 7) and Henry Villard (1958)—argued that oligopoly market structures were more conducive to innovation than either monopoly or pure competition. But there had emerged in the debate precious little that could pass for "theory" by the standards accepted in other parts of the economics discipline. The main early theoretical contributions—by Fellner (1951), Arrow (1962), and Horowitz (1963)—all attempted to determine the maximum amount a firm could afford to invest in R & D, given the size of the market and the pricing behavior adopted under diverse assumptions. Only Horowitz paid any attention to the interactions among firms in their R & D rivalry, and none had an explicit model of R & D investment behavior.

There were two main directions in which such theory building could proceed. One was to investigate how rivalry affected the quality goals R & D decision makers set—for example, how far cost-reduction efforts were to be carried, or how large an advance to seek in the technical attributes of a new product. The other was to ask how rapidly firms move toward a given set of quality objectives. Obviously, it would be desirable to treat both variables simultaneously, but first steps demanded a less ambitious approach. My weapons systems and civilian sector innovation case studies convinced me that the timing question was the crucial one. They also provided a key to the needed breakthrough. In one of our early case studies, J. W. Schaefer, "inventor" of the Nike Ajax missile system concept and now (1983) a Bell Telephone Laboratories executive, suggested that there was for any given R & D project a trade-off between time and cost: the pace of development can be accelerated, but normally only at increasing total development cost. Further case studies revealed that different systems developments, military and civilian, resolved this time-cost trade-off in strikingly different ways, and that quite generally, the more "urgent" the need was, the more one accepted higher costs to save time. M. J. Peck and I articulated the concept of the time-cost trade-off function further and were able in our 1962 book to show that the deeper the stream of anticipated benefits from a successful R & D project, the faster was the optimal development schedule. This was essentially a "game against nature" solution, which we knew did not correctly characterize the rivalrous cases we had studied. But the rivalry problem was left for a later assault, that is, when I finished my graduate studies.

Before that effort could proceed, a preliminary hurdle had to be cleared. There was considerable skepticism concerning the time-cost trade-off concept, particularly from the Rand Corporation, where an extraordinarily talented group of economists had found a common interest in questions of research and development strategy. In 1961 Richard Nelson published an important article denying the empirical significance of the trade-off under technological uncertainty (p. 362) and setting up as his objective minimization of *either* expected cost or expected time. I was convinced this approach missed the central point. One reason was my work on the simple calculus of optimal time-cost trade-offs. In addition our group had studied the innovation (Bell Telephone Laboratories' TH microwave radio relay system) Nelson held up as an example of successful development strategy. Unlike the Rand group, however, we had also made a comparative study of Bell's earlier TD-2 system development, in which a quite different, much faster development strategy had been pursued. The reason for the strategy differences lay in the payoffs, not in the intrinsic technological uncertainties: without TD-2, the Bell System risked losing a whole lucrative market, whereas delays in the availability of TH only meant foregoing modest potential operating cost savings. To show that the logic of time-cost trade-offs held up under conditions of high technological uncertainty, I wrote the selection reprinted as chapter 4.

The next and crucial step entailed "inventing" a plausible but tractable formulation of how the payoffs from product R & D are affected by inter-firm rivalry. Product R & D rather than cost-saving process R & D was the focus because most industrial R & D was product oriented and also because, for reasons suggested by Lange (1943), process R & D seemed from observation to be more frequently a straightforward game against nature without important rivalry attributes. The selection reprinted as chapter 5 was my basic solution to the problem. Presented at the March 1966 conference culminating our Ford Foundation program, it is the scholarly contribution in which I take the greatest pride. Its good features, and especially its attempt to blend rigor and realism, must speak for themselves. Rather than dwelling on them, I must unfurl some loose ends and (alas) errors.

The limitation emphasized by conference discussant Carl Kaysen was the lack of any explicit treatment of uncertainty. As chapter 4 shows, there is no inherent reason why uncertainty cannot be introduced. The problem was simply that the mathematics seemed formidable, especially if a realistic payoff structure was to be retained. Important advances came first in a series of papers of unusual technical virtuosity by Kamien and Schwartz between 1971 and 1978. More recently, many other scholars have published papers in which uncertainty plays a prominent role, sometimes with a rich treatment of market structural relations at the same time.

Another loose end was my arbitrary assumption that development begins at time $t = 0$ whereas, as I acknowledged in chapter 5, firms might prefer to delay initiating a development until exogenous technical progress has occurred. Yoram Barzel made the first important advance on this problem (1968). His method was to ignore the time-cost trade-off relationship and analyze the problem of firms deciding at what moment to seize a development possibility whose cost was fixed at a moment in time but declined over time. My own efforts to rise to the bait of note 11, chapter 5, developing a "more general dynamic theory" with technology-push and demand-pull effects, are summarized best by the selection in chapter 6, which was presented at an exchange symposium in Moscow. It draws among other things upon Barzel's insights. However, no conclusive integration of technology-push, demand-pull, and time-cost trade-offs was achieved. The problem is, if a firm had sufficient foresight and market control, it would always start its development early enough to proceed at a leisurely, low (but not minimum) cost pace and still maximize profits in the Barzel monopoly sense. But if there is rivalry, the firm is almost certain to be preempted if it pursues such a strategy. Rivalry may accelerate both the starting date and the speed of development so much that innovators' profits are wiped out. However, the zero-profit result depends on both the time that has elapsed allowing benefit functions to diverge dynamically from cost functions and the number of rivals, and with small numbers of rivals, sudden transitions from one behavioral regime to another can occur.

One way out is to go to a full-blown equilibrium model in which the solution is forced to the zero-profit condition, letting the number of rivals and perhaps also their pricing behavior as well as R & D outlays be endogenous. This has been the method of recent work, such as by Loury (1979) and Dasgupta and Stiglitz (1980). It is reasonable enough to suppose that "large" new product markets (large in the sense that benefits under monopoly greatly exceed development costs) will attract more R & D rivals than "small" markets, all else equal. However, the notion of an R & D rivalry converging inexorably to a symmetric zero-profit equilibrium stands Schumpeter, who above all emphasized disequilibrium and the role of entrepreneurship, on his head. It is also so patently at odds with what one observes in the real world that I find it too much to swallow. Surely here, any good Schumpeterian must interject, "theory" may have to step aside for "history" in the form of structural or behavioral criteria nominating one firm or another to take the lead. On this problem in a more general context, see Richardson (1960). Or alternatively, one might attack the problem of structural endogeneity at an acceptable level of realism with the kind of rich evolutionary (i.e., nonmaximizing) model pioneered by Nelson and Winter (1982, chs. 12–14).

My 1967 rivalry paper assumed development cost functions to be independent of other firms' behavior. This assumption could be wrong if technical problem solving by the first innovator eases the task of later imitators. That possibility was first explored, and the logic of "fast second" strategies made clear, by Baldwin and Childs (1969). Later works have observed that development possibility functions shift not only because of exogenous technical change but also as a result of prior development efforts, so that chainlike dynamic cost interdependences exist. The chain problem is very difficult mathematically, but progress on it has been made, most notably by von Weizsäcker (1980).

That there must be an explicit functional relationship between R & D outlays and resulting end product quality was postulated by Peck and me (1962, p. 469) and numerous others. However, the first to do anything interesting with the concept from a Schumpeterian perspective was Nordhaus (1969, ch. 5). His theory of optimal patent life was the seminal contribution in a sequence that now has experienced quite rich elaboration. My own contribution, chapter 7, was modest. It did two things. It translated Nordhaus's rather nonintuitive mathematics into more understandable geometry. And more important, it extended a key finding of my 1967 paper to Nordhaus's problem. In evaluating incentives for R & D, two quite distinct phenomena must be weighed: whether the expected value of quasi rents less R & D costs is positive, so that the firm has an incentive to invest, and whether *marginal* changes in market parameters (e.g., the number of rivals, their development speed, or the length of a patent's life) marginally stimulate or retard more active innovative effort. By analyzing a special case, Nordhaus was able to ignore the first condition. My paper identified other cases where the first (positive profit expectation) condition may be more important than marginal stimulus effects.

An important parameter in my 1967 model was the permanent erosion coefficient ε, which governed the extent to which the first firm onto the market with a new product gains a lasting market share advantage over later imitators. More recent empirical research has shown that this "first-mover" advantage can be extremely important in terms of both market shares and sustainable price premiums, especially in such fields as pharmaceuticals. See Bond and Lean (1977). Schmalensee (1982) has pioneered a rigorous explanation of why such first-mover advantages persist. One implication is that innovation may prove profitable even in the absence of patent protection. The theory of optimal patent protection originated by Nordhaus must still be extended to take into account first-mover advantages other than winning the race to the Patent Office.

In my view, the least satisfactory aspect of my 1967 rivalry article is the discussion of welfare implications. Indeed, parts are simply wrong. There are two main problems. First, the analysis should have weighed the *marginal* cost of accelerated development against the marginal social benefit from earlier product availability. More important, it sidestepped the fact that, for rivalry to have its schedule-accelerating effect, it may be necessary to pay the marginal cost not only of accelerated development but also of duplicating (or multiplying) the costs of development relative to what they would be under monopoly. More recent work has put great emphasis on this cost of duplication, which can make rivalry much less attractive on balance than my article intimated (see, e.g., Loury 1979, Dasgupta and Stiglitz 1980).

Further reflection has led me to conclude that the pure duplication models go too far in the opposite direction. Modern marketing theory, recognizing the advantages of a first mover and the characteristically poor showing of latecomer "me too" products, advises firms to differentiate their products by seeking market segments not yet served by existing or anticipated rival products. To be sure, duplication may occur inadvertently, but more often than not, even new products introduced simultaneously tend to have differentiating characteristics. To the extent that this is true, the correct basis for welfare judgments is a spatial differentiation model, not a "me too" model. My contribution to the burgeoning literature of that genre is chapter 8.

That "product variety" model will win no first-mover prizes. Most of its conclusions can be found in earlier papers by Lancaster (1975), Archibald and Rosenbluth (1975), and Spence (1976), among others. It does, however, have two main differentiating characteristics. Most of the literature on optimal product variety has been written at such a high level of abstraction that it is difficult to tell what is driving the results. By casting the analysis in a framework of simple surplus integrals over a geometric product characteristics space, I have tried to make the whole business more intelligible. Equally important, my objective, consistent with my Schumpeterian bias toward a marriage of theory with history and statistics, was to apply the analysis to an actual case. With an explicit grounding in potentially observable demand and cost functions, the theory becomes operational. A contribution by Steven Wildman (1984) has made the link to conventional demand analysis even more explicit and in the process pointed out an error I committed in my estimate of how cereal price and profit increases affected total welfare.

Near the top of the agenda of work still needed is merging the theory of optimal product variety with the theory of R & D project acceleration and "duplication" under rivalry. Bringing together two strains of analysis, each mathematically complex if an acceptable degree of realism is to be maintained, poses formidable difficulties. Still in view of the ingenuity economists have displayed in advancing the relevant theory over the past fifteen years, I am confident the job will be done.

References

G. C. Archibald and Gideon Rosenbluth. The "New" Theory of Consumer Demand and Monopolistic Competition. *Quarterly Journal of Economics* (November 1975): 569–590.

Kenneth J. Arrow. Economic Welfare and the Allocation of Resources for Invention. In the National Bureau of Economic Research conference report, *The Rate and Direction of Inventive Activity*. Princeton University Press: 1962, pp. 619–625.

Yoram Barzel. Optimal Timing of Innovations. *Review of Economics and Statistics* (August 1968): 348–355.

W. L. Baldwin and G. L. Childs. The Fast Second and Rivalry in Research and Development. *Southern Economic Journal* (July 1969): 18–24.

Ronald Bond and David Lean. *Sales, Promotion, and Product Differentiation in Two Prescription Drug Markets.* Federal Trade Commission staff report. Washington D.C.: 1977.

Partha Dasgupta and Joseph Stiglitz. Uncertainty, Industrial Structure, and the Speed of R & D. *Bell Journal of Economics* (Spring 1980): 1–28.

William Fellner. The Influence of Market Structure on Technological Progress. *Quarterly Journal of Economics* (November 1951): 560–567.

J. K. Galbraith. *American Capitalism.* Boston: Houghton Mifflin, 1952.

Ira Horowitz. Research Inclinations of a Cournot Oligopolist. *Review of Economic Studies* (June 1963): 128–130.

Morton I. Kamien and Nancy Schwartz. Expenditure Patterns for Risky R & D Projects. *Journal of Applied Probability* (March 1971): 60–73.

Morton I. Kamien and Nancy Schwartz. Timing of Innovations under Rivalry. *Econometrica* (January 1972): 43–60.

Morton I. Kamien and Nancy Schwartz. Potential Rivalry, Monopoly Profits, and the Pace of Inventive Activity. *Review of Economic Studies* (October 1978): 547–557.

Kelvin Lancaster. Socially Optimal Product Differentiation. *American Economic Review* (September 1975): 567–585.

Oscar Lange. A Note on Innovations. *Review of Economic Statistics* (February 1943): 19–25.

Glenn C. Loury. Market Structure and Innovation. *Quarterly Journal of Economics* (August 1949): 395–410.

Richard R. Nelson. Uncertainty, Learning, and the Economics of Parallel Research and Development Projects. *Review of Economics and Statistics* (November 1961): 351–368.

Richard R. Nelson and Sidney Winter. *An Evolutionary Theory of Economic Change.* Cambridge Ma.: Belknap, 1982.

William D. Nordhaus. *Invention, Growth, and Welfare.* Cambridge, Ma.: The MIT Press, 1969.

M. J. Peck and F. M. Scherer. *The Weapons Acquisition Process: An Economic Analysis.* Boston: Harvard Business School Division of Research, 1962.

G. B. Richardson. *Information and Investment.* New York: Oxford University Press, 1960.

Richard Schmalensee. Product Differentation Advantages of Pioneering Brands. *American Economic Review* (June 1982): 349–365.

Michael Spence. Product Selection, Fixed Costs and Monopolistic Competition. *Review of Economic Studies* (June 1976): 217–235.

Henry Villard. Competition, Oligopoly, and Research. *Journal of Political Economy* (December 1958): 483–497.

C. C. von Weizsäcker. *Barriers to Entry.* New York: Springer-Verlag, 1980.

Steven S. Wildman. A Note on Measuring the Surplus Attributable to Differentiated Products. *Journal of Industrial Economics* (1984), in press.

4 Time-Cost Trade-offs in Uncertain Empirical Research Projects

4.1 Introduction

Recently the relationship between time and cost in research and development projects has attracted considerable interest. Empirical estimation of the time-cost trade-off function is exceptionally difficult, since R & D projects can seldom be replicated under precisely controlled conditions. PERT-type analytic studies have suggested a convex relationship, with total cost decreasing at a decreasing rate as time is increased.[1] Most of the results presented thus far, however, depend upon an initial basic assumption that diminishing returns set in as more work force is applied to individual project tasks. While plausible, this is surely not the only and perhaps not the most important mechanism causing cost to vary with time. Notably, the role of technological uncertainty cannot be overlooked.

In this paper the relationship between time and cost in what may be called uncertain empirical research and development projects is explored. Specifically, we consider situations where a large number of potential technical approaches can be identified and where several of these approaches may lead to successful solutions, even though *ex ante* no single approach promises anything close to certainty of success. Many illustrations come to mind. Edison, for example, is said to have tested 1,600 different filament materials before finding one that satisfied his incandescent lamp requirements, although his carbon filament solution was not the only one that ultimately proved workable. The discovery of aureomycin followed testing of several thousand microorganisms, but later work disclosed a whole class of organic molecules with roughly similar therapeutic properties. Numerous different materials were tried in the search for suitable Jupiter IRBM reentry body ablative coatings and for a high-strength, low-weight Polaris rocket motor casing. Similarly, in the Polaris program a variety of approaches to the problem of thrust vectoring were pursued, and several acceptable solutions emerged.

Given the difficulty of ascertaining actual time-cost trade-off relationships empirically, an effort is made here to proceed as far as possible on the basis of elemental a priori assumptions. Qualifications associated with real-world complications will be added later. The following greatly simplifying assumptions will be made initially: first, we assume that each approach to a technical problem has the same prior subjective probability of success p, where $0 < p < 1$. From this, we define $q = 1 - p$ to be the

Source: *Naval Research Logistics Quarterly* 13 (March 1966): 71–82.

probability of failure for a given approach. Second, we assume that the success probability of any specific approach is independent of the number and sequence of other approaches pursued. Third, it is assumed that any successful approach will solve the required problem, and that additional successes are redundant. Fourth, we assume that each approach has the same dollar cost M of execution, which is independent of the number and sequence of other approaches pursued. Finally, it is assumed that each fully staffed approach normally takes exactly one time period to execute.[2]

4.2 Setting the Number of Approaches

Under these assumptions, the probability of overall project success is defined by:

$$P(p, N) = 1 - q^N, \tag{1}$$

where N is the number of approaches executed. The more approaches pursued, the higher the probability of overall project success will be. To decide how large N will be, one must weigh the expected cost M of each additional approach against the expected gain from pursuing that approach. If B is the discounted present value of the benefits realizable upon successful solution of the technical problem, the expected value $E(B)$ of a project with N approaches is $P(p, N)B = (1 - q^N)B$. As a first approximation (to be modified later), expected profits will be maximized by authorizing additional approaches as long as the cost M of the Nth approach is less than the incremental gain from conducting that approach, which is defined by:[3]

$$\Delta E(B) = [(1 - q^N) - (1 - q^{N-1})]B = q^{N-1}(1 - q)B. \tag{2}$$

For any given q and B, $\Delta E(B)$ must decline as N increases. For any given q and N, $\Delta E(B)$ increases with B. Therefore the greater are the benefits B realizable upon successful project completion, the more approaches it will pay to authorize.[4]

4.3 Properties of the Time-Cost Trade-off Function

Let us now assume provisionally that the number of approaches authorized N and hence the probability of overall project success $P(p, N)$ is decided on. It is still necessary to determine how the execution of those N approaches will be phased over time. One possibility is to run the approaches serially, that is, one after the other. Another is to run all the approaches concurrently in the first period, guaranteeing project completion (with probability $P(p, N)$ of success) by the end of that period. Many other distributions are possible when N and the number of periods are fairly large.

Three quantities vary with the choice of a time sequence of approaches: (1) the number of periods T required to execute all N approaches, and hence the planned time before the probability of project success $P(p, N)$ is expected to attain its full anticipated value; (2) the expected value $E(T)$ of the time required to achieve a successful solution or terminate the project (the latter after N unsuccessful approaches); and (3) the expected cost $E(C)$ of the project. These three are functionally related, defining two different time-cost trade-off functions: the relationship between T and $E(C)$, and the relationship between $E(T)$ and $E(C)$. Let us consider first the relationship between T and $E(C)$.

Plainly, if the N approaches are distributed over T periods, T periods are required before the anticipated probability of project success $P(p, N)$ is assured in an *ex ante* sense. For example, if 10 approaches, each with p of 0.20, are to be pursued, one can expect the overall success probability of 0.89 to be attained one period hence if all 10 approaches are run concurrently in the first period, but only 10 periods hence if the approaches are run serially. The expected cost of project execution must be $10M$ in the fully concurrent strategy, since all 10 approaches will have been run before any approach is completed under the present assumptions. But expected cost must be lower if the series approach is pursued. This is so because success *may* come in an early period, making it unnecessary to continue with the remaining, originally planned approaches.

To study the properties of the function linking T and $E(C)$ further, let us begin with a special assumption: the N planned approaches are to be distributed evenly over the planned project duration T so that in any single period N/T approaches will be executed.[5] If the cost per approach is M, expected cost as a function of T is given by

$$E(C) = \frac{NM}{T} + q^{N/T}\left(\frac{NM}{T}\right) + \cdots + (q^{N/T})^{N-1}\left(\frac{NM}{T}\right). \tag{3}$$

Letting t be a running integral time variable, this simplifies to

$$E(C) = \sum_{t=0}^{T-1} (q^{N/T})^t \left(\frac{NM}{T}\right). \tag{4}$$

Now the larger T is, the smaller the cost per period NM/T will be, but the more periods there will be in the summation. If the $(q^{N/T})$ term were equal to 1.0, which is possible only when $N/T = 0$, $E(C)$ would be constant with respect to T, since increases in T would simply mean dividing NM into T equal parts and summing T of those parts. $E(C)$ can increase with T only when $(q^{N/T}) > 1$, which is impossible, since $0 < q < 1$ in any uncertain approach worth trying. It must decrease with T when $(q^{N/T}) < 1$. And this must normally be true, since N must be positive and T is not likely to be infinite in any research project worth conducting. Therefore expected project cost $E(C)$ must decline as T is increased. Or conversely, the more rapidly the project is to be conducted, the higher its expected cost will be.

If the probability of overall project success $P(p, N)$ is to be held constant, q and N must be held constant. Given q and N constant, the greater T is, the smaller N/T is and so the closer we approximate the constant cost case of $q^{N/T} = 0$. Thus as T increases, $E(C)$ decreases, but at a diminishing rate. This proves that for the special case of approaches distributed evenly over time, the T, $E(C)$ trade-off function is strictly convex to its origin. Computed trade-off functions for $P(p, N)$ of 0.99, 0.95, 0.90, and 0.80, each assuming an individual approach success probability p of 0.05 with a cost per approach of $1,000, are illustrated in figure 4.1.[6]

Unfortunately for the cause of simplicity, the equal-number-of-approaches-per-time-period scheduling strategy is generally not the most efficient strategy if one is interested primarily in achieving a certain probability of project success $P(p, N)$ by time T. Where N_i is the number of approaches scheduled for the ith time period, the problem of efficient scheduling in this case is to minimize the more general expected cost function:

$$E(C) = MN_1 + q^{N_1} MN_2 + \cdots + (q^{N_1 + \cdots + N_{T-1}}) MN_T \tag{5}$$

subject to the constraint

$$\sum_{i=1}^{T} N_i = N,$$

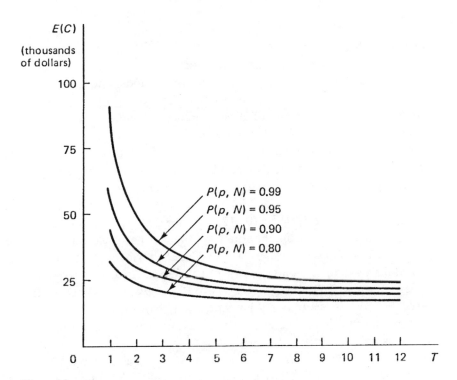

Figure 4.1
Time cost trade off curves for selected cumulative success probabilities

with N set at a level that yields the desired probability of overall project success. Under these assumptions the most efficient strategy is to schedule a greater number of approaches in each successive time period. To see this, the scheduling problem can be viewed as a problem of allocating resources (N approaches) to T activities (periods). Cost is generally minimized in such a case with an allocation that lets each activity come as close as possible (within limits imposed by the integral number of projects) to having the same incremental cost.[7] In the present instance, where ΔN_i is the marginal allocation of resources to the ith period, expected marginal costs are equalized when:

$$M\Delta N_1 q^0 = M\Delta N_2 q^{N_1} = \cdots = M\Delta N_T(q^{N_1 + \cdots + N_{T-1}}). \qquad (6)$$

Since the M's cancel out, and since each successive q term is smaller than its predecessor, each successive ΔN_i term must be larger to preserve the equality. And since this must be true for any N (i.e., at any overall level of resource allocation), each successive period i must have a higher total allocation N_i (the sum of its marginal allocations ΔN_i) than the preceding period $i-1$. In common sense terms this means that when interested in achieving success by the end of two or more periods, one saves the bulk of the trials for later periods, hoping that the few early trials will yield a success making the expense of later approaches unnecessary.

A numerical example of equation (5) was computed by dynamic programming methods [2, 14–18]. A 0.05 individual approach success probability was assumed, N was set at 60 to yield an overall project success probability of 0.95, and optimal schedules were computed for T from two through six periods. The most efficient six-period schedule was found to require a 6, 7, 8, 10, 12, 17 time pattern of approaches—a substantial departure from the equal-approaches-per-period strategy. The computation, however, also revealed that normally this additional scheduling sophistication does not buy a particularly large reduction in costs. For $p = 0.05$ and $N = 60$, the optimal two-period schedule has expected costs $E(C)$ only 5.9 percent lower than the equal-approaches-per-period schedule. The percentage saving from optimal scheduling declines as T increases; thus with $T = 6$, the optimal strategy yields an $E(C)$ only 3.3 percent less than the equal-approaches strategy.[8]

Recognition that $E(C)$ is minimized for any T by scheduling more approaches in later than in earlier periods does not alter the previous conclusion about the time-cost trade-off function's convexity. For the $T = 1$ case, there can be no difference in scheduling strategies, and so $E(C)$ is unaltered. But as T increases, strategies superior to the equal-approaches method can be found. It follows that expected cost must decrease as T increases even more under the efficient strategy than under the equal-approaches strategy of equation (4). And since the percentage gain from efficient as opposed to equal-approaches scheduling declines as t increases, the convex curvature must be more pronounced with the efficient strategy.

Convexity of the trade-off function is also preserved when all costs are discounted to present value by a multiplier such as $1/(1 + r)^t$, where r is the appropriate interest rate. The greater T is, the more the cost of the last period's approaches will be discounted, and so discounted expected cost must decrease as T increases. But because the second derivative of the discount multiplier with respect to $t = T$ is positive, the rate of decrease in cost must decline as T increases.

In sum, under the assumptions set forth thus far, we find that expected project cost $E(C)$ decreases at a declining rate with increases in the number of periods T over which the project's technical approaches are distributed.

The task remains of deducing the properties of the function relating expected time and expected cost. This is perhaps a more empirically meaningful relationship; decision makers are probably concerned more about the expected or average length of time to project completion than they are with the maximum time T required to reach a predetermined confidence level $P(p, N)$, assuming the worst possible luck in early approaches. "Project completion" in this context means either the achievement of a successful approach or abandonment of the project after N unsuccessful trials. Expected time to project completion $E(T)$ is defined as

$$E(T) = 1 + q^{N_1} + \cdots + q^{N_1 + \cdots + N_{T-1}}. \tag{7}$$

Intuitively, $E(T)$ is the sum of the units of time for each of the T periods, each unit deflated by the probability that a prior success will have made that period's effort unnecessary.

Since $E(T)$ increases monotonically with T, given N and q, the function relating $E(C)$ and $E(T)$ must have a shape similar to the function relating $E(C)$ and T. The values of the $E(C)$, $E(T)$ relationship are simply shifted nearer the $E(C)$ axis for all values of $E(T) > 1$. Therefore $E(C)$ must decrease as $E(T)$ increases, although the fall in $E(C)$ per unit of $E(T)$ will be more rapid than the fall in $E(C)$ per unit of T. And as in previous cases, the decline in $E(C)$ as $E(T)$ increases must occur at a diminishing rate.[9]

4.4 Modifications of the Basic Model

The time-cost trade-off functions studied thus far have been based on assumptions that obviously violate reality through oversimplification. Most fundamental have been the assumptions of equal success probabilities for each approach, equal costs per approach, independence of approach success probabilities and costs, and redundancy of second and subsequent successes.[10] Let us consider now whether the time-cost trade-off function's convexity is preserved when these assumptions are relaxed.

If the probability of success p varies from approach to approach, the conclusion that $E(C)$ decreases at a declining rate as $E(T)$ increases remains unaltered. The principal change is that the time savings attainable by increasing $E(C)$ will be less than in a comparable equal-success-probabilities case. To illustrate, we may compare two projects, one with N approaches whose failure probabilities q are all equal and the other with N approaches whose failure probabilities $q_1, \ldots, q_N$ are unequal. Let the overall probability of project success be held constant; that is, let

$$1 - q^N = 1 - \prod_{i=1}^{N} q_i.$$

Assume also that the cost per approach is constant in both cases. If in each situation all N approaches are scheduled concurrently for the first period, $E(T) = 1$ in both cases. If, on the other hand, one wishes to minimize expected cost, the approaches must be scheduled serially. In the unequal probabilities case it will furthermore be advantageous to schedule the approach with the highest success probability first, and so on. Since the probability that approaches in any subsequent period will have to be executed must be lower in the unequal probabilities case than in the equal probabilities case, $E(T)$ for the minimum-cost serial strategy with unequal probabilities must also be lower.[11] Thus the $E(C)$, $E(T)$ trade-off function will initially have a steeper slope in the unequal probabilities case, but it still must be of the general convex form illustrated in figure 4.1.

The same conclusion applies when the costs of different approaches, or both costs and success probabilities, vary from approach to approach. Here the analysis becomes much more complicated, since an unusual nonlinear integer programming problem must be solved. But as long as at least some approaches may be deferred to later periods, $E(C)$ must decline as $E(T)$ increases. This is so quite generally because, whenever the probability of incurring a cost can be reduced by deferring the planned incurrence of that cost, expected cost will be reduced, even though expected time to incurrence of all planned costs must be increased.

A third modification in the direction of greater realism is to assume that the probability of success or the cost of any given approach is related in some systematic way to the execution of previously executed approaches, that is, that learning takes place. Each approach carried out may, for instance, raise the probability of success for subsequent approaches or permit the identification of approaches with higher success probabilities. It is not necessary to explore specific Markov process models of this phenomenon to see that expected cost must continue to be inversely related to expected time. If benefits are to be realized through learning, two things are necessary: at least one approach must be scheduled for the first period, and there must be approaches scheduled for later periods whose subjective success probabilities will be enhanced or whose costs will be reduced by the prior experience. No learning is assumed to take place with the minimum-time strategy, with all approaches scheduled concurrently during the first period.[12] Only as trials are deferred into later periods, increasing $E(T)$, can the cost-reducing (and to some extent also time-reducing) benefits of learning be reaped. Therefore $E(C)$ must decline as $E(T)$ increases. What learning does is shift the curves such as those in figure 4.1 to the left for values of $E(T)$ (on the horizontal axis) greater than 1.

A fourth possibility is that the success probabilities of individual approaches, or their costs, may be interdependent within a single time period. Beneficial cross-fertilization of ideas may occur between concurrently scheduled approaches; specialized equipment or talent may be available on favorable terms only if some critical scale of concurrently executed approaches is exceeded; or incentives for vigorous creative effort may be enhanced as the number of competing approaches is increased. Any of these influences might cause approach success probabilities to rise or approach costs to fall as one moves from serial toward some concurrent scheduling. As a result there may be a tendency for $F(C)$ actually to fall as $E(T)$ is decreased within certain limits, notably, within the range of relatively high $E(T)$ values. The final result depends on the strength of these tendencies compared to the strength of the opposing probabilistic tendencies explored in the section entitled "Properties of the Time-Cost Trade-off Function." This is essentially an empirical question on which relatively little evidence is available. However, there are a priori grounds for believing that the forces causing $E(C)$ to decline with $E(T)$ are not overpowering. Cross-fertilization over time (e.g., interactions following from learning) is probably more effective than cross-fertilization within a single time period. Specialized talent can often be hired advantageously on a consulting basis, and independent research organizations offer access to special experimental equipment. I have argued elsewhere [8, pp. 44–49] that the incentive benefits of competition reach a peak with relatively few competing R & D projects and probably decline when more projects vie for a single prize. And when approaches to a technical problem are pursued concurrently within the confines of a single organization, there is a propensity for all to hew to a fairly narrow conceptual line favored by the organization's professional leaders.[13] If promising but unconventional approaches are thereby excluded from the menu, the overall probability of success will fall and expected cost to successful completion will rise as a result of concurrent scheduling. In short, though institutional and organizational factors may well cause the time-cost function to bend back upward beyond some value of $E(T)$, in contrast to the continuously declining configuration shown in figure 4.1, it is not likely that cost will become a continuously increasing function of time.

Finally, we must relax the assumption that only the first successful solution obtained in a multiple-approach project is not redundant. If many approaches are pursued concurrently, more than one success may emerge, and the quality of the solutions meeting minimum standards of success will undoubtedly vary.[14] Presumably, the more solutions meeting minimum standards one achieves, the higher will be the quality of the best solution. In this respect minimum-time strategies and series strategies cannot be completely comparable, since the concurrent execution of many or all approaches will yield more successes than will series execution of the same approaches, with project termination after the first success. Indeed, the fundamental cost-saving property of the series strategy is the opportunity it provides for avoiding additional trials after one success emerges. Potential quality variation therefore raises definite complications for the analysis given here. Nevertheless, the series approach does allow greater flexibility to forego planned future approaches once a high-quality solution is in hand, and so expected cost must continue to decrease as expected time is increased, quality being held constant. The most that can presently be said in addition is that the more important better-than-minimum quality is to the decision maker, the more advantageous concurrent scheduling is likely to be, other things being equal.

In sum, the time-cost trade-off function appears to be convex for a much broader set of assumptions than those on which the analysis in the third section was based, although in certain cases an increasing cost–increasing time relationship may set in for higher time values.

4.5 Choosing an Optimal Schedule

If the relationship between time and cost is in fact generally convex—that is, if within some range decreases in expected time to project completion can be secured only by accepting accelerating increases in expected project cost—then trade-offs between conflicting cost minimization and time minimization desires must be made. For a preliminary insight into these trade-off decisions, let us assume (risking minor errors) that expected cost $E(C_d)$, discounted to present value at an appropriate interest rate, is a smooth continuous function of expected time $E(T)$, holding the probability of overall project success $P(p, N)$ constant:

$$E(C_d) = f[E(T)|P(p,N)]. \tag{8}$$

For the range within which expected cost decreases as expected time increases, the first derivative of (8) with respect to $E(T)$ is negative. When, assuming strict convexity, the decrease in $E(C)$ occurs at a declining rate, the second derivative of (8) with respect to $E(T)$ is positive.

To determine how far expected time should be compressed by increasing expected cost, we must know how much will be gained by saving time. Typically, the benefits realizable from a successful research project will flow in for many periods after the project's completion. We may therefore approximate the benefit stream by the expression:

$$B[E(T), t] = P(p, N) \int_{E(T)}^{h} b(t)e^{-rt}\,dt, \tag{9}$$

where $b(t)$ is the instantaneous rate at which benefits are received per unit of time, h is the decision maker's horizon or the last year during which positive benefits can be reaped, and r is the interest or discount rate.[15] The conventional criterion of economic rationality calls for maximization of discounted benefits minus discounted costs: $B[E(T), t] - E(C_d)$. The first-order condition for a local maximum in this case is

$$f'[E(T)|P(p,N)] = P(p,N)b[E(T)]e^{-rT}. \tag{10}$$

Intuitively, the expected increase in benefits due to anticipating research project completion one period earlier must, at the optimum, equal the expected increase in project cost due to compressing the schedule by one period. As long as the second derivative of (8) is positive, the second-order conditions for a local maximum will normally be satisfied. If so, then the greater the $b(t)$ is in the neighborhood of the optimal $E(T)$—or, the deeper the stream of potential benefits—the lower the optimal $E(T)$ will be. In other words, the greater the payoff in future time periods contingent upon successful research project completion, the more concurrent rather than series scheduling of research approaches should be emphasized.

One final complication must now be introduced. The preceding case assumed the probability of overall project success to be given. In the second section it was tentatively suggested that $P(p, N)$ be determined by equating the expected cost of the last approach with the expected gain from conducting that approach. But this optimizing method breaks down when $E(T)$ is variable, since the total amount of benefits to be realized (equation 9) varies inversely with $E(T)$. The deeper the stream of benefits, the shorter the optimal $E(T)$ will be, *ceteris paribus*. But the shorter the $E(T)$, the longer the benefits will be reaped, and so the more approaches it will pay to authorize. And the greater the N, the higher the $P(p, N)$ will be, and so the deeper the expected (probability-weighted) stream of benefits will be. A simultaneous determination of N and T is required, unless one is willing to set N (and hence the level of confidence in eventual success) on the basis of purely subjective attitudes toward risk.

This simultaneous decision-making problem can be formulated as follows: where t is a running integral time variable, B_t is the dollar value of the benefits realizable in the tth period contingent upon success, M is the cost per approach, q is the probability of failure of each approach, N is the number of approaches, and r is the interest or discount rate. we wish to maximize net present value, defined as

$$V = \sum_{t=2}^{T} [1 - q^{N(t-1)/T}]\left(\frac{1}{1+r}\right)^t B_t + \sum_{t=T+1}^{h} (1 - q^N)\left(\frac{1}{1+r}\right)^t B_t$$
$$- \sum_{t=1}^{T} [q^{N(t-1)/T}]\left(\frac{1}{1+r}\right)^{t-1}\left(\frac{NM}{T}\right), \tag{11}$$

with respect to N and T. Since this expression is impregnable to analytic methods, a numerical simulation analysis to determine the properties of optimal solutions was executed. The value of (11) was computed for a wide range of possible combinations of N and T for each of eight benefit stream depths (assumed constant per period through 25 periods) for success probabilities of 0.01, 0.05, 0.10, and 0.20. M was assumed to equal $1,000 per approach and the discount rate r was 0.06. The results can be summarized as follows: first, for any given success probability, the optimal N increased monotonically with the value of the benefits B_t realizable per time period. No such consistent pattern was evident with respect to the optimal T's. Second, for any given q and B_t, many different combinations of N and T tended to give net present values very close to the maximum observed value. In other words, project profitability was insensitive to certain changes in the schedule variables. But third, profitability was very sensitive to changes in N/T, that is, to the number of approaches scheduled per time period. As long as the optimal N/T ratio was maintained, net present value V did not depart much from its maximum because N and T were varied together by substantial proportions away from their optimal values. Movement away from the optimal N/T ratio, on the other hand, caused a rapid decline in V.[16] Finally, the deeper the stream of benefits B_t was, given any q, the more approaches per period it was profitable to schedule. This last finding is illustrated in figure 4.2, which plots the

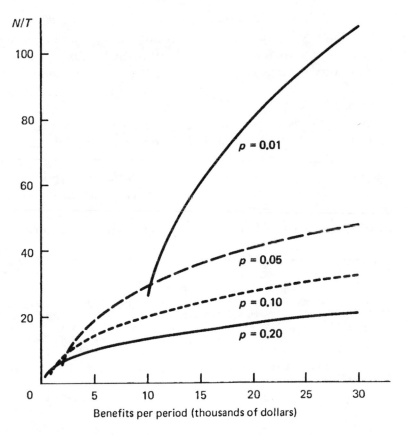

Figure 4.2
Optimal scheduling as a function of individual project success probabilities and the depth of the benefits stream

optimal N/T ratios as a function of dollar benefits per period B_t for four different approach success probabilities.

Thus we find our previous conclusion essentially unaltered in the more complex case of permitting N and T to vary simultaneously. The deeper the stream of benefits, the more approaches one should schedule per time period, and therefore the sooner successful project completion can be expected.

4.6 Implications

Even though the models discussed here are gross simplifications of the real world, they seem to suggest definite implications for the budgeting of actual research projects. Convexity of the relationship between time and cost tends to emerge from the existence of substantial empirical uncertainties. And when the time-cost trade-off function is convex, concurrent scheduling of all approaches to a technologically difficult problem is not necessarily optimal, despite frequent assertions to this effect, especially in military circles. Nor is serial scheduling necessarily a good thing. It all depends on the stream of benefits realizable through a successful solution: the deeper the stream, the more desirable concurrent scheduling is, and the shallower the stream, the more desirable the series strategy is. Even when success probabilities and payoffs are difficult to estimate (as they always are), rough and ready recognition of this simple principle will undoubtedly lead to improved allocation of scarce research resources.

Notes

The research for this paper was supported by a grant from the Inter-University Committee on the Microeconomics of Technological Change, sponsored in turn by the Ford Foundation. Use was also made of computer facilities supported in part by National Science Foundation grant NSF-GP579. I am indebted to Harold W. Kuhn and S. P. Burley for helpful comments.

1. For a survey of the PERT literature, see [6]. Other approaches to the problem are found in [5, ch. 9] and [7].

2. An alternative formulation might be to define p as the probability of success associated with a single year of research effort. This approach would not alter the results presented here.

3. If the failure probabilities are not identical for all approaches, and if each approach has the same cost, approaches should be selected in the order of lowest failure probabilities first. If costs vary from approach to approach, a nonlinear programming problem must be solved, although the basic result is similar to the solution in this simpler case.

4. It is conceivable that decision makers also value certainty of success for its own sake. Then the optimum depends not only on the cost and value of incremental approaches but also on the decision maker's subjective preferences. In this case, which will not be explored further, the number of approaches usually will exceed the number authorized in the pure profit-maximizing case.

5. Note that fractional approaches may be required; this violates an initial assumption but does not seem unreasonable. An approach may be stretched over more than one period, even though it cannot be conducted in less than one period.

6. The tendency for $E(C)$ to be less variable for lower $P(p, N)$ is quite general. For p ranging from 0.01 to 0.50, the ratio of $E(C)$ for $T = 1$ to $E(C)$ for $T = 25$ was found to be approximately 4.3 for $P(p, N) = 0.99$, 3.0 for $P(p, N) = 0.95$, 2.5 for $P(p, N) = 0.90$, 2.0 for $P(p, N) = 0.80$, and 1.4 for $P(p, N) = 0.50$. Thus the more confident of ultimate project success one seeks to be, the more sensitive one's costs are to scheduling decisions.

7. See, for example, [1, 21–22].

8. The percentage saving from optimal scheduling increases rapidly as higher success probabilities $P(p, N)$ are sought. For instance, the saving jumps to about 16 percent in the two-period case if N is increased to 100, letting $P(p, N) = 0.994$.

9. It is appropriate once again to ask, Is there a strategy better than the equal-approaches-per-period strategy? That is, is there a strategy maintaining the same value of $E(T)$ with a lower $E(C)$? The problem is one of minimizing $E(C)$, subject to N and also to $E(T)$ (as defined in equation (7)) being held constant. The two-period case of this problem turns out to be overdetermined. Cases for $T > 2$ are determinate but too complicated to yield much in the way of analytic insights. Numerical trials involving many different scheduling strategies for the $N = 60$ case suggested that the equal-approaches strategy is inferior to a strategy that has the number of approaches scheduled in successive periods decline slightly. The difference in costs is quite small, however.

10. The assumption that approaches must be conducted in exactly one time period has already been relaxed in note 5. It does, however, raise an economies-of-scale question similar to the one to be explored shortly in connection with the independence assumptions.

11. A proof of this assertion is developed easily from equation (7) and from the fact that the sum of variables (the failure probabilities) whose product is constant is minimized when the variables are equal.

12. Richard Nelson [4] has formulated a somewhat different model of uncertain hardware development in which learning occurs within each approach. He considers only the cost-reducing and time-reducing benefits of running approaches concurrently when internal learning takes place, and not the benefits of series scheduling. But in fact, when the latter possibility is introduced into his model, one finds a relationship between expected cost and expected time similar to the one obtained here. Using his numerical example, and assuming that all but terminal projects are abandoned unless a first flight is made within 20 months, $E(C)$ for the two-approach case is $84 million with series scheduling compared to $88 million with concurrent scheduling. For $N = 3$, $E(C)$ is $80.4 million with series as opposed to $91 million with concurrent scheduling. For $N = 4$, the comparable cost figures are $78.2 million and $96.5 million. Naturally, $E(T)$ increases as one moves from Nelson's concurrent strategy to series scheduling. But that is precisely the point: that trade-offs between time and cost exist and must be made.

13. The Air Force's early emphasis on heat sink reentry techniques is a glaring example.

14. For example, if $p = 0.05$ and $N = 50$, the probability that at least one success will be had is 0.92, assuming that all 50 approaches are executed. But there is also a 0.10 probability of five or more successes.

15. This formulation assumes that the project is to be initiated at $t = 0$. A different assumption would require only a slight change in notation.

16. The optimum was sensitive to changes in N/T, but not to proportional changes in N and T, because what happens in the later years of an uncertain planned project has little bearing on originally expected costs and returns. This is so because the costs and contingent returns associated with later years are discounted heavily by both the probability of success in prior periods and by the conventional interest discount term. The most important feature of optimal project scheduling appears to be that of having the correct number of approaches per time period in early periods, whose costs and contingent benefits are only weakly discounted. This clearly facilitates a dynamic, heuristic approach to R & D scheduling. One does the best one can this year, and then reoptimizes next year on the basis of new data and expectations.

References

1. Baumol, W. J. *Economic Theory and Operations Analysis.* Englewood Cliffs, N. J.: Prentice-Hall, 1961.

2. Bellman, R. E., and S. E. Dreyfus. *Applied Dynamic Programming.* Princeton, N. J.: Princeton University Press, 1962.

3. Josephson, Matthew. The Invention of the Electric Light. *Scientific American* (November 1959): 98–118.

4. Nelson, R. R. Uncertainty, Learning, and the Economics of Parallel Research and Development Projects. *Review of Economics and Statistics* (November 1961): 351–368.

5. Peck, M. J., and F. M. Scherer. *The Weapons Acquisition Process: An Economic Analysis.* Boston: Harvard Business School Division of Research, 1962.

6. Rosenbloom, R. S. Notes on the Development of Network Models for Resource Allocation in R & D Projects. *IEEE Transactions on Engineering Management* (June 1964): 58–63.

7. Scherer, F. M. Government Research and Development Programs. In *Measuring Benefits of Government Investments*, Robert Dorfman, ed. Washington, D.C.: Brookings Institution, 1965, pp. 34–56.

8. Scherer, F. M. *The Weapons Acquisition Process: Economic Incentives.* Boston: Harvard Business School Division of Research, 1964.

5 Research and Development Resource Allocation under Rivalry

Even the most casual observer cannot escape noticing the invigorating effect rivalry commonly has on industrial firms' research and development efforts. In this paper an attempt is made to analyze the phenomenon of research and development rivalry in a dynamic profit maximization framework and to predict the market structural conditions most conducive to rapid technological progress.

We begin by formulating models of the firm's optimal R & D resource allocation problem for a specific innovative project under nonrivalrous and rivalrous conditions. Alternative solutions to the duopolistic rivalry case are examined. Cournot-type reaction patterns under various assumptions about key parameters are then studied. Finally, welfare implications and opportunities for further research are identified.

5.1 Returns and Costs in the Nonrivalrous Case

Research and development projects are like other investment projects—more uncertain, to be sure, but conceptually similar. A profit-maximizing firm will conduct its R & D projects so as to maximize the surplus of expected revenues over expected costs, each stream discounted to present value. The revenues from successful R & D project completion depend upon the date of completion, the quality of the end product (related in turn to its ability to satisfy existing or latent demands), and the reactions of rivals. The costs of an R & D project depend upon the state of technology, the quality of the end product, and the speed of development. Let us begin by specifying the cost side in more detail.[1]

The research and development required to attain a given end product involves a stream of costs extending over several time periods. Empirical studies reveal that the time pattern of R & D outlays is typically bell shaped, with the peak rate of spending occurring at the time when the end product is put into production.[2] (Expenditures after production begins are mainly for debugging and improvements; these will not concern us here.) There is, however, no unique time pattern of R & D expenditures for a particular project. Management can choose to spend at higher rates in early periods, bringing the end product to the point of production and commercial introduction at an early date, or at lower rates, accepting a

Source: Reprinted from *Quarterly Journal of Economics* 81 (August 1967): 359–394. Copyright, 1967, by the President and Fellows of Harvard College.

longer span of development and hence later product introduction. When time is saved by increasing the *rate* of spending beyond a level sufficient to sustain scale economies, the *total cost* of development increases. This is so because three types of diminishing returns to time compression set in:

1. R & D is in many ways a heuristic process. Each sequential step provides knowledge useful in the next step. Time can be saved by overlapping steps, but then one takes actions (e.g., conducts tests) without all the knowledge prior steps have furnished. As more and more actions are based on a given amount of prior knowledge, more and more costly mistakes are made.

2. R & D often involves significant uncertainties about feasible solutions. Alternative technical approaches with finite success probabilities can be explored in series until a success emerges, but this takes time. Expected time to successful solution can be reduced by running technical approaches concurrently, but this increases the expected value of project cost because more approaches, which will ultimately prove unnecessary, will be run.

3. Development time can be compressed by allocating more and more technical personnel to each task, but here the classical diminishing returns tendency operates.

Consequently the relationship between the expected value of development time and the expected value of total development cost is generally convex to time and cost coordinates. As time is compressed, total development cost rises at an increasing rate.

The functional relationship between development time to product introduction T and total expected development cost C, given quality objective Q, can be written

$$C = \int_0^T c(t, T, Q) \, dt, \tag{1}$$

assuming that the development effort begins at time $t = 0$. Its convexity property requires that $\partial C/\partial T < 0$ and $\partial^2 C/\partial T^2 > 0$. For many analytic purposes this general specification is sufficient. However, for computer simulations the following explicit time-cost trade-off function was assumed:

$$C = \$10^3 \int_0^T \frac{3,500}{-25.5 + 10T - 0.5T^2} e^{-[(t-T)^2/2T] - rt} \, dt, \quad T \geq 3, \tag{2}$$

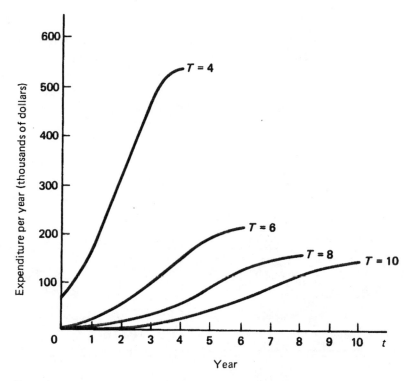

Figure 5.1
R & D spending rates as a function of expected development time

with r an appropriate discount rate. Figure 5.1 shows how the rate of spending (the integrand of equation 2) varies over time t for development schedules T of 4, 6, 8, and 10 years, assuming $r = 0$. Figure 5.2 presents a "collapsed static" view of the time—*total* cost trade-off function, again assuming a zero discount rate. Given the parameters assumed in equation (2), three years is the absolute minimum time for product introduction (with infinitely high development costs), while $T = 8.5$ years is the development schedule that minimizes undiscounted total costs.[3] These parameters were chosen to reflect as realistically as possible the circumstances in an actual development project of moderate technological difficulty.

The cost variables of equations (1) and (2), like the benefit variables in subsequent equations, must be viewed as "best guess" or expected value estimates, subject to a sometimes considerable variance. Uncertainty may under this simplification be cast in a role less important than it deserves,

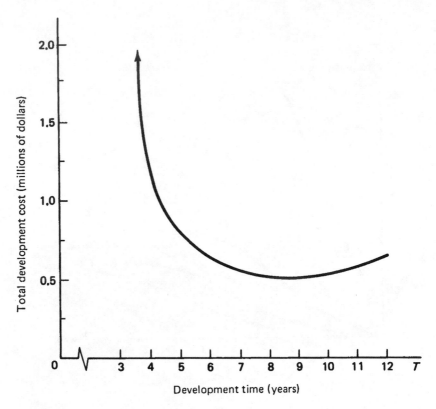

Figure 5.2
The time-total cost trade-off function

but it is not left in the wings. Hedging against uncertainty by running parallel approaches concurrently is one of the main bases of the time-expected cost trade-off function's convex shape. Furthermore, as Mansfield and Brandenburg have shown in their pathbreaking empirical study, the uncertainties encountered in most industrial research and development projects are apparently not so severe as to preclude a profit-maximizing approach to R & D resource allocation.[4]

Normally, total development cost varies with Q as well as T over a three-dimensional trade-off surface. This relationship can be represented in an elaboration of figure 5.2 by a family of time-cost trade-off curves, with curves farther from the origin reflecting more ambitious quality objectives.[5] Here we shall focus, for reasons to be given shortly, on the case of a single expected quality level objective.

Confronted by a time-cost trade-off relationship such as equation (2), a firm must decide how rapidly to execute its development project. Early commercialization is possible but only at high total development cost. The firm's optimal schedule depends on the payoffs from saving time. The simplest choice problem arises when rival reactions are of no consequence, that is, when research is strictly a game against nature. Examples include the introduction of new cost-reducing processes by a monopolist or pure competitor or by an oligopolist reluctant to change its output sufficiently to induce rival reactions,[6] and the introduction of a new product with patent protection which will block imitation completely. Here the innovator must estimate (however roughly) the stream of quasi rents $v(t)$ flowing from the innovation. Each interval's quasi rents are discounted to present value at the rate r, reflecting the opportunity cost of committing scarce R & D resources to the project and perhaps also a premium for uncertainty.[7] Assuming that the development project is initiated at time $t = 0$, is brought to the point of commercialization in T years, and that the end product becomes obsolete at time $t = H$, the total expected benefits flowing from the project are given by

$$V = \int_T^H v(t)e^{-rt}\,dt. \tag{3}$$

A profit-maximizing firm will adjust its development schedule so as to maximize the surplus π of discounted expected returns V over discounted expected development costs C with respect to T. The first-order condition for a maximum is

$$v(T)e^{-rT} = -\frac{\partial C}{\partial T}. \tag{4}$$

Intuitively, the discounted increase in quasi rents due to introducing the product one period earlier must at the optimum equal the discounted increase in cost due to completing the development effort one period earlier.[8] With a typically convex trade-off relationship between C and T, the right-hand side of (4) increases as T is reduced. It follows that the deeper the stream of benefits $v(t)$ in the neighborhood of the optimal T, the shorter the optimal T will be. This result is consistent with observation and common sense: the bigger the payoff from an R & D project, the more willing firms are to bear the costs of a minimum-time "crash" development program.

5.2 The General Rivalry Problem

With modifications only in detail this game-against-nature model can explain the choice of an optimal scheduling strategy in a significant class of R & D programs, including most cost-saving developments. Nevertheless, surveys reveal that internal process (cost-saving) development efforts consume less than a fourth of all U.S. industrial R & D expenditures, the remaining three-quarters going into product development and improvement.[9] And in the new product category, few positions impregnable to the imitation of rivals are attainable; it is possible to "invent around" all but the most basic patents. Therefore it is important to consider how technological leadership enhances the market positions of innovating firms and how rivals react to the threat of being left behind.

In a quite general model of new product rivalry each firm's expected development costs would depend, as before, on its own product quality index objective Q, the time when development is initiated, and the degree to which it compresses its development time T. But into the quasi-rent term new variables enter. A firm's expected quasi rents depend not only upon its own quality and introduction date but also on its rivals' qualities and introduction dates. The task of the firms involved in a new product rivalry is to maximize, either collectively or in some individual sense, their profits with respect to the time and quality variables they either control directly or indirectly influence. The solution to the resulting system of first-order equations would then be solved for the time paths of the firms' R & D expenditures.

Unfortunately, this approach to the problem of R & D rivalry is too general and complex to yield useful insights. If analytic progress is to be made, we must specify the behavioral equations with some precision and accept a number of simplifying assumptions.

The first and most severe simplification is to assume that only one new product quality level is considered; all firms have the same quality objective. This is clearly not always so; many new product rivalries involve more leapfrogging than matching. The U.S. strategy in the supersonic transport rivalry is a good example of leapfrogging, although the subsonic jet airliner race among Boeing, Douglas, General Dynamics, Sud Aviation, and de Havilland more closely approximated a quality-matching game. Quality goals are held to a single value here mainly because it is difficult to specify realistically the interactions associated with quality differentials, and also because even a simple quality differential model would be too complex to yield clear analytic insights.[10] The quality-matching assumption has several positive justifications. First, many new product rivalries, especially in consumer goods markets, *are* of the quality-matching type, partly because the technological opportunities for achieving significant quality differentials are limited and partly because consumers are unable to discriminate among fine quality variations. Simply having a workable automatic transmission, rectangular picture tube, zig-zag stitcher, or liquid detergent is the most important *technological* aspect of consumer product rivalry; the rest can be left to Madison Avenue. Second, in an environment of technological uncertainty some quality differentials observed *ex post* are the result of chance, rather than *ex ante* planning. The Comet I experience is a good negative illustration. Third, the quality-matching assumption at least provides a point of depature for analyzing more complex new product strategies. A firm must in any event consider the quality-matching alternative; whether better strategies can be found depends on comparative incremental costs and gains.

Consistent with this restriction to a single quality objective, we assume that rivals have identical time-cost trade-off functions (i.e., the same parameters for equation 2). Relaxation would alter the results only quantitatively and not qualitatively.

Third, it is assumed that at least one of the firms begins development at time $t = 0$. Obviously, the actual starting time of a new product rivalry is seldom precisely determinate because of institutional lags. The assumption made here implies that t is calibrated to zero whenever, and for whatever reason, a new product rivalry begins.

Firms might in certain cases prefer to delay initiating a new development project because the exogenous advance of technical knowledge will shift their time-cost trade-off curves toward the origin (of figure 5.2).[11] But when a project appears profitable at time $t = 0$, the shift would have to be quite strong to warrant delayed project initiation, since if a given product introduction date is to be maintained, delayed initiation forces costly compression of the development schedule. And if, alternatively, the product introduction date is postponed, payoffs fall. Another possibility in the same vein is that laggards will learn from the developmental mistakes and successes of leaders, thereby experiencing a favorable shift in their time-cost trade-off functions. In such cases the result may again be delayed initiation of R & D, but the opportunities for pursuing this strategy are limited by the security measures firms employ to guard their R & D know-how and by patent barriers against the copying of specific design features. These cost function complications, which in some instances are undoubtedly important, must be ignored in the subsequent analysis.

We assume next that each firm follows throughout the course of its development effort a single time path of R & D expenditures, the time path associated with its optimal equilibrium value of T. For instance, if the equilibrium development schedule is four years, the firm will adhere to the path $T = 4$ in figure 5.2. This is fully compatible with schedule interactions only if all schedule adjustments are made in a very short interval, so that equilibrium is attained soon after time $t = 0$. Although reaction lags may in reality be substantial, the assumption of rapid convergence on the equilibrium path seems warranted at least as a first approximation.[12] Since any acceleration of the development schedule, whenever made, requires accepting higher *incremental* development costs, it retains the heart of the firm's schedule choice problem, even when misrepresenting the quantitative niceties.

A further, obvious assumption is that each firm must conduct its own R & D project in order to innovate or imitate. Licensing is excluded as an alternative because royalties exceed development costs, because innovators are unwilling to help rivals imitate, or because the know-how essential to producing a complex new product can only be secured through one's own development efforts, and not from a sheaf of blueprints. Empirical support can be found for all three explanations.

Finally, we shall confine our attention initially to rivalry between only two firms.

5.3 Specific Duopoly Models

To formulate specific models of product research and development rivalry, further assumptions are required. We shall strive for maximum realism within the broad framework outlined thus far.

Two main types of product innovation rivalry can be identified: the introduction of product improvements that, if not matched, lead to changes in participants' market shares within a market of given size and the introduction of new products that either establish wholly new demand functions or shift existing demand functions to the right. Most actual cases are an amalgam of these pure types. For instance, rivalry in the automobile industry generally centers on market shares, but if no technical and styling changes were made, some consumers would replace their autos less frequently, and so innovation also shifts demand curves to the right. These two pure types, called the "market sharing" and "new market" models, will be analyzed separately. The models can readily be combined to describe any special case, and, as we shall see, they have similar analytic properties.

An essential component of any innovation model must be a potential for profits, due in turn to entry barriers, imitation lags, or other imperfections. Let the potential quasi rents attainable from the sale of a new product (i.e., total revenues less costs, including amortization of non-development new investment) be estimated at $\$V$ per year. We assume at this stage either constant costs and joint profit-maximizing pricing or markup pricing to deter entry, so that prices and hence V do not depend upon the number of firms.[13] Future returns must of course be discounted to present value at the opportunity cost of capital r. In addition the profit-making potential of a new product is likely to decline over time due to exogenous technological obsolescence at a rate of 100σ percent per year. The discounted quasi-rent potential for year t will therefore be $\$Ve^{-\rho t}$, with $\rho = r + \sigma$.

An innovator will not realize all of this quasi-rent potential for two main reasons. First, new markets must be cultivated and won. It takes time to overcome consumers' resistance to change and to develop the market's full potential. Where 1.0 represents full potential realization, this gradual penetration process can be represented by letting the innovator's discounted total quasi-rent realizations in the absence of imitation be written

$$V_L = \int_{T_L}^{\infty} [1.0 - e^{-\gamma(t - T_L)}] V e^{-\rho t} \, dt, \tag{5}$$

where T_L is the innovator's product introduction date (following T_L years of research and development) and γ is a "penetration coefficient" indicating the proportion of the unexploited quasi-rent potential captured each year. (The subscript L, for leader, will be used to identify the variables of the firm leading a new product race, while the subscript F will be used to identify the follower's variables.) The value of γ depends on the receptiveness of customers to new products, the degree of qualitative superiority

the new product has over existing substitutes, the amount of sales promotion effort put forth, and so forth.

Second, imitation will deprive the innovator of some quasi rents. An
imitator's quasi rents depend on its "target" share of the new market
and the rate at which it can build up sales to reach that target share.
For totally new products the imitator's target share may depend mainly
on its imitation lag. Few actual innovations are so radical, however.
Normally we should expect the imitator's target share S_F^* to depend
primarily on the firm's share of related markets, the strength of its
distributional organization, its advertising coverage, and so forth. We
assume also that the imitator moves toward full realization of its share
at a rate of 100μ percent per year following imitation. Therefore the
imitator's total quasi-rent realizations V_F can be written

$$V_F = \int_{T_F}^{\infty} [S_F^* - S_F^* e^{-\mu(t-T_F)}] V e^{-\rho t}\, dt, \tag{6}$$

the process beginning at the imitator's time of new product introduction
T_F and continuing until the product becomes obsolescent.[14] Although the
imitator's entry may accelerate exploitation of the new market somewhat,
it is more likely that its post-imitation gains V_F will be an offset against
the quasi rents the innovator would reap under monopoly conditions,
given by equation (5). We obtain therefore the following revised quasi-
rent equation for the innovator:

$$V_L = \int_{T_L}^{\infty} [1.0 - e^{-\gamma(t-T_L)}] V e^{-\rho t}\, dt - \int_{T_F}^{\infty} [S_F^* - S_F^* e^{-\mu(t-T_F)}] V e^{-\rho t}\, dt. \tag{7}$$

Figure 5.3 illustrates a case where $V = \$2$ million per year, $\gamma = 0.30$,
$\mu = 0.30$, $\rho = 0.15$, and $T_L = 4$ years. The innovator's discounted quasi-
rent stream is given, assuming no imitation at all by its rival, imitation
at $t = 8$ years, and at $t = 6$ years.

Equation (6) implies that the imitator eventually can realize its original
target share of the new market, no matter how great its imitation lag is.
This is not unrealistic; Procter & Gamble's experience in the liquid
household detergents field and IBM's experience vis-à-vis Remington-
Rand's Univac are good examples of strong finishes following slow starts.
On the other hand, it is conceivable that hesitancy by Philco, Zenith,
General Electric, and others in the color television field has caused those
firms to enjoy shares more or less permanently lower than their shares

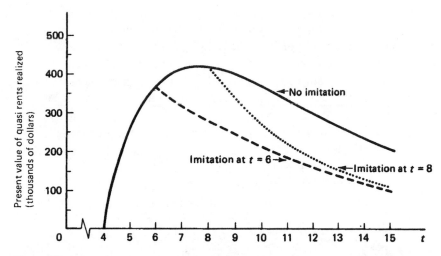

Figure 5.3
Innovator's benefits flow for diverse imitation scenarios

in the black-and-white market. Similarly, Gillette's share of the stainless steel razor blade market has apparently stabilized at about 60 percent, compared with its 90 percent share of the carbon steel blade market, due to its 18 month lag behind the stainless innovators.[15] This case can be represented by letting the imitator's target share decay 100ε percent for every year of imitation lag. For the imitator we obtain the new, more general quasi-rent equation:

$$V_F = \int_{T_F}^{\infty} \left[S_F^* e^{-\varepsilon(T_F - T_L)} - S_F^* e^{-\varepsilon(T_F - T_L) - \mu(t - T_F)} \right] V e^{-\rho t}\, dt. \tag{8}$$

The innovator's quasi-rent equation becomes

$$V_L = \int_{T_L}^{\infty} \left[1.0 - e^{-\gamma(t - T_L)} \right] V e^{-\rho t}\, dt - \int_{T_F}^{\infty} \left[S_F^* e^{-\varepsilon(T_F - T_L)} \right.$$
$$\left. - S_F^* e^{-\varepsilon(T_F - T_L) - \mu(t - T_F)} \right] V e^{-\rho t}\, dt. \tag{9}$$

Equations (8) and (9) are identical to equations (6) and (7) when $\varepsilon = 0$, that is, for the special case of no permanent market share erosion.

We turn now to the market-sharing rivalry model. During its period of technological leadership an innovator in a market-sharing game captures more and more of its rival's market share, and hence a larger and larger share of the total market quasi-rent potential V. Let δ be the rate at which the laggard's pre-innovation market share is temporarily taken over by the innovator per year of technological lag. Let β be the rate at which the imitating firm recovers its market share once it has imitated. This recovery may in time be complete, or leadership may confer on the innovator a permanent market share gain increasing with the imitation lag. As in the new market model, let ε represent the rate at which the imitator's market share erodes permanently per year of lag. An innovator cannot take over permanently a portion of its rival's share larger than the portion it captures temporarily during its leadership period; thus $\varepsilon \leq \delta$.

For the general market-sharing case, the innovator's quasi-rent equation is as follows, where S_F is the imitating firm's original market share:

$$V_L = \int_{T_L}^{T_F} [S_F - S_F e^{-\delta(t-T_L)}] V e^{-\rho t} \, dt + \int_{T_F}^{\infty} [S_F - S_F e^{-\varepsilon(T_F-T_L)}] V e^{-\rho t} \, dt$$

$$+ \int_{T_F}^{\infty} [-S_F e^{-\delta(T_F-T_L)} + S_F e^{-\varepsilon(T_F-T_L)}] e^{-\beta(t-T_F)} V e^{-\rho t} \, dt. \qquad (10)$$

The first term is the innovator's gain during its leadership period, the second its gain following imitation due to the permanent erosion of its rival's market share, and the third its temporary gain following imitation before the imitator fully recovers its new permanent share. Since the leader's gain must be the laggard's loss in a pure market-sharing rivalry, the imitator's quasi-rent equation is simply the negative of equation (10). When the rivals have identical product introduction dates ($T_1 = T_2$), no change in market shares occurs, and so $V_1 = V_2 = 0$.

The principal parameters of these two basic models of duopolistic new product development rivalry can be summarized as follows:

$V \equiv$ total market quasi-rent potential per year,
$S_F^* \equiv$ the imitator's target share in a new market,
$S_F \equiv$ the imitator's original share in an existing market,
$\rho \equiv$ the discount rate, including opportunity cost and obsolescence terms r and σ,
$\varepsilon \equiv$ the imitator's permanent share erosion rate,
$\gamma \equiv$ the innovator's new market penetration rate,
$\mu \equiv$ the imitator's new market entry rate,
$\delta \equiv$ the innovator's market takeover rate in a market-sharing rivalry,
$\beta \equiv$ the imitator's share recovery rate in a market-sharing rivalry.

5.4 Solution Concepts

In any product rivalry situation the profit equations of the firms involved are interdependent, since each firm's quasi rents depend on both its own product introduction time and its rivals' times. For the duopoly case this interdependence can be shown graphically by means of von Stackelberg isoprofit maps.[16] Figure 5.4 is a typical illustration. It assumes a new market rivalry with $V = \$2$ million per year, $S_1^* = S_2^* = 0.50$, $\gamma = 0.40$, $\mu = 0.40$, $\varepsilon = 0.25$, $\rho = 0.15$ (with $r = 0.10$ and $\sigma = 0.05$), and a time-cost trade-off function given by equation (2). It assumes further that each firm begins development at time $t = 0$. Firm's 1's product introduction date (and hence its development time T_1) is measured on the horizontal axis and Firm 2's on the vertical axis. Four representative isoprofit curves for Firm 1 are drawn in light solid lines; Firm 2's isoprofit curves are given by light dotted lines. The longer Firm 2's development time T_2 is, the higher Firm 1's profits are for any value of T_1. Given any value of T_2, Firm 1's profits first increase as T_1 is reduced (moving from east to west on the map), but eventually they decline as further development time compression becomes increasingly costly.

As in all analyses of duopoly behavior, we are interested in a simultaneous "solution" to the firms' profit equations. And as always, no unambiguous solution exists. The outcome depends on the specific assumptions made with respect to rival reactions. Here four leading solution concepts are considered: minimax, joint maximization, the Cournot assumption, and von Stackelberg leadership.

The minimax strategy is deficient as a solution approach for several reasons. First, the payoff matrices of R & D rivalries are typically of the nonconstant-sum variety, and so the compulsion toward minimaxing associated with zero-sum games is absent. Second, the assumption that one's rival will choose the strategy *most* damaging to one's own interest (i.e., compressing development time to its minimum technically feasible value) is much too pessimistic, since the costs to rivals of adopting this strategy are prohibitive. This pitfall can be avoided by eliminating from consideration dominated rival strategies, but only at the risk of making the minimax solution depend in certain cases on the order in which dominated strategies are discarded.[17] Third, even when nondominated rival minimax strategies can be identified, a firm may benefit by proceeding at least initially on the assumption that, because of inertia, miscalculation,

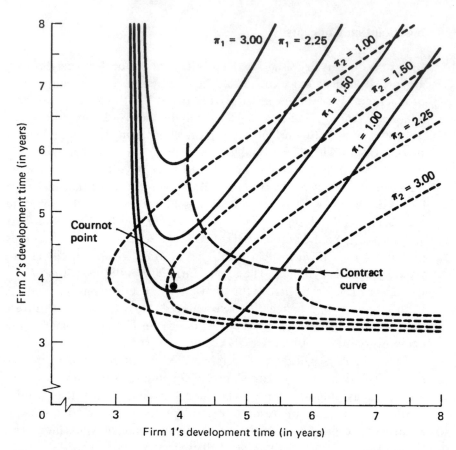

Figure 5.4
Von Stackelberg isoprofit curves for a new market rivalry

or a cooperative attitude, rivals will choose a relatively unaggressive schedule. The very fact that research and development projects extend over a substantial period makes it possible to avoid the minimax approach unless rival actions take an aggressive turn.

A strict minimaxer would choose at once the development schedule making the best of its rival's most damaging nondominated strategy. But in actual R & D rivalries, firms appear typically to react in a series of steps to rival schedule moves. The Cournot assumption is clearly superior to minimax in explaining reactive behavior of this type. Cournot behavior has the additional virtue of not being overly pessimistic: decisions are based on the best current estimate of rival development time (derived from intelligence on rival spending rates) and not on some projection of what might be, assuming the worst. At the same time it hedges against the adverse consequences (being caught in a position of technological inferiority) flowing from overly optimistic assumptions concerning rival schedules, for evidence of vigorous effort in the rival's laboratories can be viewed as a signal to accelerate one's own effort. In support of this assertion, computer simulations of both the new market and market-sharing models over a wide range of parameter values yielded Cournot equilibrium solutions at worst only slightly inferior to the minimax outcomes.

The Cournot assumption is vulnerable to the criticism of myopia in ignoring subsequent rival reactions to one's own decision variable changes and, as a consequence, in generating an equilibrium outcome which fails to maximize either individual or collective profits. Structurally, R & D rivalries fall into the classic Prisoners' Dilemma mold. To illustrate, the Cournot equilibrium, Pareto-optimal, and two other outcomes attainable under the parameter assumptions of figure 5.4 are presented in the following payoff matrix, with Firm 1's net profits (in millions of dollars) listed before and Firm 2's after the comma in each element:

Firm 2's development time strategy
3.8 years   4.5 years

Firm 1's time strategy		3.8 years	4.5 years
	3.8 years	1.52, 1.52	2.19, 1.35
	4.5 years	1.35, 2.19	1.74, 1.74

It is evident that for both firms, $T = 3.8$ years is a dominant strategy. Yet both firms could become better off, realizing net profits of $1.74 million each, if they chose the less pessimistic strategy $T = 4.5$. Still to achieve this mutually advantageous outcome the firms must trust each other to cooperate and not to seek unilateral gains. For if Firm 1 sets its T_1 at 4.5 when $T_2 = 3.8$, it receives a payoff $170,000 less than the worst payoff it can expect playing the Cournot game through to its equilibrium.[18]

This result is illustrated more generally in figure 5.4. The heavy dashed line is the contract curve—the locus of tangency points of the two firms' isoprofit curves. The Cournot equilibrium point $T_1 = T_2 = 3.8$ years lies off the contract curve. Both firms can gain by moving to the contract curve, if means of cooperation can be devised. The $T_1 = T_2 = 4.5$ years outcome maximizes joint profits, subject to the condition that the firms have symmetric development times. Even higher joint profits can be achieved by movement along the contract curve toward unequal development times. Joint profits attain their unconstrained maximum when only one firm engages in development, setting its $T = 4.1$ years and if need be pooling quasi rents to secure compliance of the other firm.

Market-sharing rivalries differ only in a few details, as the following payoff matrix illustrates, assuming $V = 2 million per year, $S_1 = S_2 = 0.50$, $\varepsilon = 0.25$, $\rho = 0.15$, $\delta = 0.40$, and $\beta = 0.40$:

		Firm 2's development time strategy		
		3.9 years	6.0 years	No development
Firm 1's time strategy	3.9 years	$-1.10, -1.10$	$+0.43, -1.96$	$+1.58, -2.70$
	6.0 years	$-1.96, +0.43$	$-0.43, -0.43$	$+1.55, -1.98$
	No development	$-2.70, +1.58$	$-1.98, +1.55$	$0, 0$

The Cournot equilibrium schedule of 3.9 years dominates the alternatives, yet both firms would be better off if they could agree on longer development times, and they would maximize their joint profits by refraining from development altogether! This is so because the quasi-rent gains and losses from innovation and followership offset each other with no expansion of the market, while development costs persist. The pure market-sharing rivalry is zero-sum in quasi rents, but negative-sum in terms of gains less development costs. The main difference between new market and market-sharing rivalries is that with the former there can be at least some time-matching (diagonal) outcomes more profitable than development of the new product by neither firm.

Clearly then, firms are better off cooperating to maximize joint profits than they are adhering to the Cournot assumption. Are real-world firms in fact able to exercise the necessary restraint? In some instances they undoubtedly can and do.[19] But Cournot-type behavior appears much more likely for three main reasons. First, each R & D project differs in numerous respects from all previous projects. Because of this uniqueness, opportunities for tacit learning, the development of quantitative precedents, and the dynamic use of threats to elicit cooperation are minimized. Each R & D rivalry is in a sense the last of its kind, with especially weak inhibitions against uncooperative behavior.[20] Pricing decisions iterated weekly or daily are quite different in this respect, and so it should not be surprising that joint profit maximization is observed much less frequently in R & D rivalry than in oligopolistic price competition. Second, R & D projects are typically so complex, and intelligence information on rival strategies so imperfect, that the mutual coordination and trust required for joint profit maximization cannot easily be maintained.[21] Here again we find a distinct contrast with pricing behavior, especially under the "open price" approach to tacit coordination.[22] Third, as Fellner has suggested, some firms overestimate their own ability and underestimate their rivals' ability to succeed at the innovation game, and therefore they adopt an uncooperative, independent stance.[23] If only one firm proceeds in this manner, it can pull all its rivals along into a series of Cournot reactions.

Because it appears most consistent with the structure and dynamics of real-world new product rivalries, we shall stress the Cournot assumption and the reactions to which it gives rise in the remaining sections. We shall consider, among others, the following questions: Does a stable Cournot equilibrium exist? How does the equilibrium solution vary with changes in the principal parameters of the R & D rivalry model? And do firms react to rival schedule accelerations by accelerating their own efforts, or by slowing them down?

One further solution concept—unilateral or mutual von Stackelberg leadership—deserves brief mention. A von Stackelberg leader attempts to set that value of its own T which maximizes its profits, given its rival's Cournot reaction function. Geometrically, it tries to reach its highest isoprofit curve touching the rival's reaction function. This solution is less interesting than the Cournot solution, since knowledge of rivals' reaction functions is apt to be scant in R & D rivalry. Furthermore, because nearly all Cournot reaction functions undergo a sign change where $T_1 = T_2$, as we shall see, and because of the characteristic V-shape of the isoprofit curves for both new market and market-sharing rivalries, the von Stackelberg leadership point coincides with the Cournot point in all market-sharing and in many new market games where the rivals commence development at about the same time and with equal target market shares. The leadership case is therefore trivial in symmetric duopoly situations. Attractive leadership possibilities do exist when initial market positions are asymmetric, but these will be examined only briefly due to space constraints.

5.5 Specific Cournot Reaction Patterns

We now explore the properties of Cournot solutions to the two main rivalry models. Each firm is assumed to maximize its own profit with respect to its own development time, taking its rival's development time as a parameter. For the general case where innovator firm L leads the way into a new market, we obtain by differentiating equation (9) with respect to T_L the first-order condition:

$$\frac{\partial C_L}{\partial T_L} = V \left[-\frac{\rho e^{-\rho T_L}}{\rho} + \frac{\rho e^{-\rho T_L}}{\gamma + \rho} - \frac{S_F^* \varepsilon e^{-\varepsilon(T_F - T_L) - \rho T_F}}{\rho} \right.$$
$$\left. + \frac{S_F^* \varepsilon e^{-\varepsilon(T_F - T_L) - \rho T_F}}{\mu + \rho} \right] \tag{11}$$

For the general case where innovator Firm L leads the way in a market-sharing rivalry, we obtain by differentiating equation (10) the first-order condition:

$$\frac{\partial C_L}{\partial T_L} = S_F V \left[-\frac{\rho e^{-\rho T_L}}{\rho} + \frac{\rho e^{-\rho T_L}}{\delta + \rho} + \frac{\delta e^{-\delta(T_F - T_L) - \rho T_F}}{\delta + \rho} \right.$$
$$\left. - \frac{\delta e^{-\delta(T_F - T_L) - \rho T_F}}{\beta + \rho} - \frac{\varepsilon e^{-\varepsilon(T_F - T_L) - \rho T_F}}{\rho} + \frac{\varepsilon e^{-\varepsilon(T_F - T_L) - \rho T_F}}{\beta + \rho} \right] \tag{12}$$

The Overall Speed of Development

Consider first how the overall speed of development (i.e., the optimal T_L for any given rival T_F) varies with key parameters of the model. It is readily ascertained that the right-hand sides of both (11) and (12) are always negative for positive values of ρ, γ, μ, ε, δ, and β. The longer the development period T_L, the lower is the total payoff V_L, given any T_F. Similarly, the left-hand side term $\partial C_L/\partial T_L$ is always negative within the range of meaningful time-cost trade-offs, that is, when it costs money to save development time. From the convexity of the time-cost trade-off function we know also that $\partial^2 C_L/\partial T_L^2 > 0$. It follows that if $|\partial V_L/\partial T_L|$ increases as any relevant parameter Z increases (i.e., if $\partial^2 V_L/\partial T_L\partial Z < 0$) the profit-maximizing development time T_L must fall, *ceteris paribus*. Conversely, when $\partial^2 V_L/\partial T_L\partial Z > 0$, the profit-maximizing T_L will rise as Z increases.

Since the first derivatives with respect to T_L of the quasi-rent integrals (equations 9 and 10) are negative, and since V appears as a positive pre-multiplier in both cases, $\partial^2 V_L/\partial T_L\partial V < 0$ for both the new market and market-sharing models. The deeper the potential stream of quasi rents at stake, the shorter an innovating firm's optimal time of development T_L will be, *ceteris paribus*. This result parallels the game-against-nature result of section 5.1.

Turning to the market share parameters, we find that $\partial^2 V_L/\partial T_L\partial S_F^*$ and $\partial^2 V_L/\partial T_L\partial S_r$ are both negative. The larger its rival's actual or target market share, the stronger an innovator's incentive to conduct its development project rapidly is. This result provides a first insight into the relationship between market structure and technological progressiveness. Ignoring complications to be introduced later, firms with small actual or target market shares leading the way to a new product should be expected to conduct their developments more rapidly than innovating firms with large market shares.

Reaction Function Slopes

Similar reasoning applies in establishing the effects of rival schedule changes on a firm's Cournot-optimal development schedule. If the cross-partial term $\partial^2 V_1/\partial T_1\partial T_2 > 0$, the slope of Firm 1's quasi-rent function becomes steeper as Firm 2's development time is reduced, and Firm 1 will react aggressively to Firm 2's speedup, accelerating its own development schedule. Geometrically, when Firm 1's development time is given on the horizontal axis of a von Stackelberg map and Firm 2's time on the vertical (as in figure 5.5), Firm 1's reaction function will have a positive slope. If $\partial^2 V_1/\partial T_1 \partial T_2 < 0$, the obverse is true: Firm 1 will react submissively to Firm 2's speedup, slowing down its own development pace.[24] If $\partial^2 V_1/\partial T_1 \partial T_2 = 0$, Firm 1 will not react at all to changes in its rival's schedule; its reaction function is parallel to the rival's development time axis.

Four cases for an innovating firm can now be examined. First is the new market rivalry with no permanent target share erosion ($\varepsilon = 0$). Differentiating quasi-rent equation (7) with respect to T_L and T_F, we obtain

$$\frac{\partial^2 V_L}{\partial T_L \partial T_F} = 0. \tag{13}$$

The innovator will not react at all to the imitator's schedule changes in the new market model with no permanent share erosion. Second is the new market model *with* permanent share erosion ($\varepsilon > 0$). Differentiating equation (9) with respect to T_L and T_F, we get

$$\frac{\partial^2 V_L}{\partial T_L \partial T_F} = V S_F^* \left[\frac{\varepsilon(\varepsilon + \rho)e^{-\varepsilon(T_F - T_L) - \rho T_F}}{\rho} - \frac{\varepsilon(\varepsilon + \rho)e^{-\varepsilon(T_F - T_L) - \rho T_F}}{\mu + \rho} \right] \tag{14}$$

The numerators within the brackets are identical, and so as long as the imitator's entry coefficient μ is positive, the whole expression is positive. An innovating firm will react to rival schedule accelerations by accelerating its own schedule. Third is the market-sharing model with no permanent share erosion. Setting $\varepsilon = 0$ in equation (10) and differentiating with respect to T_L and T_F, we obtain

$$\frac{\partial^2 V_L}{\partial T_L \partial T_F} = V S_F \left[\frac{\delta(\delta + \rho)e^{-\delta(T_F - T_L) - \rho T_F}}{\beta + \rho} - \frac{\delta(\delta + \rho)e^{-\delta(T_F - T_L) - \rho T_F}}{\delta + \rho} \right] \tag{15}$$

Here the conclusion is less clear-cut. When $\delta = \beta$, there is no reaction at all. When $\delta > \beta$ (i.e., when the innovator takes over a laggard's market share at a faster rate than the imitator recovers its share later), the innovator will react to rival schedule accelerations by accelerating its own schedule. When $\delta < \beta$, the innovator will react submissively to its rival's speedups. Finally, we have the market-sharing model with permanent share erosion, yielding the cross-partial expression:

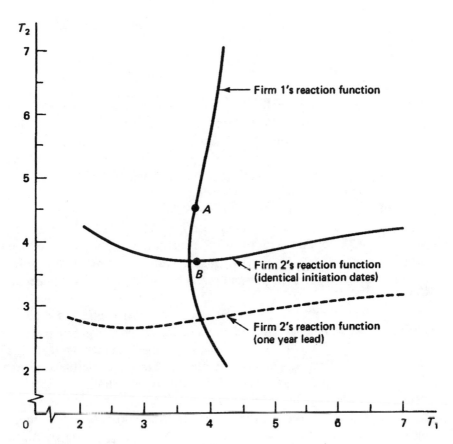

Figure 5.5
Reaction function relationships

$$\frac{\partial^2 V_L}{\partial T_L \partial T_F} = V S_F \left[\frac{\delta(\delta + \rho)e^{-\delta(T_F - T_L) - \rho T_F}}{\beta + \rho} - \frac{\delta(\delta + \rho)e^{-\delta(T_F - T_L) - \rho T_F}}{\delta + \rho} \right.$$

$$\left. + \frac{\varepsilon(\varepsilon + \rho)e^{-\varepsilon(T_F - T_L) - \rho T_F}}{\rho} - \frac{\varepsilon(\varepsilon + \rho)e^{-\varepsilon(T_F - T_L) - \rho T_F}}{\beta + \rho} \right]. \tag{16}$$

This equation is still more difficult to interpret. The sum of the third and fourth bracketed terms, which represent the only change from equation (15), is clearly positive when $\beta > 0$. Considering also the first two terms, it is evident that the whole expression is positive, and therefore aggressive reactions will be the rule, whenever $\delta \geq \beta$. Only when $\beta > \delta$ is a submissive reaction possible. Numerical simulation of the $\beta > \delta$ case for a wide range of parameter values showed that submissive reactions appear only for low values of ε and δ combined with high values of β. For example, when $\beta = 0.30$, equation (16) turns negative in the neighborhood of $\delta = 0.13$ when $\varepsilon < 0.40$. But generally, positive values of ε make submissive reactions in the market-sharing game much less likely and, if they occur, much weaker.

We find then that the permanent share erosion coefficient ε has a critical influence on innovator reactions in both new market and market-sharing rivalries. The higher the ε, the more likely aggressive reactions to rival accelerations are, and the stronger the reactions will tend to be. This conclusion, while not obvious, is intuitively appealing. When permanent instead of only temporary slices of an existing or new market are the prize for technological leadership, innovators should naturally be more inclined to fight to preserve their leadership positions against the reactions of rivals.[25]

The results given thus far apply only when the firm whose reaction function is being derived has an expected product introduction date earlier than its rival's anticipated date, e.g., when $T_1 < T_2$ if Firm 1's reaction function is of interest and both firms began development at time $t = 0$. When the *imitator's* quasi-rent equations (e.g., equation 8 in the new market case and the negative of equation 10 in the market-sharing case) are differentiated with respect to T_F and T_L, we obtain the mirror image of innovator cross-partial equations (13) through (16). The bracketed terms are identical, but all signs modifying the bracketed terms are reversed. If forced to follow, a firm will slow down its development effort in response to its rival's acceleration, whereas with identical parameter values, it would have accelerated its efforts if it could assume a leadership role. In other words, except when $\partial^2 V_1/\partial T_1 \partial T_2 = 0$, the reaction function of Firm 1 has a kink where that firm's product introduction date equals its rival's expected introduction date. The sign of the reaction function's slope reverses at the equal-times point, as illustrated in figure 5.5 for a market-sharing rivalry with $V = \$2$ million, $S_1 = S_2 = 0.50$, $\delta = 0.75$, $\beta = 0.50$, $\varepsilon = 0.50$, and $\rho = 0.15$.

This finding does not mean that, to enter a new product rivalry, the second firm must always behave submissively. To see why, consider the dynamics of reaching equilibrium in figure 5.5. Suppose Firm 2 begins development at time $t = 0$. In the absence of any effort by Firm 1, its Cournot-optimal T_2 will be roughly 4.5 years. Now if Firm 1 observes its rival on an expenditure path leading to $T_2 = 4.5$ and reacts immediately, it will move to point A on the leadership segment of its own reaction curve, setting $T_1 = 3.8$ years. Firm 2 will react by shifting to point B on its reaction curve, where $T_2 = 3.7$ years. In just three steps the rivals have come very close to the Cournot equilibrium point, and at each step each firm was able to move to the leadership segment of its reaction curve.

Only when a firm delays initiating its countervailing development project well beyond $t = 0$ will that firm be denied the use of its leadership segment. This case can only be approximated with figure 5.5. We assume that the time index t is set at zero when Firm 1 begins its development, and that Firm 2 began its development earlier, at $t = -1$. The vertical axis now measures Firm 2's product introduction date correctly but overstates that firm's development time by one year. Now Firm 2's reaction function (dotted lines) must lie below its reaction function for symmetric development initiation dates, and the Cournot equilibrium finds Firm 1 on the submissive segment of its reaction function.[26]

Rival Reactions Associated with Corner Solutions

The analysis of reaction patterns up to this point has ignored the possibility of corner solutions due to kinks and discontinuities in the quasi-rent functions. As we have seen, a firm's quasi-rent function as innovator differs from its function as imitator, and so it should not be surprising that Firm 1's V_1 function is kinked at the point where $T_1 = T_2$ so that a discontinuity exists in $\partial V_1/\partial T_1$ at $T_1 = T_2$. To see this for the market-sharing case, let $(T_2 - T_1) \rightarrow 0$ so that the lag terms in the exponents of quasi-rent equation (10) and its negative vanish.[27] Differentiating the modified (10), we obtain Firm 1's slope as innovator in the neighborhood of $(T_2 - T_1) \to 0$:

$$\frac{\partial V_1}{\partial T_1} = VS_2\left[\frac{\rho e^{-\rho T_1}}{\delta + \rho} - \frac{\rho e^{-\rho T_1}}{\rho}\right] \tag{17}$$

Similarly, differentiating the modified negative of equation (10), we obtain Firm 1's slope as imitator in the neighborhood of $(T_1 - T_2) \to 0$:

$$\frac{\partial V_1}{\partial T_1} = VS_1\left[\frac{\rho e^{-\rho T_1}}{\delta + \rho} - \frac{\rho e^{-\rho T_1}}{\rho}\right]. \tag{18}$$

The two expressions differ only in their market share premultipliers. The quasi-rent functions have no kink at $T_1 = T_2$ only in the symmetric market structure case of $S_1 = S_2$. Otherwise a kink exists, and $\partial V_1/\partial T_1$ has a discontinuity. When $S_2 > S_1$, the slope $\partial V_1/\partial T_1$ is steeper when Firm 1 expects to be first on the market with its new product than when it expects to trail its rival. Thus duopolists with minority market shares will tend to conduct their developments more rapidly in an innovative role than in an imitative role. The opposite is true when a firm occupies a dominant role in its industry. This result is generally consistent with intuition. In a market-sharing game the (relatively) small firm has much to gain by cutting into its bigger rival's market position through innovation but less to lose when it trails its rival.[28] A dominant firm has little to gain by innovating, but much to lose when its position is attacked by a smaller innovator.

Because of these differences, a small firm's reaction function typically exhibits a pronounced submissive discontinuity where it crosses the equal-time diagonal, as shown by the dotted function in figure 5.6 for a market-sharing rivalry with $S_1 = 0.20$, $V = \$2$ million per year, $\delta = 0.30$, $\beta = 0.30$, $\varepsilon = 0.10$, and $\rho = 0.15$. On the other hand, a dominant firm's reaction function bends and follows the equal-time diagonal along a substantial stretch before bending back at a lower development time, as illustrated with a solid reaction function in figure 5.6, assuming the same parameters except that $S_2 = 0.80$.

These asymmetries lead to interesting reaction dynamics. Suppose small Firm 1 initiates its development at a $T_1 = 4.5$ year rate. Dominant Firm 2 moves to point A on its reaction function, with $T_2 = 4.4$ years. Firm 1 reacts by moving to point B, with $T_1 = 4.0$ years. Firm 2 reacts aggressively, moving to C, with $T_1 = 4.0$ years. Now Firm 1 reacts submissively, shifting to D, with $T_1 = 5.2$ years, causing Firm 2 to relax its pace back to $T_2 = 5.0$ years (point E). If reactions occur instantaneously, as we have

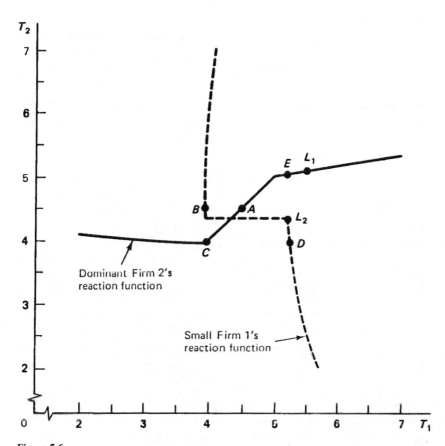

Figure 5.6
Reaction functions of dominant and fringe rivals

assumed thus far, perpetual oscillation will result in place of the three-step convergence toward stable equilibrium illustrated in figure 5.5.[29] Obviously, one is not apt to find perpetual schedule oscillations in many actual R & D projects. Rampant instability is prevented by the finite information and institutional lags accompanying actual reactions, and perhaps also because it is difficult organizationally to slow a project down once it gains momentum. For this and other reasons discussed in section 5.2, the analysis here can be only an approximation to the actual dynamics of scheduling rivalry.

Is it absurd to expect any such oscillation in R & D scheduling? This is an empirical question and the evidence is meager, but I have studied one such case in detail. During the late 1940s, AT & T accelerated the development of TD-2, a long-range microwave radio relay system, partly in response to the initiation and acceleration of developments by several firms hoping to command a share of the television signal relay business. AT & T's vigorous program in turn discouraged completely the efforts of some firms and induced Western Union to slacken its development pace.[30] As a second illustration, representatives of the German chemical industry reported in interviews that during the 1920s and 1930s small firms frequently discontinued research and development projects when I. G. Farben responded aggressively with an imitative effort.

Duopoly Market Structure and Technological Vigor

Let us assemble now some of the pieces hewn thus far. We have found that in both new market and market-sharing rivalries, duopolists with minority market shares have stronger incentives than dominant firms to innovate vigorously. This is so in two respects. First, in the innovative phase relatively small firms have steeper quasi-rent function slopes with respect to their own development times, and so they have an incentive to conduct their developments more rapidly than dominant firms for all but the shortest rival development times, *ceteris paribus*. Second, their cross-partial terms $\partial^2 V_S / \partial T_S \partial T_D$ are larger in absolute value than dominant firms' cross-partials, and so in the innovative phase they react more strongly to rival schedule accelerations. On the other hand, because of a kink in the quasi-rent function at $T_S = T_D$, small firms are more apt to scurry for cover when a dominant firm takes the lead. But this last result implies a disadvantage only in the imitative, and not the innovative, realm. All in all, the analysis suggests that relatively small firms would tend to be more vigorous technological innovators than firms that dominate their markets. The latter, on the other hand, can be expected to react strongly when smaller innovators threaten their market positions.

It would be unwise to place too much reliance for policy purposes on conclusions from this mathematical model when subjective and random elements bulk so large in the process of technological innovation. Yet the implications of the model agree surprisingly well with observations of real-world behavior. The superior innovative records of smaller (and newer, e.g., with $S^* = 0$) firms stand out in Passer's study of late nineteenth century electrical manufacturing, Maclaurin's study of radio and television innovations, Bright's analysis of the electric lamp industry, Mansfield's quantitative analyses of product innovations in the steel (but not the petroleum) industry, and fragmentary evidence on innovation in the automobile industry.[31]

Despite its apparent consistency with available evidence, the model might nevertheless misspecify the interactions of firms in certain situations. One alternative formulation deserves special attention. The exponential decay form of quasi-rent equations (9) and (10) assumes that the innovator's sales growth is dependent mainly upon the amount of unexploited market potential. Maximum absolute growth and the highest growth rates are realized immediately after innovation, when unexploited potential is highest. But even though the potential exists for rapid sales growth following innovation, firms may be unable to tap it fully because physical and organizational bottlenecks constrain the rate at which they can expand production and sales. For a firm with a 20 percent market share to capture 25 percent of the remaining market in the year following innovation ($\delta = 0.25$), it must expand its sales by 100 percent. And if this is impossible, the small firm's incentive for accelerated development will surely not be so strong as the previous analysis indicates.

Conceivably, a small innovator's market penetration may be governed by internal growth limits initially, and by unexploited market potential only when a certain critical relative size is attained. If so, the innovator's market penetration path over time can be described by an S-curve of the logistic form. Although the equations for this formulation are rather complex, the essence of the problem can be grasped through a simplification. Consider a firm (subscript L) innovating in a market-sharing situation and subjected throughout the limited duration of its leadership period only to the constraint on its own sales growth. Unexploited potential is great enough throughout this period so that the takeover relationship emphasized previously (involving δ) is not binding. Specifically, we assume that its market share growth cannot exceed 100α percent per year. Neglecting the possibility of permanent rival share erosion, Firm L's quasi-rent function can be written as

$$V_L = \int_{T_L}^{T_F} S_L e^{\alpha(t-T_L)} V e^{-\rho t}\, dt + \int_{T_F}^{\infty} (S_L e^{\alpha(T_F-T_L)} e^{-\beta(t-T_F)} V e^{-\rho t}\, dt;$$

$$S_L e^{\alpha(T_F-T_L)} < 1.0. \tag{19}$$

Differentiating with respect to T_L, we obtain

$$\frac{\partial V_L}{\partial T_L} = S_L V \left[-\frac{\alpha e^{\alpha(T_F-T_L)-\rho T_F}}{\alpha - \rho} + \frac{\rho e^{-\rho T_L}}{\alpha - \rho} - \frac{\alpha e^{\alpha(T_F-T_L)-\rho T_F}}{\beta + \rho} \right] \tag{20}$$

which is negative for positive α, β, and ρ. Since S_L is a positive premultiplier, $\partial^2 V_L/\partial T_L \partial S_L < 0$. The larger the innovator's market share is, the stronger its incentive to conduct the development rapidly; the smaller S_L is, the weaker that incentive will be. This is a reversal of the earlier conclusion in favor of relative smallness. Differentiating (20) with respect to the rival firm's development time T_F, we obtain the cross-partial:

$$\frac{\partial^2 V_L}{\partial T_L \partial T_F} = S_L V \alpha e^{\alpha(T_F-T_L)-\rho T_F} \left[-1 - \left(\frac{\alpha - \rho}{\beta + \rho} \right) \right] \tag{21}$$

This must be negative for positive α, β, and ρ, and so when the laggard rival accelerates a countervailing development project, Firm L will react submissively and relax its own development pace.

Thus we find that relatively small firms subjected to sales growth constraints are not nearly the innovative tigers they are when their penetration into dominant firm positions is limited only by the customer loyalties and similar frictions summarized in the takeover coefficient δ or the penetration coefficient γ. Whether this or our earlier model better describes the actual position of small firms is an empirical question. The experiences of Xerox, Schering (with its cortical steroids), and Adell Chemical (manufacturer of Lestoil) suggest that sales growth constraints are not necessarily highly restrictive, although they certainly might be in certain cases.[32] Growth constraints are also not apt to be restrictive for medium- and large-size conglomerate firms innovating in markets where they have only small shares.

A further qualification must be treated more briefly than its potential significance warrants. The derivative of equation (11) with respect to γ is unambiguously negative, and the derivative of (12) with respect to δ is negative over most plausible values of δ, β, T_L, and T_F. This means that the more rapidly a firm is able to penetrate new markets or take over existing markets through innovation, the shorter its optimal development time will be, *ceteris paribus*. Now it is conceivable that large firms, enjoying well-established channels of distribution and economies of scale in promotion, have higher values of γ and δ than small firms. If so, their incentives to innovate vigorously will be strengthened relative to the incentives of small firms, other things being equal. Supporting this inference from the theory, several company executives remarked in interviews that the most important single factor inhibiting small firms from undertaking certain ambitious R & D projects is their inferiority relative to large rivals in marketing the new products emerging from successful technical efforts.

5.6 The N-Firm Problem

Thus far we have limited the analysis to duopolistic new product rivalries. Actual duopolies are few and far between in manufacturing industry. Generalization to the N-firm case is therefore important. Nevertheless, a highly realistic analysis is beyond the reach of this article. We must settle for modest gains—presentation of a naive model and identification of one path toward a more faithful representation of the real world. Only the new market analysis will be given, since the behavior of the market-sharing model is identical.

The main new simplifying assumption is that in making its development scheduling decisions, potential innovator Firm i takes into account parametrically only the product introduction date (and when all firms begin development at $t = 0$, the development time) T_j of a representative rival firm j. This could mean that Firm j has the average introduction date in a frequency distribution of actual dates, or that all of Firm i's rivals behave symmetrically. We assume also that each potential new market entrant has the same target market share. Then if there are N potential entrants, each firm's target share is $1/N$, and the aggregate target share of all Firm i's rivals is $(N - 1)/N$. Let V again be the total quasi-rent potential per year of the new market. As before, Firm i is assumed to be able to exploit the full market potential until representative

Firm j imitates, and so up to time T_j its quasi-rent function is

$$\int_{T_i}^{T_j} [1.0 - e^{-\gamma(t-T_i)}] V e^{-\rho t} dt. \tag{22}$$

This really overstates its probable gain, since some firms will normally be ahead of the representative firm (and perhaps also Firm i) in their introduction dates. On the other hand, the estimate for the post-T_j period understates Firm i's gains, since not all firms will have imitated at T_j and hence will not yet have squeezed into the market. The complete estimated quasi-rent function for Firm i can be written as follows:

$$\begin{aligned} V_i = &\int_{T_i}^{\infty} [1.0 - e^{-\gamma(t-T_i)}] V e^{-\rho t} dt \\ &- \int_{T_j}^{\infty} \left[\left(\frac{N-1}{N} \right) e^{-\varepsilon(T_j - T_i)} \right. \\ &\left. - \left(\frac{N-1}{N} \right) e^{-\varepsilon(T_j - T_i) - \mu(t-T_j)} \right] V e^{-\rho t} dt. \end{aligned} \tag{23}$$

Differentiating with respect to T_i, we obtain

$$\begin{aligned} \frac{\partial V_i}{\partial T_i} = V \left[-\frac{\rho e^{-\rho T_i}}{\rho} + \frac{\rho e^{-\rho T_i}}{\gamma + \rho} \right. \\ - \left(\frac{N-1}{N} \right) \frac{\varepsilon e^{-\varepsilon(T_j - T_i) - \rho T_j}}{\rho} \\ \left. + \left(\frac{N-1}{N} \right) \frac{\varepsilon e^{-\varepsilon(T_j - T_i) - \rho T_j}}{\mu + \rho} \right] \end{aligned} \tag{24}$$

The larger the N, the larger $(N-1)/N$ will be, and so the larger $\partial V_i/\partial T_i$ will be for any T_i. Hence the greater the number of firms, the stronger an incentive Firm i has to conduct its development rapidly, realizing as much profit as it can before imitators swarm in and cut into its market position. Differentiating (24) again with respect to T_j, we obtain the cross-partial:

$$\frac{\partial^2 V_i}{\partial T_i \partial T_j} = \frac{V(N-1)}{N} \left[\frac{\varepsilon(\varepsilon + \rho) e^{-\varepsilon(T_j - T_i) - \rho T_j}}{\rho} - \frac{\varepsilon(\varepsilon + \rho) e^{-\varepsilon(T_j - T_i) - \rho T_j}}{\mu + \rho} \right], \tag{25}$$

which is positive, indicating an aggressive reaction to rival accelerations in the innovative stage. The larger the N, the larger $\partial^2 V_i/\partial T_i \partial T_j$ will be, and so the stronger Firm i's reactions to representative rival firm schedule accelerations will be. Thus the model indicates that the greater the number of potential new market entrants, the stronger the incentive an innovating firm will have to develop its new product quickly and to accelerate its development effort in response to rival accelerations.

Taken at face value, these results support the case for atomistic market structure, just as the duopoly results supported the case for relative smallness. However, certain additional qualifications must be introduced. For one, the quasi-rent potential V may not be parametric, as assumed thus far, but may vary inversely (and possibly discontinuously) with N because recognition of mutual interdependence in pricing breaks down as the number of firms increases. This effect would, if foreseen, weaken an innovator's incentive to execute its development rapidly and react sharply to rival accelerations when N is large. On the other hand, increases in N no doubt raise the probability that some firm will in its R & D decisions conform at an early date to the Cournot assumption, ignoring future rival reactions and triggering a race toward early product introduction. Once this happens, other firms are forced to react with their own accelerated development efforts, especially when the rivalry has some market-sharing properties.

It must also be made clear that in this and the preceding section we have been concerned primarily with marginal conditions, that is, with finding *local* profit maxima. But especially in new market rivalries, cases may arise where the global Cournot optimum occurs at a corner (i.e., with a decision not to engage in development at all). The expected value of Firm i's *total* quasi rents (equation 23) *falls* with increases in N as more and more firms divide up a given market potential. Consequently, even though the *marginal* profit incentive for rapid development (equation 24) is strengthened by a high N, the probability of satisfying a positive total profit condition is reduced. And when firms recognize that overcrowding of a new market means losses for all, they may well choose to redirect their R & D resources into less competitive fields. In short, increases in N beyond the value that permits all participants to anticipate earning positive profits could discourage vigorous research and development. The higher the market's overall quasi-rent potential V, and the lower each firm's expected development costs, the higher N can be without having this adverse impact.[33] The crossover point obviously depends on conditions unique to each specific project, although there is reason to believe that more frequently than not N can be reasonably large (e.g., well in excess of four firms) before technological rivalry is inhibited. One bit of supporting evidence is provided by a recent statistical study showing that the ratio of scientific and engineering employment to total employment in American manufacturing industries during 1960 attained a maximum at four-firm concentration ratios of approximately 55 percent.[34]

Richer insights into research and development rivalry might be derived by elaborating the presently naive N-firm model along more complex and realistic lines. One promising approach is to substitute a distributed lag imitation function, possibly based upon available empirical data, for the representative firm device.[35] This task lies beyond the reach of the present paper.

5.7 Welfare Implications

If the preceding analysis is at all near the mark, rivalry normally accelerates the pace of technological research, development, and innovation, as long as the number of firms competing is not excessive. When quasi-rent cross-partial terms $\partial^2 V_i / \partial T_i \partial T_j$ are positive, Cournot reactions will carry firms to equilibrium development schedules shorter than the schedules optimal under monopoly. Negative cross-partial terms appear only in market-sharing rivalries where ε is small and $\beta > \delta$, or when bottlenecks constrain small innovators' sales growth. Asymmetries in duopoly market shares and (within limits) increases in the number of rivals also heighten incentives for accelerated development.

Of course this acceleration of technological progress has its price. From the standpoint of the firms involved, rivalry that leads to Cournot or minimax equilibria fails to maximize joint profits. Still it is more important to answer the question: Is the social welfare enhanced by the accelerated development of new products due to rivalry, despite the increased development costs arising from duplication and schedule compression? Here we draw upon a proposition recently proved elegantly by Dan Usher.[36] Even when there are no external economies of the sort frequently associated with the advance of technology, any commercially profitable product or process innovation necessarily confers a net benefit or consumer surplus upon society which cannot be appropriated by the innovator(s) except under a first-degree discriminating monopoly. More simply, if the innovators benefit privately from an innovation, society must also benefit.

Two separate cases must be examined. First, in the new market case rivalry-induced acceleration of development is definitely desirable socially. This is so because unprofitable investment in new product research and development is inconsistent with Cournot equilibrium, at least in an *ex ante* expected value sense. If rival reactions drive any firm into a position where its expected development costs exceed expected quasi rents, the firm can react submissively, cancelling its development project and realizing the "nothing ventured, nothing gained" zero-profit outcome.[37] If then development is profitable at the accelerated schedule equilibrium, a consumer surplus must be realized, and so the schedule under rivalry cannot be socially undesirable. It must indeed be socially desirable, for consumers receive the new product at the same price and in the same quantities earlier (assuming that *pricing* decisions are not affected by the date of introduction) and therefore realize their consumer surplus over a longer period.[38]

The pure market-sharing case is quite different. An innovator's quasi-rent gains are the losses of imitators, for by definition no expansion of the overall market results from the product change. Therefore firms cannot avoid losses simply by cancelling their development projects, unless rivals do so too. Furthermore, since quasi-rent gains and losses sum to zero, any finite development schedule must be unprofitable in the aggregate, and shorter, more expensive development schedules mean higher aggregate private losses than more leisurely schedules. Still as Usher demonstrates, privately unprofitable innovations may nevertheless confer net social benefits. No clear-cut judgment is possible without information (on consumer and social indifference curves) that is never practically available.

Since most new product rivalries are a blend of the pure new market and market-sharing types, we can reach no simple generalization concerning the social desirability of accelerated innovation induced by rivalry. In some cases, especially when significant new markets are opened up, acceleration is clearly beneficial. But in other cases the welfare effects of rivalry could on balance be unfavorable, and contrary to widespread belief, private incentives may cause too much money to be spent on research and development.

5.8 Conclusion

This paper is offered more in the spirit of a beginning than an end. Numerous extensions of the basic model can be visualized, such as to allow quality leapfrogging and finite reaction lags and to permit a more complete treatment of the N-firm problem. An adaptation to qualitative arms races is conceivable. And perhaps most important, the rivalry parameters δ, β, γ, μ, ε, and α might all be estimated through empirical studies, if the ubiquitous *cetera* can be successfully impounded *in paribus*. Hopefully, economists undertaking studies of industries prone to new product rivalry will make the attempt.

Notes

Work on this paper was supported by a grant from the Inter-University Committee on the Microeconomics of Technological Change and Economic Growth, sponsored in turn by the Ford Foundation. Use was also made of computer facilities supported in part by National Science Foundation Grant NSF-GP579. The author is indebted to W. O. Criminale, R. E. Quandt, and Carl Kaysen for helpful comments.

1. For a more complete discussion, see my Government Research and Development Programs, in Robert Dorfman (ed.), *Measuring Benefits of Government Investments* (Washington, D.C.: Brookings Institution, 1965), pp. 34–56; and Time-Cost Tradeoffs in Uncertain Empirical Research Projects, *Naval Research Logistics Quarterly* 13 (March 1966): 71–82.

2. See M. J. Peck and F. M. Scherer, *The Weapons Acquisition Process: An Economic Analysis* (Boston: Harvard Business School, Division of Research, 1962), p. 311.

3. Total undiscounted costs begin to increase as T is stretched beyond 8.5 years because economies of specialization are lost when the project is conducted at too small a scale in any time period. The minimum cost point shifts to higher values of T as r is increased, and when $r > 0.15$ the backward bend disappears.

4. See Edwin Mansfield and Richard Brandenburg, The Allocation, Characteristics, and Outcome of the Firm's Research & Development Portfolio: A Case Study, *Journal of Business* 29 (October 1966): 447–464.

5. See Peck and Scherer, *The Weapons Acquisition Process*, pp. 254–281. For an application to military contracting policy, see N. S. Weiner, Multiple Incentive Fee Maximization: An Economic Model, *Quarterly Journal of Economics* 77 (November 1963): 604–616.

6. See Oscar Lange, A Note on Innovations, *Review of Economic Statistics* 25 (February 1943): 19–25, who argues that process innovations by oligopolists will usually be of this type.

7. Though conventional, this treatment of the discounting problem implies the partial equilibrium assumption that the project is small enough relative to the firm's overall R & D portfolio that changes in its resource allocations do not induce overall R & D portfolio changes, and hence affect the value of the firm's opportunity cost.

8. Second-order conditions for a maximum will normally be satisfied if there is a physical limit to the compression of development time. Note also that no provision for new capital

investment at the time of commercialization has been made here. Inclusion of an investment term would not alter the results significantly. On both points, see my Government Research and Development Programs, pp. 48–51.

9. See W. Eric Gustafson, Research and Development, New Products, and Productivity Change, *American Economic Review* 52 (May 1962): 178–179; F. M. Scherer, Size of Firm, Oligopoly, and Research, *Canadian Journal of Economics and Political Science* 31 (May 1965): 260–261; and Pouring More Billions into R & D, *Business Week* (May 7, 1966): 165.

10. For one attempt to do so in the weapons development field, see Peck and Scherer, *The Weapons Acquisition Process*, pp. 632–638.

11. Continuous exogenous technological progress can be represented by an additional term $-\lambda t$ in the exponent of equation (2). Developments made worthwhile mainly because a shift in the time-cost trade-off function has occured can be called "technology-push" innovations. Those made worthwhile because firms find themselves entering a period of especially high $r(t)$ values can be called "demand-pull" innovations. On these two notions a more general dynamic theory of technological innovation can be built, although the task lies beyond the scope of the present paper. For a penetrating empirical analysis of supply and demand influences in technological change, see Jacob Schmookler, *Invention and Economic Growth* (Cambridge: Harvard University Press, 1966).

12. Ideally we should like to build a model that incorporates explicit reaction lags. This is not possible because the mathematics would become formidable, and because correct specification of a completely dynamic cost function requires insights presently unavailable. Suppose that a firm proceeds along path $T = 8$ in figure 5.2 for two years and then accelerates its effort (e.g., to path $T = 4$). Where will it enter the $T = 4$ path? Clearly not at $t = 2$, for in two years along the $T = 8$ path the firm will hardly have completed as much of the required R & D work as it would have by *starting* along the $T = 4$ path. Realized development costs and time must evidently be some weighted average of the values associated with each "pure" path followed. The question is, is progress toward completion in an R & D effort proportional to the percentage of a schedule's time consumed, or to the amount of planned expenditure actually achieved? If the former, the firm starting along the $T = 8$ path will have attained 25 percent completion in two years, but if the latter, it will have attained only about 4 percent completion. The actual relationship is undoubtedly a blend of these extremes. Progress in solving conceptual problems (research?) is probably more closely proportional to time than to expenditures, while progress in reducing concepts to practice (development?) may be more closely proportional to effort. Until we know more about these dynamic relationships, some misspecification is unavoidable.

13. V is, of course, a function of many things such as consumer tastes, the product price, the prices of other substitute products, advertising outlays, and consumer income. But exclusion of these variables from the present analysis poses no problems as long as they are not related functionally to the decision variables—the rivals' development schedules.

14. Note that if we are analyzing the problem from the imitator's point of view, $t = 0$ must be calibrated so as to make T_F reflect the imitator's development time as well as its product introduction date. But when we are analyzing the problem from the innovator's point of view, T_F can reflect the imitator's introduction date but not its development time, if the imitator begins development later than the innovator (e.g., at time $t > 0$). This complication will be ignored in many of the following analyses through the assumption of symmetric development initiation dates, although the symmetry assumption will be relaxed at a later stage.

15. How Gillette Has Put on a New Face, *Business Week* (April 1, 1967): 58.

16. Heinrich von Stackelberg, *Marktform und Gleichgewicht* (Vienna and Berlin: J. Springer, 1934), pp. 44–53.

17. See T. C. Schelling, *The Strategy of Conflict* (Cambridge, Ma.: Harvard University Press, 1960), p. 156n.

18. It is worth noting that the lower the discount rate ρ, the more strikingly the profits from a joint-maximizing strategy diverge from those achieved with any given inferior strategy.

19. The automobile manufacturers apparently tried hard to avoid rivalrous handling of safety innovations. They experienced some success during the late 1950s and early 1960s, but since the recent surge of interest in safety, cooperation has proved more difficult. See The Face in the Mirror at General Motors, *Fortune* 71 (August 1966): 209, and Safety Executive at Ford Asks End of "One-Upmanship," *New York Times* (February 27, 1966).

20. See R. D. Luce and Howard Raiffa, *Games and Decisions* (New York: Wiley, 1957), pp. 98–102, and L. B. Lave, An Empirical Approach to the Prisoners' Dilemma Game, *Quarterly Journal of Economics* 76 (August 1962): 424–436.

21. A similar argument emphasizing the complexity of ballistic missile deployment decisions is employed by Martin McGuire to support the use of the Cournot assumption. *Secrecy and the Arms Race* (Cambridge, Ma.: Harvard University Press, 1965), pp. 166–167.

22. For illustrations drawn from the atomic and hydrogen bomb development histories, see F. M. Scherer, Was the Nuclear Arms Race Inevitable?, *Co-Existence* (January 1966): 56–59.

23. William Fellner, The Influence of Market Structure on Technological Progress, *Quarterly Journal of Economics* 65 (November 1951): 574–575.

24. This concept of "submissiveness" was first employed by Lewis F. Richardson in his study of quantitative arms races. *Arms and Insecurity* (Chicago: Quadrangle, 1960), pp. 52–60. See also K. E. Boulding, *Conflict and Defense* (New York: Harper, 1962), ch. 2.

25. "Permanent" market share erosion does not necessarily mean erosion for ever and ever, but only in a *ceteris paribus* sense. Although a laggard may lose market position permanently if it never goes further than belatedly matching the innovator's new product quality, it might recover by innovating in a new game at a higher quality level. Here quality leapfrogging rivalries, which cannot be analyzed directly with the present model, may become especially relevant.

A related complication also warrants attention. Quasi-rent equations (9) and (10) both have infinite upper limits. This does not lead to absurd results because of the discount terms, but it might misrepresent the case where decision makers have finite horizons, perhaps because future product rivalry is expected to negate the effects of the current rivalry. To explore this case, both models were analyzed assuming finite horizons. Analytic generalization becomes more difficult, since the finite horizon analogue of cross-partial equation (14) has four terms and the analogue of (16) seven terms. Generally, imposition of a finite horizon makes submissive reactions somewhat more likely. However, a numerical analysis of some 4,000 values of the finite horizon version of equation (16) for a wide range of critical parameter values showed that the finite and infinite horizon results differ only slightly for horizons as short as twelve years.

26. The illustration is only an approximation because Firm 2 has proceeded with its development at a low rate for a year before Firm 1 reacts, and so we run into the cost function definition problems discussed in note 12. Firm 2's reaction function has been drawn in figure 5.5 on the assumption that the firm can adjust the level of its R & D effort for *every* period, which is obviously incorrect. The dotted reaction function therefore *overstates* Firm 2's reaction possibilities. A more accurate, fully dynamic function should lie further north at least in the neighborhood of its lowest time values. The longer the lag before the imitator begins its imitating development, the more constrained the leader's reaction possibilities are, until, when the imitator's lag equals the innovator's original development time, no opportunity for a leader reaction remains.

27. The new market case has similar properties but is more complex. A proof is omitted to conserve space.

28. One qualification is in order. Even though the potential *absolute* gain for a small firm exceeds the potential absolute loss, utility-maximizing small firm managers may be more concerned about *relative* position losses. In other words, losing half a $5 million market may be just as disturbing as gaining half of a $20 million market is satisfying. To the extent that this is true, small firms will be more vigorous technologically than the present profit-maximizing analysis suggests.

29. Reaction functions like those shown in figure 5.6 also make von Stackelberg leadership attractive. L_2 in figure 5.6 shows the dominant firm's von Stackelberg leadership point, and L_1 the small firm's leadership strategy.

30. F. M. Scherer, The Development of Microwave Radio Relay Systems in Bell Telephone Laboratories, unpublished case study. The example is not perfect because regulatory constraints on network interconnection also discouraged potential newcomers.

31. H. C. Passer, *The Electrical Manufacturers* (Cambridge, Ma.: Harvard University Press, 1953), esp. pp. 358–360; W. R. Maclaurin, *Invention and Innovation in the Radio Industry* (New York: Macmillan, 1949); A. A. Bright, *The Electric Lamp Industry* (New York: Macmillan, 1949); Edwin Mansfield, Size of Firm, Market Structure, and Innovation, *Journal of Political Economy* 71 (December 1963), 561; and How Chevrolet Sets the Pace for Detroit, *Business Week* (December 4, 1965): 62.

32. Adell Chemical more than doubled its sales each year from 1955 to 1960. But four years after Procter & Gamble and then Lever Brothers retaliated with their own household liquid detergents, Lestoil's share of the relevant market had dropped from nearly 100 percent to 12 percent—a nice example of high μ and low ε coefficients. See Lestoil: The Road Back, *Business Week* (June 15, 1963): 118–124; and Two Small Companies Move in Big on the $100-Million Liquid Cleaner Market, *Business Week* (December 17, 1966): 140.

33. It is worth noting that when time-cost trade-off functions shift continuously toward the origin, as assumed in note 11, and when demand-induced shifts in V are also continuous, there will be room for only one firm to carry out the development profitably when an innovation first becomes profitable. It follows that when the quasi-rent potential is sufficient to sustain profitable development by more than one firm, there must either have been a lag in recognition of the profit potential, or a discontinuous shift in the cost or quasi-rent functions.

34. F. M. Scherer, Market Structure and the Employment of Scientists and Engineers, *American Economic Review* 57 (June 1967).

35. See Edwin Mansfield, The Speed of Response of Firms to New Techniques, *Quarterly Journal of Economics* 67 (May 1963): 290–309; and Intrafirm Rates of Diffusion of an Innovation, *Review of Economics and Statistics* 45 (November 1963): 348–359.

36. The Welfare Economics of Invention, *Economica* 31 (August 1964): 279–287.

37. This reaction turned up frequently in computer simulations of the new market case with low values of V or high values of ε. It should be noted that the abandonment alternative will involve no losses at all only if reactions are instantaneous, so that firms realize their efforts will be unprofitable before heavy development costs have been sunk. This is obviously never strictly true, but we have seen that convergence may come very close to Cournot equilibrium in only three steps, and if these steps are taken early in the development effort, when spending rates are low, the sunk expenditures will be small relative to total potential development costs (see figure 5.1).

38. To be sure, this welfare judgment ignores income redistribution considerations. The higher costs of accelerated research and development programs benefit individuals in white coats at the expense of stockholders.

6 The Microeconomics of Decision Making for Innovation

In most sectors of the U.S. economy, decision making for technological innovation is carried out by private enterprises seeking to maximize their profits, taking into account market supply and demand conditions. A rich body of economic theory and empirical evidence on these decision-making processes has been accumulated over the past two decades.

Technological innovation can be characterized as responding to both technology-push and demand-pull influences.[1] Technology push occurs when changes in scientific and engineering knowledge make new products or processes feasible or reduce their costs. Demand pull occurs when the market for an innovation expands, causing the benefits realizable through innovation to exceed costs. The role of technology-push stimuli has long been known. Pioneering statistical research by Jacob Schmookler has shown more recently that demand-pull influences are also very important.[2] Specifically, Schmookler demonstrated that changes in innovative activity, as measured through a count of capital goods invention patents, are highly correlated with changes in investment. He has shown furthermore that peaks and valleys in inventive activity typically *lag* changes in investment, rather than preceding them in time.[3] Schmookler argues that invention rises in response to a demand increase because there are more people engaged in production and hence a higher probability of chance invention, more abundant sources of capital, and higher profitability for any given invention.[4]

It has often been argued that uncertainty and risk are too great to permit rational decision making with respect to technological innovation. Research by Edwin Mansfield has shed much light on the costs and risks of industrial research and development (R & D) projects, which are the principal institutionalization of technological innovation in a market economy. In various samples of electrical equipment, proprietary drug, and chemical R & D projects, the average probability of successful technical completion varied between 0.52 and 0.68.[5] Only 16 percent of the electrical equipment R & D projects were cancelled owing to unanticipated technical difficulties. However, projects that are technically successful often experience a lack of acceptance in the marketplace. The fraction of projects that ultimately resulted in a profit on the market ranged from 8 to 29 percent in three business firms studied by Mansfield.[6]

Source: In *The Economics of Technological Progress*, Lloyd Reynolds, ed. (U.S.–U.S.S.R. Symposium, privately published, 1976), pp. 99–112.

Enterprises pursue diverse strategies to cope with the technological uncertainties of research and development. One is to delay the initiation of costly development work until inexpensive applied research has pointed the way to solutions. Another is to proceed step by step in development, making sure that each earlier step has resolved all relevant uncertainties. A third is to pursue multiple approaches simultaneously to ensure that at least one approach will be successful. The more parallel projects the enterprise supports and the greater the degree to which development tasks are carried out concurrently rather than in series, the sooner successful technical completion will occur, but the more costly the development effort will be.[7] These time-cost trade-off possibilities can be characterized mathematically in terms of the "development possibility function"

$$C = C(T_0, T_E, t), \tag{1}$$

where C is the discounted total cost of development, T_0 is the time at which development is begun, T_E is the expected date of successful completion, and t is a running time variable. The phenomenon of technology push is characterized by the relationship $\partial C / \partial t < 0$. The time-cost trade-off relationship tends to have the properties $\partial C / \partial (T_E - T_0) < 0$ and $\partial^2 C / \partial (T_E - T_0)^2 > 0$.

To maximize its profits, a capitalist enterprise seeks to maximize the difference between the discounted private benefits from an innovation and development cost, where the benefits reflect either the net cost savings afforded by a process innovation or the surplus of new product sales revenues less production and marketing costs. Let the expected benefit in year t be $b(t)$. Assume, for the sake of simplicity, that the stream of potential benefits over time is of constant depth, so that $\partial b / \partial t = 0$ and demand-pull stimuli are absent. Assume also that the decision to commence development is taken at time $t = 0$ so that the expected duration of the development period is given by T_E. Then the enterprise's problem is to choose that development strategy characterized by a value of T_E that maximizes its expected profits:

$$\pi = \int_{T_E}^{\infty} b(t) e^{-rt} dt - C(T_E), \tag{2}$$

where r is the enterprise's cost of capital or rate of time discount. Then the first-order condition for maximum profits is

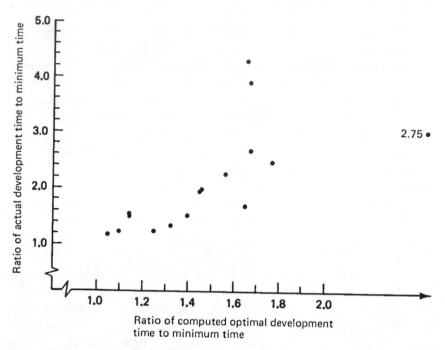

Figure 6.1
Comparison of Mansfield's actually observed with computed optimal development times

$$\frac{\partial \pi}{\partial T_E} = -b(T_E)e^{-rT_E} - \frac{\partial C(T_E)}{\partial T_E} = 0. \tag{3}$$

Since $\partial C(T_E)/\partial T_E < 0$, this means that the profit-maximizing development period T_E will be shorter, the larger $b(t)$ is (i.e., the more lucrative the benefits from development are). This is an intuitively appealing result: important projects—those that yield large payoffs—should be conducted more rapidly and with more generous resource support than unimportant projects.

Mansfield and colleagues have estimated the shape and magnitude of the time-cost trade-off functions and marginal benefits for sixteen chemical, machinery, and electronics research and development projects.[8] They then computed the optimal development time for each. Analysis of their data reveals that projects do in fact tend to be conducted more rapidly and at higher cost, the higher the value of $b(T_E)$ is relative to the minimum possible development cost. Figure 6.1 relates the ratios of actual-to-minimum to computed optimal-to-minimum development times. The simple correlation between the logarithms of the two sets of ratios is $+0.75$.

That the derivative of $\int_{T_E}^{\infty} b(t)e^{-rt}\,dt$ with respect to T_E is negative means that the discounted benefits function $B(T_E)$ has a negative slope when it is plotted on present money value and development time coordinates, as in figure 6.2a. The development cost function $C(T_E)$ likewise has a negative slope, and the optimal development time T_E^* occurs where the vertical distance between the two curves is minimized. This assumes a vantage point in time $t = T_0 = 0$, and development is commenced immediately. But as running time t advances, the relative positions of the two curves may change. Figure 6.2b shows a shift in the development cost function from one possible starting date to another owing to the exogenous advance of scientific and engineering knowledge. At the vantage point in time for which development cost function $C(\cdot, \cdot, 1)$ is constructed, no schedule of development is profitable. But technology push has made development profitable from the later vantage point for which $C(\cdot, \cdot, 2)$ has been constructed. Analogously, an exogenous increase in demand may shift the $B(T)$ curves outward, as in figure 6.2c, making development profitable when previously it was not. Such a shift exemplifies the demand-pull effect.

When either the benefit or cost curves are shifting continuously over time, a profit-maximizing firm must determine the best moment when to commence development as well as the best time schedule to use for conducting development. The mathematics for this problem can become quite complex.[9] If one assumes, for simplicity, a fixed period of active development or that discounted development costs are invariant with respect to the length of the development period, but that development costs decline continuously at the rate of 100δ percent per year as the starting date is deferred, and assuming further that benefits continue to be realized into perpetuity, it can be shown that it is profitable to delay the initiation of development until the benefit in the year of completion $b(T_E)$ is equal to $(\delta + r)$ times the discounted cost of development.[10] On the other hand, development is barely profitable (i.e., at the breakeven point) when its initiation is deferred only until $b(T_E)$ equals r times the discounted cost of development. Thus the enterprise that anticipates a continuing

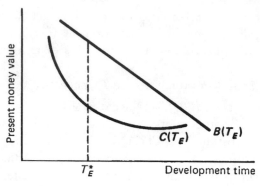

a.

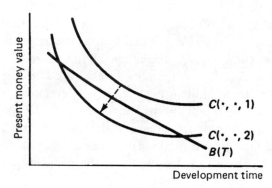

b.

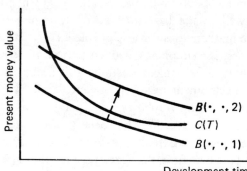

c.

Figure 6.2
Time-cost trade-off and benefits function relationships: (a) the static optimum, (b) the
technology-push case, (c) the demand-pull case

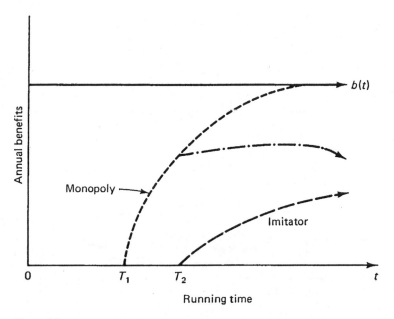

Figure 6.3
Innovator and imitator benefit flows

exogenous technology push will not commence development at the moment when an innovation first becomes profitable but will wait until it can expect above-normal economic profits. Such a strategy of delay is feasible only if the firm has an insulated monopoly position. Competition among enterprises to be first in the market with a new product or process will tend to accelerate the initiation of development to an earlier, less profitable date. If the private benefits to the innovator are less than the overall benefits to society from having the new product or process, as is typically the case, such acceleration is desirable in terms of increasing social welfare.[11] It is not necessarily true, however, that acceleration of innovation to the point at which innovators realize zero economic profits is socially optimal.[12] A zero-profit result is optimal only when the ratio of social to private benefits $k = (\delta + r)/r$.

Another view of the role of competition can be obtained by assuming that development begins at time $t = 0$ and expanding the benefit function $b(t)$ to reflect the fact that the first enterprise on the market with a superior new product gains a market share advantage which is larger and endures

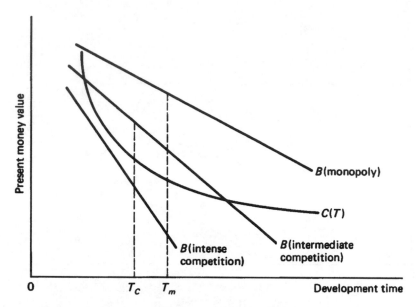

Figure 6.4
How the speed of innovation depends on market structure

longer, the greater is the first firm's product introduction date lead over rival imitators. The mathematics again can become fairly complex, so a geometric overview will be provided instead.[13] Let $b(t)$ now represent the *potential* benefits derivable from introducing a new product, rather than the benefits actually realized. Assume that this potential is constant over time, as with the solid horizontal line $b(t)$ in figure 6.3. No innovator is likely to realize this potential fully immediately after introducing its new product; it takes time to penetrate and cultivate the market. For an enterprise that introduces the product at time T_1 and then remains a monopolist, the time trajectory of its benefits realization is likely to approximate the dotted line labeled "monopoly" in figure 6.3. However, if competitive imitation occurs at time T_2, the second firm into the market may realize a benefits stream shown by the dashed trajectory labeled "imitator" in figure 6.3, and the would-be monopolist's benefits are eroded accordingly, as described by the dot-dash line branching off from the monopolist's benefit stream.

Mathematical manipulations too intricate to reproduce in this short paper reveal that, rather generally, the introduction of competition into a new product development situation which otherwise would be monopolized has two main effects.[14] These are describable geometrically through figure 6.4, which is similar to figure 6.2, with the present value of expected benefits and costs on the vertical axis and the length of the development period on the horizontal axis. First, competition steepens a firm's discounted expected benefit function, leading to an acceleration of the profit-maximizing development schedule (e.g., from T_M to T_C). Second, competition shifts the discounted expected benefit function toward the origin. This need cause no special problem. But it can if the shift is sufficiently large that the benefits function lies at all points below and to the left of the discounted development cost function. Then development is perceived to be unprofitable and does not occur (e.g., with the lowest of the three benefits functions, marked "intense competition" in figure 6.4).

We find therefore a kind of paradox. Up to a point, competition leads to an acceleration in the pace of technological innovation, both by ensuring that some enterprise will commence research and development at an early date and by stimulating a fast pace of development. But too much competition in too small a market may stifle incentives for development. What is needed for a rapid rate of technological advance is the proper blend of competition and monopoly.

This insight has further implications in the technology-push and demand-pull phenomena. When an innovation is not profitable even to a monopolist, it may become profitable if demand increases or research and development costs fall. A sharp drop in development costs associated with a scientific or technological breakthrough or a sudden spurt in demand can make development profitable even for fragmented, highly competitive industries as well as for monopolized industries. Then the propensity of competitive industries to exploit new development possibilities quickly is unambiguously favorable. When on the other hand exogenous scientific progress occurs only gradually and continuously or demand grows slowly, monopolists will for a time be uniquely able to exploit the technical possibilities profitably, and, despite their lack of stimulus, they may innovate sooner than firms in a more competitively structured but otherwise identical industry would. Although the evidence available on this phenomenon thus far has been meager, two statistical studies of the relationship between market structure and the vigor of research and development effort suggest that monopolistic structure is most conducive to technological innovation in fields with a slow pace of scientific advance or limited opportunities for product differentiation, whereas the effect of monopoly power is weak or even negative in high-opportunity fields.[15] Thus the most favorable market structure for technological innovation depends on such variables as the rate of exogenous scientific advance.

Such models of technological rivalry among private enterprises can also be extended to shed light on the nature of qualitative arms races between nation states.[16]

Notes

1. See Richard R. Nelson, The Economics of Invention, *Journal of Business* (April 1959): 101–127.

2. Jacob Schmookler, *Invention and Economic Growth* (Cambridge: Harvard University Press, 1966).

3. Ibid., pp. 115–136.

4. Ibid., pp. 109–115.

5. Edwin Mansfield, *Industrial Research and Technological Innovation* (New York: Norton, 1968), p. 59; and Edwin Mansfield, John Rapoport, Jerome Schnee, Samuel Wagner, and Michael Hamburger, *Research and Innovation in the Modern Corporation* (New York: Norton, 1971), pp. 35–36 and 41–42.

6. *Research and Innovation in the Modern Corporation*, pp. 55–57.

7. Compare Richard R. Nelson, Uncertainty, Learning and the Economics of Parallel Research and Development Projects, *Review of Economics and Statistics* (November 1961): 351–364; M. J. Peck and F. M. Scherer, *The Weapons Acquisition Process: An Economic Analysis* (Boston: Harvard Business School Division of Research, 1962), pp. 254–268; F. M. Scherer, Time-Cost Tradeoffs in Uncertain Empirical Research Projects, *Naval Research Logistics Quarterly* (March 1966): 71–82; and Mansfield et al., *Research and Innovation in the Modern Corporation*, pp. 110–156.

8. *Research and Innovation in the Modern Corporation*, pp. 152–155.

9. See Carole Kitti, *Patent Policy and the Optimal Timing of Innovations*, Ph.D. dissertation, University of Chicago, 1973.

10. Where C is the cost of development at time 0, the development cost declines at the rate 100δ percent per year, and the benefits realized each year after successful development are b, one maximizes

$$\int_{T_0}^{\infty} be^{-rt}dt - Ce^{-(\delta+r)T_0}$$

with respect to T_0. The first-order condition for a maximum is

$$be^{-rT_0} = (\delta + r)Ce^{-(\delta+r)T_0}.$$

11. See Edwin Mansfield, John Rapoport, Anthony Romeo, Samuel Wagner, and George Beardsley, Social and Private Rates of Return from Industrial Innovations, *Quarterly Journal of Economics* (May 1977): 221–240.

12. See Yoram Barzel, Optimal Timing of Innovation, *Review of Economics and Statistics* (August 1968): 348–355; and Morton Kamien and Nancy Schwartz, Timing of Innovations under Rivalry, *Econometrica* (January 1972): 43–60.

13. See F. M. Scherer, Research and Development Resource Allocation under Rivalry, *Quarterly Journal of Economics* (August 1967): 359–394.

14. Ibid.; Morton I. Kamien and Nancy L. Schwartz, On the Degree of Rivalry for Maximum Innovative Activity, *Quarterly Journal of Economics* (May 1976): 245–260; and Kamien and Schwartz, Potential Rivalry, Monopoly Profits and the Pace of Innovative Activity, manuscript, Northwestern University Graduate School of Management, February 1976.

15. See F. M. Scherer, Market Structure and the Employment of Scientists and Engineers, *American Economic Review* (June 1967): 524–530; and William S. Comanor, Market Structure, Product Differentiation, and Industrial Research, *Quarterly Journal of Economics* (November 1967): 639–657.

16. See Peck and Scherer, *The Weapons Acquisition Process*, ch. 9 and appendix 9A; and Martin McGuire, *Secrecy and the Arms Race* (Cambridge: Harvard University Press, 1965).

7 Nordhaus's Theory of Optimal Patent Life: A Geometric Reinterpretation

For more than a century the patent system has been studied with remarkable care by economists.[1] Yet only recently, in a contribution by William Nordhaus, has formal economic theory been brought to bear successfully on the central policy issue of the patent system—*how much protection* should be accorded inventors and innovators. This article extends Nordhaus's pioneering work and corrects what in some cases is a significant interpretational error. Nordhaus's original presentation was largely algebraic, but certain problems he left unsolved can be tackled more directly through the geometric approach taken here. This mode of attack has the fringe benefit of making what in the original paper was a rather forbidding tangle of mathematical notation more comprehensible intuitively.

7.1 The Basic Model

I begin by observing, as Nordhaus did, that inventions and innovations are not free goods. To make and introduce an invention that reduces unit production costs, research and development (RD) outlays must be incurred. For any given production task there exists at some moment in time an "invention possibility function" (*IPF*) which relates the percentage unit production cost reduction B achieved (the "output" of an inventive effort) to the expenditure on RD. The more research input, the greater will be the cost saving, *ceteris paribus*. For mathematical convenience Nordhaus considers only the very simple invention possibility function $B = \beta RD^{\alpha}$, which with $\alpha < 1$ implies continuously diminishing marginal returns to inventive effort. However, it seems more plausible (and as we shall see, more flexible) to assume an inflected function like $B(RD)$ in figure 7.1, where at first there are increasing returns to the research effort, after which diminishing returns set in.

The benefits to the firm depend in a slightly more complex manner on the cost savings facilitated. Following Kenneth Arrow, Nordhaus assumes that production is initially carried out under competitive conditions at constant unit cost and price $0C_0$, as shown in the conventional supply and demand diagram figure 7.2.[2] The firm that secures exclusive patent rights on an invention reducing unit costs to $0C_1$ can either drive

Source: *American Economic Review* 62 (June 1972): 422–427. Journal of the American Economic Association.

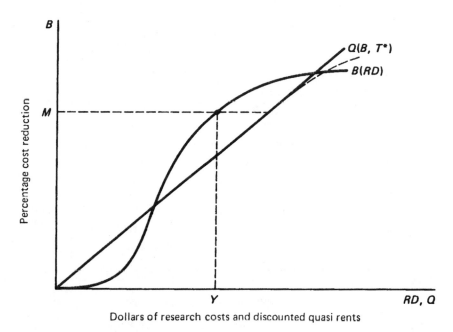

Figure 7.1
The invention possibility and discounted quasi-rent functions

other firms out of business, producing the whole former output $0X_0$ and commanding a monopoly rent of $C_0 EAC_1$ per year, or it can license the patent to existing producers, charging a royalty that extracts the same surplus $C_0 EAC_1$ from them. Note that even though the patent confers some monopoly power, it does not permit the patent holder to charge a price above the cost $0C_0$ associated with the (now inferior) competitive process. Because of this, and if demand is not very elastic in the neighborhood of the competitive price, the optimal postinvention price and quantity under a patent monopoly will be identical to those in the preinvention equilibrium. However, if the invention reduces cost by so much (i.e., to $0C_2$) that the new long-run cost curve cuts the monopolist's marginal revenue curve MR to the right of the old competitive output $0X_0$, the patent holder will find it advantageous to see that price is reduced below $0C_0$ and that output is expanded beyond $0X_0$. Nordhaus assigns the name "run-of-the-mill" to inventions that reduce cost insufficiently to induce a price reduction and output expansion, as with process $0C_1$ in

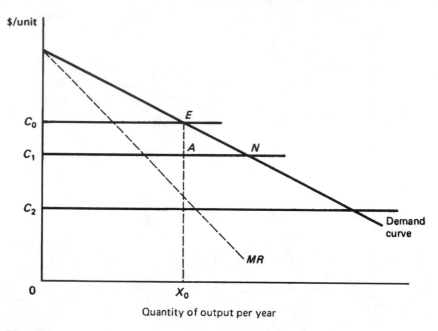

Figure 7.2
Output and quasi-rent effects of a cost-reducing invention

figure 7.2. Following Nordhaus, I shall focus here on the run-of-the-mill case, touching only peripherally on the case of "drastic" price-reducing process inventions like those leading to unit cost $0C_2$ in figure 7.2.

Since there is no output expansion effect with run-of-the-mill inventions, the annual monopoly rent to the patent holder is a linear function of the percentage cost reduction B. For a given patent life $T = T^*$, the patent monopolist's total discounted quasi-rent function $Q(B, T^*)$ can therefore be shown as a straight line in the coordinates of figure 7.1.[3] (If the cost reduction effort is pursued into the stage where the "drastic" invention case holds, the quasi-rent function begins to curve rightward, as shown by the dashed offshoot from $Q(B, T^*)$ in figure 7.1.) Given the market demand and competitive supply conditions, the invention possibility function $B(RD)$, and some patent life T^*, the firm maximizes its profits by extending its RD expenditures to that level where the horizontal distance between the "cost of invention" function $B(RD)$ and the quasi-rent function $Q(B, T^*)$ is a maximum (i.e., at RD outlay $0Y$ and percentage cost reduction $0M$ in figure 7.1).

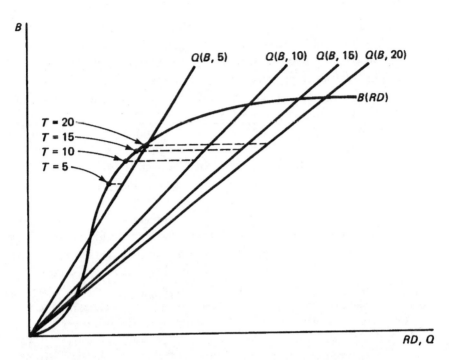

Figure 7.3
How the extent of invention depends on patent life

The patent grant's duration T is usually fixed by the government. This means that T is a parameter to the inventor-innovator (though some exceptions exist). But to the government the patent life is a policy variable, normally decided on for broad classes of inventions, though case-by-case determination is not inconceivable. As the government increases the patent grant's life under given technological and market conditions, the number of years over which the patent recipient can command monopoly rents rises, and the quasi-rent function $Q(B, T)$ shifts to the right. For simplicity, I (and Nordhaus) assume that the patent holder reaps the full monopoly potential of its invention while the patent is in force and that competitive imitation wipes out supranormal rents completely at the patent's expiration date. Thus we tentatively ignore imitation lags, reputation effects, and the obsolescence that occurs due to exogenous technological change and competitive "inventing around" one's patent. Given these assumptions and constant market demand, the existence of a positive discount rate ensures that the rightward shift of $Q(B, T)$ with increases in T exhibits diminishing returns, since the gains from incremental patent life extensions are discounted more and more heavily. Figure 7.3 illustrates the relationships between run-of-the-mill invention quasi-rent functions for various patent lives, assuming constant demand and continuous compounding at a 12 percent discount rate. As the period of patent protection rises, the equal-slope, maximum profit point on the invention possibility function shifts to the right, as indicated by arrows designating the several patent holder's optima in figure 7.3. The longer the patent's life, the farther a profit-maximizing firm will carry its cost-reducing RD expenditures.

How far should this cost-reducing effort proceed if society's interest is to be served? To find out, Nordhaus uses a standard technique of welfare economics. Returning to figure 7.2, we observe that while a run-of-the-mill invention leading to unit cost $0C_1$ enjoys patent protection, the patentee realizes each year a producer's surplus $C_0 E A C_1$ equal to the cost saving on the preinvention output. When the patent expires, competition drives the price down to $0C_1$, output is increased, the producer's surplus is wiped out, and society gains a new consumers' surplus $C_0 E N C_1$. Ignoring the redistributive implications of this change (or assuming constant and equal marginal utilities of income between the patent holder and society in general), the "price" society pays to induce a reduction in unit costs from $0C_0$ to $0C_1$ is essentially the sacrifice of the "welfare triangle" $EAN (= C_0 E N C_1 - C_0 E A C_1)$ from the time the invention is introduced until the date of patent expiration, plus the inventor's RD costs. To find the socially optimal patent life, one must balance the marginal deferrals of this welfare triangle surplus EAN and the (rising) RD costs against the increasing amount of cost reduction (and hence increases in producer's and consumers' surplus) stimulated by longer patent lives.

Here geometry proves a blunter tool than algebra. Nordhaus determines the socially optimal patent life by maximizing with respect to T the sum of the discounted producer's surpluses $C_0 E A C_1$ from the start of the patent's life ($t = 0$) to T, plus the discounted consumers' surplus $C_0 E N C_1$ from year T to infinity, less the cost of research and development incurred; all subject to an equality constraint reflecting the inventor-innovator firm's profit-maximizing behavior in setting the slope of its IPF equal to the slope of its quasi-rent function $Q(B, T)$. The mathematics are fairly intricate and will not be reproduced. Here it suffices to characterize the heart of the determination. As the amount of induced cost reduction B rises due to a longer patent life, society must wait longer and longer to appropriate the welfare triangle EAN, though with linear demand functions the area of the triangle increases as the square of B, *ceteris paribus* (see Scherer 1970, 402). But for each additional year's wait it motivates less and less incremental cost reduction because the gain to the patent holder increases at best only linearly with increases in B, because monopoly rents of later years are discounted more heavily than those in the early years, and because additional percentage points of cost reduction are achieved only at rising research cost. Sooner or later, these diminishing-return effects overpower society's interest in stimulating additional cost reduction by extending the patent life. Therefore in all but some special limiting cases there exists a finite socially optimal patent life.

7.2 Comparative Statics Results

From the constrained welfare-maximizing conditions reflecting this balancing, Nordhaus derives three important comparative statics results. All can be comprehended intuitively from the geometric presentation.

First, the larger the arc elasticity of demand in the neighborhood of the preinvention and postinvention competitive equilibria, the shorter is the socially optimal patent life. This is so because, at least for run-of-the-mill inventions, nothing varies with elasticity but the base (and hence area) of the welfare triangle EAN. As price elasticity increases, the area of the welfare triangle increases proportionately, making society less and less willing to postpone its capture in exchange for a given incrementally induced cost reduction.

Second, the "easier" it is to achieve a given cost reduction (i.e., the steeper the IPF, and hence the larger the equilibrium induced level of cost reduction B, *ceteris paribus*), the shorter the socially optimal patent life will be. This is so because the area of the awaited welfare triangle rises quadratically with increases in B, as noted earlier, whereas the patent holder's monopoly rent $C_0 EAC_1$ rises only at a linear rate with B. Hence, when big cost reductions are likely, whether the allowed patent life is modest or long, society is less willing to defer the realization of its net welfare surplus to motivate still more cost reduction than it would be if

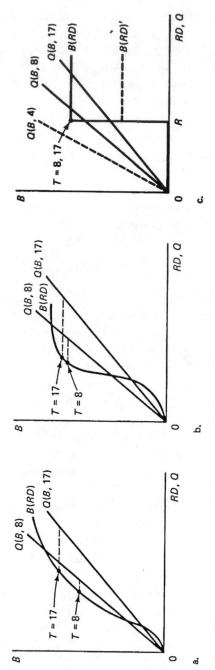

Figure 7.4
The effect of the invention possibility function's curvature: (a) highly elastic cost reduction, (b) intermediate elasticity, (c) zero elasticity

the cost savings under comparable patent life conditions and research investments were modest.

Third, the optimal patent life is shorter, the sharper the curvature of the invention possibility function in the neighborhood of the optimal RD expenditure. This result is best illustrated with a new diagram. Panels (a), (b), and (c) of figure 7.4 each have identical run-of-the-mill invention quasi-rent functions corresponding to patent lives of eight and seventeen years. The invention possibility functions, however, display increasingly sharp curvatures, analogous to declining elasticities of substitution in orthodox production function theory. The sharper the curvature, the smaller is the difference in the amount of cost reduction induced by a given increase in patent life. And as the cost reduction effect attenuates, *ceteris paribus*, society's welfare gain from deferring competitive imitation falls correspondingly, so shorter patent lives prove optimal.

From Nordhaus's equations 5.13 and 5.14 (1969, p. 78), it can be deduced that in the limiting case of a rectangular or "stair-step" IPF, as illustrated in figure 7.4c, the socially optimal patent life is zero. Here, however, the theory as developed thus far goes astray by focusing exclusively on the first-order marginal conditions for a patent holder's local profit maximum, ignoring the necessary *total condition* that expected profits be positive.[4] If the patent's life is set at zero, the quasi-rent function $Q(B, T)$ coincides with the vertical axis of figure 7.4c, lying at all points but the origin to the left of the IPF. Faced with a situation where expected quasi rents are less than RD outlays at any positive RD level, no rational firm will invest, even though the consumers' (and producer's) surpluses potentially available exceed prospective RD costs. The investment incentive is likewise stultified by short patent lives, that is, with the assumed four-year life indicated by a dotted line in figure 7.4c. And although following Nordhaus's welfare-maximizing marginal rule *necessarily* implies failure to satisfy the positive-profits condition only in this limiting stair-step IPF case, the incompatibility can also arise in other cases— notably, when the cost of achieving a given value of B is relatively high and when the invention possibility function's curvature is relatively sharp in the neighborhood of the inventing firm's equilibrium.

We see then that the patent grant really plays two investment-inducing roles, which in a different context I have called the "stimulus effect" and the "*Lebensraum* effect" roles (see Scherer 1970, p. 369). In its stimulus effect role, emphasized by Nordhaus, an optimal patent policy sees to it that the monopoly rent lure induces RD investment just sufficient to equate the marginal social gain from *further* cost reduction with marginal social cost. In its *Lebensraum* effect role, the patent grant must persuade investors that competitive imitation will be deferred sufficiently long to make discounted quasi rents exceed RD outlays for at least *some* positive RD investment level. Neither aspect can be ignored in designing an optimal patent policy.

Fortuitously, the comparative static relationships derived through Nordhaus's stimulus-effect analysis and those associated with the *Lebensraum* effect are identical for what, from a policy standpoint, is undoubtedly the most important exogenous variable—the "ease" of invention. This is demonstrated in figure 7.4c by considering two different stair-step invention possibility functions $B(RD)$ and $B(RD)'$. With "hard invention" *IPF* $B(RD)'$ (broken line), the cost saving realized by spending $0R$ dollars on research is considerably less than with "easy invention" *IPF* $B(RD)$. The *Lebensraum* condition for $B(RD)$ is satisfied with a patent life shorter than eight years, but for $B(RD)'$ even a seventeen-year life is insufficient. Quite generally, the higher the private benefit/RD cost ratio for a potential invention over some assumed period of exploitation, the shorter the allowed patent life can be while still satisfying the *Lebensraum* effect condition that expected profits be positive. This conclusion is completely consistent with Nordhaus's finding, considering marginal stimulus effects alone, that easy inventions (those yielding big cost savings in relation to the research resources invested) warrant shorter patent protection than hard inventions.

7.3 Some Implications

One immediate policy implication is that if lawmakers were to shorten the standard term of process patent grants, what would be lost would be primarily those inventions with relatively low benefit-cost ratios—those that in any event are not likely to have a great impact on social welfare. That this conclusion is based upon an extremely naive model does not necessarily nullify its thrust. Indeed, elaboration to account for a principal oversimplification strengthens the case. Contrary to what we have assumed thus far, patent protection is not the only barrier to competitive imitation. Natural inertia, secrecy, and the need to do some RD on one's own before mastering a new process all contribute to imitation lags in an atomistically structured industry.[5] When market concentration is high and nonpatent barriers to new entry are present, postinnovation pricing discipline is likely to be sufficiently firm to let an innovating oligopolist recover its *RD* investment, even if other immediate rivals imitate quickly. When any or all of these circumstances exist, the *Lebensraum* condition will tend to be satisfied with short or even zero patent lives for potential process inventions promising high benefit-cost ratios. A uniform policy of long-lived patent grants confers excessive private rewards in these cases, compensated to some unknown extent by the social benefits realized from low benefit-cost projects which otherwise would not have been undertaken and by stimulus effects at the margin of projects which would have been undertaken even with short patent lives. And although the analysis thus far has been developed only for process inventions, it is obvious that for product inventions with high private benefit-cost ratios, the *Lebensraum* condition will be satisfied at shorter patent lives than for those with low benefit-cost ratios.

A "best of both worlds" policy recognizing these relationships would tailor the life of each patent to the economic characteristics of its underlying invention. This might be achieved through a flexible system of compulsory licensing, under which the patent recipient bears the burden of showing why the patent should not expire or be licensed at modest royalties to all applicants three or five years after its issue. This burden would be sustained if the patentee demonstrated that the invention fell into one or more of the categories in which longer protection is needed to satisfy the *Lebensraum* condition (e.g., because the market is small relative to the costs of research, or because the cost savings achieved were modest in relation to research costs). When a patent-holding corporation possesses a substantial share of the relevant market and well-established marketing channels, on the other hand, there would be a presumption in favor of early patent licensing or expiration on the assumption that positive innovation profits could normally be attained without the added inducement of strong patent protection.

There is, however, one case where the implications of the modified Nordhaus theory must be regarded with special caution. Risk and uncertainty—surely significant elements in research and development decision making—have been ignored altogether. For most *RD* projects, Edwin Mansfield's studies suggest, this is probably not a fatal oversight. The uncertainties are sufficiently manageable that they can be taken into account by letting the invention possibility and quasi-rent functions be expressed in terms of expected values or certainty equivalents modified by an appropriate risk premium. Still it is at least conceivable that certain inventions with very high "best guess" benefit-cost ratios require unusually bold, farsighted, time-consuming departures from orthodox technology, with extraordinary attendant uncertainties and risks. In these cases strong patent protection offering the prospect of exceptional rewards contingent on technical and commercial success may be necessary to induce investment. Such cases are probably rare (i.e., embracing not more than a dozen or so major inventions per year) and thus cannot safely be squeezed into the mold of an orthodox profit-maximizing model like the one presented here. Nevertheless, the fact that they are exceptions makes it possible to devise a policy dealing with them as such while treating the vast majority of all patented inventions under rules which assume some fairly close approximation to profit-maximizing behavior. In particular, the presumption in favor of early compulsory licensing or short patent lives for inventions with high *ex post* private benefit-cost ratios could be waived upon a showing that the patent recipient exhibited exceptional creativity or undertook unusual technical and/or commercial risks in the invention's development.

Such a policy—flexible, but rooted in the logic of economic theory—would probably be a significant improvement over the present U.S. patent system, recognized by friends and critics alike to be arbitrary and inefficient. It warrants serious consideration.

Notes

I am grateful to William Nordhaus and the editor for helpful criticisms.

1. See the survey article by Fritz Machlup, *An Economic Review of the Patent System* (1958).

2. As long as the new process is merely used internally and not licensed to outsiders, the analysis applies equally well to the case of a monopolist or group of colluding oligopolists pricing to deter all entry in a range of relatively inelastic demand. See Scherer 1970, pp. 219–221.

3. Where r is the discount rate, $Q(B, T^*) = B(0C_0) (1 - e^{-rT^*})/r$. This formulation is used by Nordhaus after setting $0C_0 = 1$.

4. To deal with this problem algebraically, it is necessary to impose on the social welfare function being maximized an inequality constraint reflecting the necessity of positive profit expectations, along with Nordhaus's equality constraint reflecting the inventor's marginal optimizing conditions.

5. These points are developed more fully in Scherer (1970, pp. 384–390), which also deals with many of the issues raised in Nordhaus's reply to this paper.

References

K. J. Arrow. Economic Welfare and the Allocation of Resources for Invention. In *The Rate and Direction of Inventive Activity*. Nat. Bur. Econ. Res. conference report, Princeton, 1962, 619–625.

F. Machlup. *An Economic Review of the Patent System*. Study No. 15. U.S. Senate, Committee on the Judiciary, Subcommittee on Patents, Trademarks, and Copyrights. 85th Cong., 2d sess., Washington, D.C.; 1958.

E. Mansfield. *Industrial Research and Technological Innovation*. New York: Norton 1968, ch. 3.

W. D. Nordhaus. *Invention, Growth, and Welfare; A Theoretical Treatment of Technological Change*. Cambridge, Ma: The MIT Press 1969, ch. 5.

F. M. Scherer. *Industrial Market Structure and Economic Performance*. Chicago: Rand McNally 1970.

8 The Welfare Economics of Product Variety: An Application to the Ready-to-Eat Cereals Industry

8.1 Introduction

EVER since the publication of Chamberlin's *Theory of Monopolistic Competition* [6], economists have known that how well a market economy solves the three-way trade-off among product variety, economies of scale, and purity of competition critically affects the level of economic welfare. Following a long period of neglect, there has recently been an explosion of work on the theory of optimal product variety. Although unsettled questions remain, the theory reveals that whether monopolistic competition yields the welfare-maximizing amount of product variety, too little, or too much, depends on the relationships among several potentially observable variables. Except for the rather special cases of television programming and service competition among publicly regulated airlines, there has been little effort to apply the theory to real-world market situations.[1] This paper attempts to extend the set of applications to a situation where the visible hand of regulation was largely absent.

The focus is the US ready-to-eat (RTE) breakfast cereal industry, which is the subject of a major antitrust case brought by the Federal Trade Commission.[2] The FTC's complaint alleges that leading manufacturers Kellogg, General Mills, Post (i.e., General Foods), and Quaker, accounting for approximately 90 percent of RTE cereal sales during the late 1960s, collectively monopolized the industry and engaged in diverse monopolistic practices.[3] One charge is that the four respondents deterred new entry by proliferating product varieties, thereby leaving insufficient room for viable newcomers.[4] In other words, they preempted the entry of what otherwise would have been new monopolistic competitors and thereby prevented the emergence of a more atomistic market structure. The FTC did not address the question of whether product proliferation was carried beyond the point at which some plausible index of social welfare was maximized. To take that last difficult step is the aim of this paper. The paper begins by reformulating the received theory of optimal product variety in a more empirically tractable form, proceeding then to relate the available evidence to the theory.

Before we begin, an overview of the RTE cereal industry's structure and performance may be useful. The SIC industry of which it is the principal component, "cereal preparations," is one of the twenty most

Source: *Journal of Industrial Economics* 28 (December 1979): 113–134.

concentrated four-digit U.S. manufacturing industries. Among 412 to 451 four-digit industries, cereal preparations had in both 1967 and 1972 one of the ten lowest ratios of materials plus plant payroll costs to industry sales—52 percent in both years.[5] It also had less plant capital and inventory per dollar of sales than the average manufacturing industry. Thus in-plant costs were unusually low. Obversely, advertising expenditures and profits were unusually high. Among 324 to 329 four-digit manufacturing industries for which comparable input-output statistics are available, cereal preparations had the second highest ratio of advertising outlays to sales—22 percent in 1963 and 18.5 percent in 1967.[6] Accounting profits after taxes plus interest averaged 19.8 percent of assets for the RTE operations of leading firms Kellogg, General Mills, General Foods, Quaker, and Ralston between 1958 and 1970. For all manufacturing corporations, the comparable figure was 8.7 percent. Or when advertising expenditures are capitalized and depreciated at an annual exponential decay rate of 35 percent, the adjusted 1958–70 aftertax return on assets for the five RTE firms was 17.8 percent, compared to 8.4 percent for all manufacturing corporations.[7]

From the perspective of this article, an especially important feature of the RTE industry's recent history has been the introduction of numerous new product variants. Key innovations are widely considered to have been presweetened cereals, with Post's introduction of Sugar Crisp in 1950 marking the first major success; nutritional cereals (with Kellogg's Special K leading the way in 1956); and natural cereals (long available from fringe sellers but enjoying a demand surge in the early 1970s).[8] We concentrate here on the principal firms' activities following the introduction of Special K and preceding the natural cereal boom. At the end of 1957 the six largest companies had a total of 38 RTE brands in national distribution. From then to the close of 1970, they carried 51 new brands beyond the regional test stage while withdrawing 22, leaving a total of 67 brands in national distribution in December 1970. Many of the new brands failed to achieve viable market shares, and of the 51 brands launched between 1958 and 1970, only five—Kellogg's Froot Loops, General Mills' Total, Post's Alpha Bits, and Quaker's Life and Captain Crunch—succeeded in obtaining for a year or more a market share of at least 2 percent. Thus the newer products characteristically filled only small niches in the spectrum of consumer demands. In contrast, older brands showed considerable staying power. Only two pre-1958 brands were withdrawn from national distribution during the 1960s, and the 29 leading brands of 1960, with 83 percent of total industry pound volume then, retained 74 percent of the market in 1970 despite the competition of numerous products. The key question is, was the cereal makers' proliferation of product variants carried beyond the point where economic welfare was maximized?

8.2 The Theory

The problem of optimal product variety has been approached theoretically in several ways: using geographic spatial analogies following the lead of Hotelling,[9] in an orthodox consumer utility function framework,[10] with Lancasterian characteristics preference models,[11] and using demand function and consumers' surplus methods. The model employed here is a hybrid, adapting Spence's areas-under-the-demand-function focus [29], [30] to a Loesch-Hotelling [19], [12] spatial approach. As a hybrid, it sacrifices elegance to bring into clear focus relationships one can observe and attempt to measure.

Figure 8.1 provides the simplest possible view. The horizontal axis represents a one-dimensional space over which a product's real or perceived characteristics might vary, for example, in the degree of nutrient fortification, sweetness, crunchiness, or (with discrete rather than continuous variation) shape. Consumers' preferences for a given characteristic are described by their location in product characteristics space. If, for example, the relevant dimension is sweetness, a consumer who likes a relatively sweet product will have his or her preference located farther to the right (e.g., at point B) than a consumer (e.g., at A) preferring a less sweet product. We assume provisionally a uniform distribution and intensity of preferences over the relevant spatial segment, ignore the problem of finite segment bounds, and assume income effects to be insignificantly small.[12] Adapting Spence's perspective to the Loesch-Hotelling framework, the vertical ordinate of figure 8.1 for any given point in (horizontal) product characteristics space measures the integral under the inverse demand function for all consumers whose preferences (or the relevant part of whose preferences) match that point, given the prices of the product(s) purchased by those consumers and also the prices of all substitute and complement products.[13] It is convenient to net out from this value the variable costs of production and distribution. Thus figure 8.1 presents two sets of tentlike functions. The upper (solid) func-

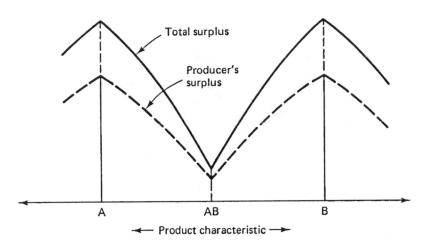

Figure 8.1
Surplus functions in product characteristics space

tion shows at any abscissa point the total surplus (consumers' plus producer's) realized from sales to consumers with preferences at any given point in product characteristics space. These ordinate values, it must be emphasized, are uniquely defined only for a specific set of products and product prices. Our analysis must deal therefore only with incremental localized product availability changes.

Figure 8.1 assumes the supply of only two products A and B. These products have characteristics exactly matching the preferences of consumers located at points A and B in characteristics space. By assumption, however, consumer preferences are distributed uniformly over space. Those whose preferences are imperfectly satisfied by A or B must either buy A or B or spend more of their income on unrepresented (perhaps quite different) products. The loss of utility experienced by a consumer with preferences at, say, boundary point AB from having to make do with imperfect substitute A or B is analogous in a geographic spatial model to the transportation cost a consumer incurs securing output from a geographically distant plant under FOB pricing. Given downward sloping demand functions, a higher delivered price in the uniform density geographic model means that less will be consumed by distant customers than by customers located near the plant, all else equal. In the variable product characteristics case the loss of utility from consuming less-than-

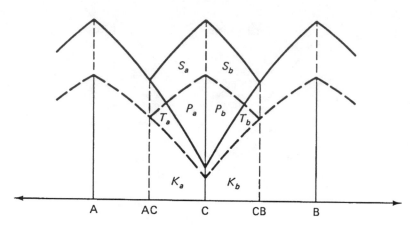

Figure 8.2
The consequences of product launching

ideal products leads analogously to a lower quantity demanded, the more distant the demander's preferences lie from the characteristics of available products. This, combined with the assumption of a uniform distribution of preferences over characteristics space, gives rise to the tent shape of the surplus functions, whose maxima are at the points in space where product characteristics exactly match preferences.

Let us consider now the introduction of a third product C at a point in characteristics space intermediate between A and B, as in figure 8.2. This means that consumer preferences in the neighborhood of C will be satisfied better, leading to an increase in consumption by those consumers, and hence to increases in consumers' and producer's surplus represented by the new tent-shaped functions with maxima above point C. Purchases will normally be divided among products at boundaries (i.e., AC and CB) where the total surplus functions intersect. Assuming uniformly distributed preferences, this implies an equal division of the market.

Whether or not product C will be offered depends critically on the fixed costs of launching it (e.g., the required investment in research and development, plant and introductory marketing) and on market structure. To mesh these pieces of the problem, it is desirable to let the producers' and consumers' surplus functions measure discounted present values rather than single-period flows. Market structure matters then in the following sense. If the market is (at least locally) monopolized and entry at C by outsiders is blocked, the relevant surplus (or more accurately, discounted present value of quasi rents) to the producer of A and B contemplating introducing C is the diamond-shaped area consisting of T_a, T_b, P_a, and P_b, where T_a and T_b represent transfers from consumers' into producer's surplus and P_a and P_b pure producer's surplus increases. On the other hand, if entry is possible, a monopolistic competitor considering offering C in competition with other firms' products A and B and assuming, Cournot-like, that C is priced at the same level as the unchanged prices of A and B, perceives itself as gaining that diamond-shaped surplus *plus* K_a and K_b, which represent transfers of quasi rents from the producers of A and B to the producer of C. Such transfers are often referred to as "cannibalization" among business people, and we shall name them accordingly.[14] The monopolistic competitor unconcerned about whence K_a and K_b come views itself as gaining a larger surplus through new product introduction than does the monopolist. It is entirely possible that fixed launching costs exceed $T_a + T_b + P_a + P_b$ but are less than that sum plus K_a and K_b. If so, product C will be introduced by a monopolistic competitor but not by a monopolist. This is the principle underlying economists' conclusion that greater product variety will emerge under monopolistic competition than under pure monopoly.[15]

Consider now a modification in the structural assumptions. If a monopolist supplies A and B but entry into C is open, the monopolist may choose also to offer C and preempt entry that would otherwise cause it to lose surplus K_a and K_b. If so, as much product variety may emerge under such entry-deterring monopoly (or oligopoly) as under monopolistic competition, other things (e.g., price) being held equal.

It remains to be seen whether the variety of products supplied under monopolistic competition or entry-deterring monopoly is optimal. Assuming that a dollar of consumers' surplus is valued equally with a dollar of producers' surplus, a new product should be introduced if its addition to surplus net of transfers (i.e., pure producers' surplus increase $P_a + P_b$ plus consumers' surplus gains $S_a + S_b$) exceeds the fixed costs of introduction. That diamond-shaped area may be either larger or smaller than the tent-shaped surplus area guiding the decisions of monopolistic competitors or entry-deterring monopolists. As figure 8.2 is drawn, the two areas are of similar magnitude, and so decisions motivated by profit maximization under actual or potential monopolistic competition will tend also to advance social welfare.

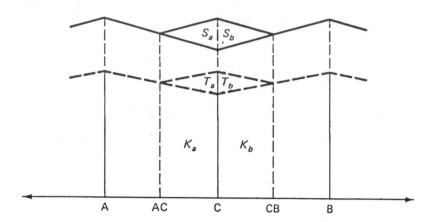

Figure 8.3
Launching of a close-substitute product

This is not necessarily so, however. Figure 8.3 provides a counter-example. The extent of cannibalization K_a plus K_b by product C is large relative to the net increase in social surplus S_a plus S_b. (Note that all producers' surplus gains now come as transfers from what was consumers' surplus when there were only two products.) If fixed costs are smaller than $K_a + K_b + T_a + T_b$ but larger than $S_a + S_b$, excessive product proliferation will occur.

Figure 8.3 differs from figure 8.2 largely in the gentler slope of its surplus functions, which in turn, given uniform preference density over characteristics space, reflects greater substitutability of the products. When products are relatively good substitutes for one another, as in figure 8.3, not much demand is choked off when consumers have to make do with a product that departs by some given amount from their "ideal" characteristics. In the limiting case of perfect substitutes (reflected by horizontal surplus functions), adding a new product has no demand-expanding effect, and so there is nothing but cannibalization. Quite generally, the better the existing substitutes and new products are for one another, the more likely it is that additional product launchings will add more to costs than to social benefits, all else equal.[16]

Cannibalization is also apt to be high relative to surplus gains net of transfers when the ratio of producers' to consumers' surplus is high. This in turn has two main determinants. First, as Spence has emphasized, when sellers maximize profits under the conventional assumptions of monopolistic competition, producer's surplus is higher relative to consumers' surplus with inverse demand functions that are concave downward (i.e., relatively flat-topped) than with convex functions.[17] Second, one would expect higher producers' surpluses, the more sellers respect their interdependence in pricing and cooperate toward joint profit-maximizing policies rather than viewing (as we have assumed thus far) the prices of spatially proximate products as insensitive to their own price- and product-launching choices.

Summing up, we have identified four potentially observable characteristics associated with a tendency toward excessive proliferation of product variants: high substitutability among the variants, modest increases in producers' surplus net of cannibalization or (assuming constant prices and unit costs) in sales volume, a high ratio of producers' to consumers' surplus, and (following from these three) extensive cannibalization. Also fixed product-launching costs must be substantial, but less than the gross producers' surplus (including cannibalization) realized by an added product variant.

Four further complications must be noted. Thus far, we have assumed that the prices of products A and B remain fixed when product C is introduced at the same price. A new entrant could, however, be greeted by a price war, or the new entry might be accommodated by the raising of existing product prices.[18] Assuming that pre-entry prices exceed marginal cost, uniform price increases reduce total surplus and hence shift the total surplus functions downward; uniform price decreases have the opposite effect (unless and until marginal cost is undercut). For non-uniform or discriminatory price changes, it is more difficult to state simple generalizations.

Second, our analysis has no way of determining what set of prices is globally optimal in either a first-best or second-best sense. It can only evaluate the desirability of marginal changes in the array of products. Given this limitation, the most that can be said is that, if the prices of preexisting products remain unchanged or increase in response to the introduction of a new product variant, the price effects of the introduction on nonlocal welfare will be either neutral or adverse incrementally. Thus any surplus of launching costs over *local* net surplus gains will not be compensated by surplus gains attributable to second-order price effects in other regions of product characteristics space.

Third, consumer preferences may not be uniformly distributed and of uniform intensity over product characteristics space. This, we shall see, will cause empirical difficulties.

Finally, we must relax the assumption of figures 8.1 through 8.3 that product characteristics space is one-dimensional. In the more realistic multidimensional case any additional product variant is apt to interact with several or many existing products, not two. This appears at first to add no important complications.[19] If the products are close substitutes, the total amount of cannibalization will be high and the net growth of producers' and consumers' surplus may be small. If they are distant substitutes and the new product fills an important unserved niche in product characteristics space, the obverse is more apt to be true. Extending this reasoning to the case of very many potential substitutes, what is sacrificed when a new product's sales come in infinitesimally small increments from products scattered throughout a preponderantly competitive economy will for the most part be units of consumption at the margins where price equals marginal cost, and no appreciable surplus, consumer or producer, is foregone.[20] If the new product yields a surplus over launching costs, welfare is undoubtedly increased. More perplexing is the situation where product interactions occur weakly over a large number of dimensions within a world of monopolies, to use Mrs. Robinson's phrase [24, p. 307]. Then the market's invisible hand may lead new product suppliers into incurring costs to swap one surplus for another, but it will be difficult or even impossible in practice to detect that welfare has been reduced.

8.3 The Cereal Industry Evidence

We turn now to the evidence, taking up in turn the costs of new RTE product launching, the extent to which sales gains were real as compared to cannibalistic, various aspects of pricing behavior, and an attempt to estimate the magnitude of added consumers' surpluses.

The Costs of New Product Launching

The earliest recognizable costs of launching a new cereal product into the market are those associated with research, development, market research, and test marketing. According to a survey of twenty-one new cereal products by Buzzell and Nourse [5, pp. 91–94], research and development costs in the 1959 to 1964 period averaged $122,000, market research costs $60,000 and the excess of other marketing costs over product sale gross margins during the period of test marketing approximately $740,000. These costs, like most others, have undoubtedly risen over time with inflation. Therefore for purposes of comparison we shall emphasize to the maximum degree possible cost and sales data centered on 1962.

Investment outlays for the equipment needed to produce a new product vary with the degree to which existing capacity can be used with minimal rebuilding. At one extreme were products such as Total or Sugar Frosted Flakes, which merely required the addition of vitamin or sugar enrobing equipment to standard wheat or corn flakes lines.[21] At the other extreme would be a product such as Quaker's Life, whose complex shape necessitated a multimillion dollar investment in newly designed machinery. Appreciable start-up costs might also be incurred in debugging production equipment, but no evidence on their magnitude is available.

For many consumer goods, and perhaps especially for ready-to-eat cereals, expenditures on introductory advertising and other types of sales promotion (e.g., special displays, free samples, and coupon campaigns) are a major element of new product-launching costs. Although considerable variation can be observed between products, the need to attain a threshold level of awareness in national "roll-out" campaigns imposes a rough lower bound on the level of introductory advertising outlays.[22] A study of twenty-five relatively successful RTE cereals introduced between 1957 and 1967 showed average advertising expenditures to have been $805,000 in the first two months of national distribution and $3.5 million over the first fourteen months, after which the average rate of spending tended to stabilize temporarily at $115,000 per month.[23] Whether in calculating introductory advertising costs one should truncate at fourteen months with the stabilization of monthly outlays is a difficult question. The same study showed that market shares stabilized at an average of 0.9 percent after two years.[24] At 1962 industry levels this implies annual sales on the order of $4.5 million per brand and, with advertising outlays averaging $1.16 million per year in the third year, an advertising/sales ratio of 26 percent.[25] Since the comparable ratio for all products, old and new, was 17 percent, this suggests that launching costs may have continued into the third year of national sales. On this and related issues more will be said later.

We find then that average launching costs in the early 1960s were at least $4.4 million per product (i.e., $122,000 + 60,000 + 740,000 + 3.5 million) and perhaps, if new production facilities were needed and extensive promotional activity other than advertising was undertaken, a good deal more.

Real Growth vs. Cannibalization

The cereal antitrust case record yields mixed and even contradictory documentary and testimonial evidence on the degree to which new products contributed to genuine market growth, as distinguished from cannibalizing existing product sales and quasi rents. In a 1966 speech to his field sales personnel, a Kellogg vice-president lamented the appearance of "so many meaningless new products" and "the futility and the wastefulness of having *too* much of a good thing."[26] The same official observed three years later that "for the past several years, our individual company growth has come out of the other fellow's hide."[27] Analyzing the sources of anticipated patronage for its OKs product, introduced nationally in 1959, Kellogg marketing staff listed as last of five in importance "people who are not eating any ready-to-eat cereals currently." Brand-switching consumers of rival products Cheerios and Alpha-Bits were listed first.[28] A 1958 Post (i.e., General Foods) memorandum observed similarly that "the pre-sweetened market is beginning to show signs of inexpansibility" and that expected rival product introductions would "further fraction the category and make the marketing of established pre-sweets more difficult in FY 1960."[29] A marketing analysis for a new pre-sweetened Post product introduced in the late 1960s estimated that half the product's sales came from cannibalization of an older Post brand, 30 percent from cannibalization of a rival Kellogg product and the rest from all other RTE cereals.[30] Similarly, a 1971 General Mills analysis found that in the highly fractionated, mature market for pre-sweetened cereals, "much of the new product growth has come at the expense of established pre-sweets, which, as a category, have shown regular declines."[31]

One can also find statements imputing to product innovation a favorable impact on overall market growth. There appears to be something approaching consensus that the appearance of the first nationally advertised pre-sweets and nutritional cereals during the 1950s had a genuine growth-stimulating effect. A 1954 statement of Post cereal-marketing philosophy indicated that "Both new products, specifically pre-sweetened cereals, and regular products have contributed to the industry growth."[32] A 1965 General Mills memorandum said that "in the early 1950s the advent of pre-sweetened cereals opened whole new avenues of volume and profit potential" and that "the sales of pre-sweetened cereals have expanded the total cereals market and have not adversely affected sales of regular cereals."[33] Discussing the forthcoming introduction of a pioneering high-nutrition cereal, a Kellogg executive predicted in 1956 that "with Special K, the possibilities are almost unlimited for getting new users who seldom use any ready to eat cereal."[34]

How does one reconcile these differing views, some of which are squarely inconsistent? One variable apparently influencing company perspectives was the overall state of demand. Over the two decades following World War II, the RTE industry experienced nearly continuous pound sales growth averaging 3.5 percent per annum. Decision makers' attitudes were buoyant, and many attributed at least a part of their good fortune to the concurrent surge of new product introductions. However, from 1966 to 1970 the growth rate dropped virtually to zero and continuing new product activity came to be viewed more skeptically, with visibly more awareness of cannibalization. Also a more sanguine view of new products' pure growth-inducing effect tended to be taken by the executives of General Mills, which gained market share during the 1960s, than by officials of Kellogg, which only maintained its share until the the late 1960s and General Foods, which lost ground. It seems clear too that industry analysts devoted inadequate attention to the simultaneous movement of demographic variables, and as a result their accounting of the sources of growth was often incomplete.

An attempt to take the fullest possible range of relevant variables into account was made by Richard Schmalensee in an unpublished statistical study of annual RTE cereal consumption per capita from 1953 to 1971.[35] Among the variables included in his time series were the following:

Q = pound sales per capita,
Y = real disposable income per capita,
Dem = population weighted by an index of cereal consumption in various age groups, divided by total population.

Using the Cochrane-Orcutt transformation (with $\rho = 0.575$) to minimize inefficiency owing to autocorrelation, he estimated the following regression, with t-ratios given in parentheses:

$$\text{Log } Q = -0.02 + 5.90 \underset{(4.89)}{\log Dem} + 0.32 \underset{(4.74)}{\log Y};$$

$$R^2 = 0.974,$$

D.W. = 1.64.

Both the income and weighted demographic variables were statistically significant. When a measure of the number of brands nationally distributed in each year was added to the regression, its t-ratio was only 0.42, suggesting that the increasing number of brands over time had no significant identifiable effect on consumption. Also insignificant was a variable measuring the proportion of working wives. Because the data were insufficient to estimate a properly identified simultaneous equation system and also because of multicollinearity, relative price indexes had implausible positive signs and were therefore excluded.

The coefficients in Schmalensee's regression can be interpreted as elasticities, and the high value of the *Dem* coefficient is puzzling. Schmalensee's *a priori* hypothesis was that its value should be near unity. One apparent reason for the unexpectedly high value was that the income and demographic variables were strongly collinear up to 1965, after which per capita income continued to grow while the growth of cereal consumption and the demographic variable slackened—the latter because children are particularly heavy RTE cereal eaters and the cohort of children twelve years old and under fell in size from 1965 to 1970. The demographic variable was therefore forced to bear the burden of explaining the post-1965 stagnation of consumption growth, taking on an implausibly large coefficient value as a consequence.

A simpler but in some ways more revealing picture of these developments by five-year intervals is provided by table 8.1. The first numerical column shows pounds of RTE cereal sold through grocery stores and the second column gives five-year growth rates. There follow two sets of demographic indexes, one using a simple population count and the other a population index with age groups weighted by relative intensity of consumption.[36] The rapid growth of cereal consumption, the stagnation of the late 1960s and (in the weighted population index) the waning of the post-World War II baby boom are all evident. What stands out is that in every five-year period but the last the rate of cereal consumption growth is more than double the growth rate of the weighted population variable.

Table 8.1
Growth trends in U.S. RTE cereal consumption and population, 1950 to 1970

Year	RTE cereal consumption (000 lb)	Percent growth, five years	Population (000)	Percent growth, five years	Weighted population	Percent growth, five years
1950	609, 800	—	150,697	—	147,896	—
1955	783,067	28.4	165,248	9.7	165,269	11.8
1960	940,584	20.1	180,670	9.3	181,456	9.8
1965	1,177,546	25.2	194,593	7.7	197,343	8.8
1970	1,183,100	0.5	204,879	5.3	204,779	3.8

Sources: Cereal consumption, CX-101E. Population, U.S. Bureau of the Census, *Current Population Reports*, Series P-25, Nos. 470 and 519; and *Statistical Abstract of the United States*: 1957.

This would appear to indicate that something more than mere demographic change—conceivably, the proliferation of pre-sweetened and nutritional cereal variants—stimulated consumption growth.

This is still not the full story, however. Consumers evidently choose RTE servings more on the basis of bulk (e.g., filling a standard 23 in³ cereal bowl) than on the basis of weight.[37] Pre-sweetening raises product weight without necessarily affecting bulk. Census data show that sugar use by the cereal industry increased from 67.8 million pounds in 1954 to 420 million pounds in 1972. RTE cereal output meanwhile grew by 613 million pounds. Thus roughly 57.5 percent of the cereal output increase consisted of sugar. Assuming that consumers would otherwise have dipped commensurately into their sugar bowls in the absence of pre-sweetening, this part of the industry's recorded output growth is merely a transfer akin to vertical integration and not real growth.[38] Applying the 57.5 percent transfer factor to the table 8.1 data for 1955 to 1970 (the period corresponding most closely to that for which Census data are available), one finds that total nonsugar growth of RTE consumption was 21.7 percent. This compares closely with the 23.9 percent growth of weighted population, suggesting that most if not all of the industry's nonsugar growth corresponded to demographic changes. Although other variables such as increasing real incomes, a rise in the proportion of working wives, a general trend toward consumption of convenience foods, the appearance of other new convenience breakfast foods, and relatively rapidly rising RTE cereal prices were at work, this plus Schmalensee's regressions suggest rather strongly that one cannot attribute much real growth of RTE cereal consumption to the proliferation of new product varieties. It follows that new products must have cannibalized the actual and potential sales and surpluses of older products extensively.

Profits and Prices

If new products cannibalized producers' surpluses from existing products while adding to fixed costs, all else equal, one might expect to observe a decline in industry profitability. No such decline is evident. If anything, the trend was toward rising accounting returns on assets during the 1960s.[39] The cereal makers avoided a decline in returns by effecting general price increases and by seeking on new products relatively high gross margins. As a 1962 General Foods marketing plan observed, the newer products carried higher profit margins to make their introduction affordable.[40] Between 1952 and 1970 the average wholesale price per pound of RTE cereals sold through grocery stores rose by 81 percent while the general wholesale price index for finished consumer food products rose by 20.4 percent.[41]

An example of the premium pricing strategy adopted for new products can be seen in Kellogg's Sugar Frosted Flakes, the best-selling pre-sweet in 1970. The product is obtained by applying a sugar frosting to the venerable corn flake. Following an increase in the price of corn flakes effective July 25, 1970, the wholesale list price of Kellogg's Corn Flakes in an 18-oz package was 34.44 cents/lb while the price of Sugar Frosted Flakes in a 20-oz package was 44.67 cents/lb. The main physical difference between the two is that the sucrose content of the Corn Flakes is approximately 7.8 percent, while it is 29.0 percent for Sugar Frosted Flakes.[42] To make a pound of Sugar Frosted Flakes, one in effect adds 0.23 lb of sugar to 0.77 lb of Corn Flakes. In mid-1970, 0.23 lb of refined cane sugar could be purchased on the spot market for 2.55 cents. Thus, using 2.55 cents worth of sugar to convert Corn Flakes into Sugar Frosted Flakes yielded additional revenue of 18.15 cents.[43] The variation of product characteristics accompanied by heavy advertising (in this case, emphasizing brand "spokesman" Tony the Tiger) made it possible to segregate markets and practice price discrimination.[44]

It is also possible, though less clearly supported, that prices on older products were raised more rapidly than corresponding increases in their cost. This is the reaction one would expect from joint profit-maximizing sellers in geographic space when new plant entrants pack the relevant space more densely.[45] Although it is uncertain whether the analogy can be extended to the case of more dense product characteristics space packing, it is clear that the cereal companies exhibited considerable concern about achieving a structure of old and new product prices that maximized collective profits.[46]

Pricing in the cereal industry was definitely more complex than our initial theoretical exposition supposed. Nevertheless, three inferences appear warranted. The average level of prices rose in real terms as a consequence of new product introductions. With uniform demand this should have shifted total surplus functions downward on average, all else equal. But there was also a probable increase in the dispersion of prices. Since some products (e.g., corn flakes, which experienced competitive pressure from private labelers) remained available at relatively low prices, it is conceivable, although by no means certain, that demands of low reservation price consumers continued to be satisfied.[47] If dead-weight welfare losses were attenuated as a result, the downward shift of total surplus functions could have been mitigated. Finally, for reasons considered in section 8.2 and also as a consequence of price discrimination, it seems likely that for any given set of total surplus functions, the ratio of producers' to consumers' surplus rose relative to what it would have been under a regime of constant and uniform prices. Substantial redistributions from consumers' to producers' surplus must have occurred. And the relatively high gross margins secured by the cereal oligopolists must have stimulated product proliferation beyond what it would have been had there been more competitive pressure on prices.[48]

Consumers' Surplus Increments

To advance farther, we must accept assumptions that cannot be conclusively supported by the available evidence. Opting to err on the side of overstating benefits, let us assume that total surplus curves were not shifted downward at all on the average as a result of the price increases attending product proliferation. Consistent with the evidence that cannibalization was extensive (and hence that spatially proximate differentiated products were fairly close substitutes) and with the related demographic evidence that product proliferation did not significantly increase physical consumption, we assume that producers' surplus gains were transfers from what otherwise would have been consumers' surplus. In other words, the situation is better described by figure 8.3, with non-cannibalized producers' surplus gains T_a and T_b reflecting transfers from preexisting consumers' surplus, than by figure 8.2, where producers' surplus gains P_a and P_b come from the growth of consumption without offsetting *old* consumers' surplus reductions. To the extent that these assumptions are valid, the increases in welfare net of transfers before launching costs are deducted must be associated solely with the consumers' surplus increments S_a and S_b.

These are not measurable in terms of the analysis presented thus far. However, they have an exact counterpart in the consumers' surplus areas under what might be called the *ceteris paribus* demand function—an inverse demand curve drawn under the assumption that all other products but the one in question continue to be available, so that what is measured is the consumers' surplus gain from having the additional product.[49] There is reason to believe that these demand functions, at least for most of the newer cereal products, tend to be concave downward, as illustrated in figure 8.4.[50] The absence of a steep slope at low quantities is suggested among other things by evidence that consumers do not exhibit much brand loyalty. Thus a Kellogg memorandum addressed to the Federal Trade Commission observed that "the fickleness of consumers toward RTE cereals means that manufacturers must continually remind consumers of their products or run the risk of being forgotten when the buying decision is made."[51] Similarly, an internal General Foods planning memorandum characterized the cereal business in 1966 as exhibiting a "multiplicity of brands and categories with little, if any, brand loyalty."[52] On the other hand, there may be a few consumers with intense loyalty to particular new products. Their existence would give rise to the convex-downward demand curve extension above the question mark in figure 8.4.[53]

Insight into the function's curvature in the vicinity of prevailing prices is provided by the testimony of cereal company executives and internal decision-making memoranda. For products that are similar to one another, but less close substitutes than, say, Kellogg's Corn Flakes and Post Toasties, retail shelf prices can apparently diverge by "a few cents a pack" without having much impact on volume.[54] But wider differentials were said in 1967 to become a potentially "significant factor in people switching," or move products into "the trouble area," or even, in the case of low-volume products, "greatly weaken our efforts" to keep them in business. [55] Cereal makers generally chose not to maintain differentials

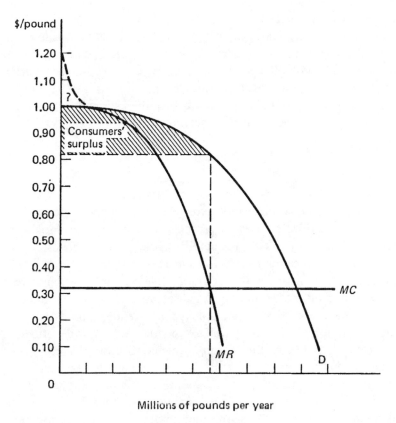

Figure 8.4
Demand function for an additional product

wider than 4 cents per pack on similar products, which means that they must have considered their demand functions to become quite elastic at prices exceeding those of the nearest substitutes by more than that magnitude.

In view of this we estimate that the *average* consumer surplus on a typical 11-oz package was 7 cents in 1970. This overstates the surplus for marginal consumers and understates it for especially loyal and/or price-insensitive inframarginal consumers. The implied consumers' surplus per pound is 10.2 cents, or 20 percent of average 1970 wholesale sales revenue per pound.[56]

We seek to compare such consumers' surpluses on new brands, representing the social gain net of transfers, with the average launching cost of a brand, estimated conservatively at \$4.4 million for 1962. We assume that the ratio of incremental consumers' surplus to wholesale sales is 0.2. If manufacturer sales volume associated with a percentage point of market share in year t is $V(t)$, the market share achieved in year t is $M(t)$, and the discount rate is r, we want to know whether the estimated discounted present value of consumers' surplus increments:[57]

$$S \equiv \sum_{t=0}^{H} \frac{(0.2)M(t)V(t)}{(1+r)^t} \gtrless \$4.4 \text{ million.} \tag{1}$$

Market share data for products introduced between 1958 and 1970 were available through 1975 at best, and there are gaps in many of the series.[58] Internal gaps were filled by linear interpolation. When the available data covered fewer than 20 years of product life, market shares were estimated through year 20 by linear extrapolation and a remainder term for years 21 to infinity was computed, assuming conservatively a continuation of year 20's observed or estimated share.[59] A discount rate of 0.09 was used, reflecting the average of values employed by Kellogg and Quaker in investment decisions.[60] This may well exceed the economywide return on investment, but it is below the marginal rate confronting a typical consumer buying on installment credit. Because the launching cost estimate is centered on 1962, the product sales data must be benchmarked accordingly, even though new products were introduced more or less continuously between 1958 and 1970, with inflation of both launching costs and sales figures occurring as time passed. This was taken into account by making two alternative sales per market share point assumptions: a \$1.0 million value associated with 1962 sales levels and a \$1.46 million value associated with 1967 sales.[61]

Inequality (1) was estimated for all new RTE cereals introduced between 1958 and 1970 experiencing any appreciable success on the market. Taking 1962 sales as the benchmark, seventeen brands satisfy the inequality; that is, they yielded estimated net consumers' surplus in excess of estimated average launching costs.[62] With 1967 sales as the benchmark, the list is expanded to twenty-two brands.[63] The other twenty-nine brands known to have been launched nationally clearly fail the test, having cost more to launch than they added to consumers' surplus. And although launching costs were presumably much lower, a similarly adverse verdict must be rendered for at least twenty-five new products whose introduction was terminated after test marketing but before nationwide distribution commenced. Thus the analysis of consumers' surplus increments suggests that product proliferation was carried well beyond the point where marginal social benefits equalled launching costs.

Among the numerous doubts one might raise concerning these calculations, only one will be added here. The "fixed" launching cost estimate is quite conservative in excluding plant investment and start-up costs and in terminating the accumulation of introductory advertising outlays at fourteen months. Sustaining advertising costs (i.e., those incurred indefinitely after the product is launched) pose peculiarly difficult welfare-accounting problems. If a potential new product were not introduced, sustaining advertising costs would not be incurred, and neither would the product's production and physical distribution costs. But given the apparently high degree of cannibalization, production costs avoided if a new product is not introduced will be offset by additional costs of turning out more of the old products. That the same offsetting will occur with respect to advertising costs is much less certain. There are threshold effects in sustaining as well as introductory advertising, and it seems reasonable to assume that with fewer products lower total advertising outlays would be required to have each product reach its threshold level of effectiveness.[69] Also many of the advertising messages concerning spatially adjacent products are mutually cancelling, conferring a net benefit on neither producers nor consumers. In view of the generally high advertising/sales ratios prevailing in the cereal industry, incremental increases in sustaining advertising and/or mutual cancellation of claims owing to brand proliferation entail costs whose present value could be large relative to the value of initial product-launching costs. To the extent that this is true, substantially larger values of S in inequality (1) may have been needed to offset the total social costs of product proliferation.

Conclusion

In drawing conclusions at the end of such an analysis, one recognizes it is not only the cereal industry's products that can be flaky. It seems undeniable that some ready-to-eat product innovations have yielded net consumers' plus producers' surpluses well in excess of launching costs. But equally clearly, conditions in the industry exhibit several hallmarks of the scenario in which the supply of product variety is overstimulated: high substitutability, extensive cannibalization, concave-downward inverse demand functions, ample producers' surplus margins (plus the monopoly power to sustain them), and substantial product-launching costs. In view of these qualitative features and the crude quantitative findings, it appears probable that product proliferation has, at least at the margin, cost more than it was worth.

Notes

The author is grateful to Ronald Braeutigam, Richard Schmalensee, John Beggs, William Burnett, and Herbert Mohring for helpful comments.

1. See Steiner [32], Spence and Owen [31], Noll *et al.* [22], and Douglas and Miller [9].

2. In the matter of Kellogg *et al.*, FTC docket no. 8883. The author appeared as an expert witness for the government on matters for the most part only indirectly related to the subject of this paper.

3. In 1978, at the conclusion of the government's case in chief, Quaker was dismissed as a respondent.

4. For the theory of this allegation, see Schmalensee [28].

5. Analysis of company data showed that the RTE subset of cereal preparations had an even lower ratio. See pp. 28, 183–195 of the FTC hearing transcript, which will subsequently be cited as TR.

6. TR 27,676–678, citing Ornstein [23, pp. 77–85].

7. Testimony of Thomas R. Stauffer at TR 19,069 ff., summarized in FTC exhibit CX-701. (The prefix CX indicates that an exhibit was introduced by complaint counsel (i.e., the FTC). A second set of initials, if any, reveals the company from whose records the document came. A third letter, if any, identifies the exhibit page.)

8. On these two, see p. Z72 of the General Foods 1967 task force study included as exhibit CX-GF-4039. The same document observes at p. Z74 that "Good ideas for new cereals are scarce."

9. See Hotelling [12], Lovell [18], Meade [20], Stern [33], and Hay [11].

10. See Usher [35], Dixit and Stiglitz [8], and Leland [17].

11. Lancaster [14], [15], [16], and Archibald and Rosenbluth [4].

12. Since RTE cereal purchases represent only a very small proportion of the average household's expenditures, ignoring income effects causes no appreciable problems. See Willig [36].

13. There is no reason why a single consumer cannot have multiple locations, reflecting a preference for variegated products.

14. See also Scherer [25, pp. 392–394], where a distinction is drawn between new market and market-sharing innovations.

15. See Lancaster [15], Archibald and Rosenbluth [4], and Spence [29], [30].

16. See also Spence [29], [30].

17. See Spence [29], [30]. With linear demand functions and constant marginal costs, consumers' surplus is a constant one-half of producers' surplus regardless of the specific parameter values, assuming conventional monopoly profit maximization.

18. For the analogous case of new plant entry into geographic space with linear point-in-space demand functions, it can readily be shown that the entry of a new plant at the boundary between two existing plants will induce an *increase* in prices if the operators of the old and new plants maximize joint profits. The proof here follows Hay [11].

Let the demand function for consumers located Z kilometers from a plant be linear, e.g.,

$$q_z = a - b(P_0 + tZ),\tag{1}$$

where P_0 is the price FOB plant and t is the transport cost per kilometer for a unit of product. Assume that demand is uniformly dense over one-dimensional geographic space. Then for a plant shipping out to M kilometers in each direction from its location, the total quantity sold is:

$$Q = 2 \int_0^M [a - b(P_0 + tZ)]dZ\tag{2}$$

$$= 2aM - 2bP_0M - btM^2.$$

With constant marginal cost c and fixed costs of F, the plant's profit is

$$\pi = (P_0 - c)(2aM - 2bP_0M - btM^2) - F.\tag{3}$$

If each plant has the same marginal production cost c and transportation cost t and if all cooperate to maximize joint profits, the optimal location of a new plant will be midway between existing plants, all sellers will charge the same price, and conjectural variations can be ignored. Under these assumptions, profits are maximized by setting $\partial \pi / \partial P_0 = 0$, from which one obtains the relationship:

$$P_0^* = \frac{a}{2b} + \frac{c}{2} - \frac{tM}{4}.\tag{4}$$

Clearly, as entry reduces the spacing M between plant boundaries, the joint profit-maximizing price P_0^* rises.

19. We ignore here the possibility that the character of pricing interactions and the strength of entry deterrence may change with N neighboring products as compared to two. On this, see Schmalensee [28].

20. For an extreme view, see Triffin [34].

21. Of course, if a new product increases company demand for the products made on such machines, as appears to have been true initially for both Total and Sugar Frosted Flakes, an investment in complete new lines may be necessary. This is not always so, however. During the late 1960s both General Mills and Post emphasized the development of new products that could use existing excess capacity.

22. On the threshold costs of launching new cigarette brands, see Scherer et al. [27, p. 249].

23. From a 1970 Quaker Oats Co. study included in the cereal case record as CX-Q-177. For similar figures, see Buzzell and Nourse [5, p. 98].

24. Had less successful brands been included, the average market share would have been much lower. The Quaker Oats study reports that between 1958 and 1970, seventy-six brands were introduced into either test market or national distribution and that only 54 percent of these remained on the market in 1970. Early market success had some impact on introductory advertising levels but not a great deal. Of the twenty-five brands analyzed, the six most successful, with an average market share of 1.67 percent at the end of the third year, had initial fourteen month advertising outlays of $4.4 million. The six least successful, with an average share of 0.34 percent, spent $3.2 million on average during their first fourteen months.

25. Applying the 0.9 percent market share, which is based on poundage, directly to total 1962 industry sales, the product sales estimate is $3.7 million. An upward adjustment was

made to reflect the fact that newer cereals were priced roughly 30 percent higher per pound than old cereals (i.e., those on the market by 1954).

26. Speech text of C. H. Tornabene, CX-K-549Q and R (emphasis in original).

27. CX-K-744B.

28. CX-K-396A.

29. CX-GF-16D.

30. CX-GF-1425I.

31. CX-GMI-2178. Other references to extensive cannibalization include CX-GF-4B, CX-GF-18L, CX-GF-325F, CX-GF-602B, CX-GF-1302B, CX-GF-1445W, CX-GF-1410O, CX-GF-3000 Z 155, CX-K-409B, CX-K-7181J, and CX-GMI-570 Z 13.

32. CX-GF-4A. But compare p. B of the same document. See also CX-GF-3000 Z 51.

33. CX-GMI-111A. See also CX-GMI-262B and CX-GMI-263A.

34. Speech text of Mard Leaver, CX-K-560C. See also CX-K-5651.

35. I am indebted to Professor Schmalensee for providing these materials.

36. With 1.000 being the average for all consumers, the weights by age group are: 12 years and under, 1.417; 13–19, 1.023; 20–44, 0.699; and 45 and older, 0.973. The source is CX-GF-3000K.

37. See CX-GMI-279D and testimony at TR 14,454 and 17,445.

38. The assumption is debatable. Many pre-sweetened cereals consist of 40 percent or more by weight of sucrose—the equivalent of adding two and a half heaping teaspoons of sugar to an average 1.4 oz serving of unsweetened puffs or flakes. To the extent that consumers would not consciously have added as much sugar, the problem of unknowing overdose raises doubts about the premise accepted here that consumers know what they are getting. On this, see CX-GF-4039 Z 7.

39. CX-701 C-P.

40. CX-GF-17E. See also p. L of the same document, noting that General Foods set a gross margin target of 16 cents/lb for older *exclusive* products and 21 cents/lb on new products. The average wholesale price per pound of all General Foods RTE cereals at the time was 32 cents/lb.

41. Cereal sales and quantity data are from CX-101 E and F; wholesale price index data are from the *Economic Report of the President*.

42. From measurements by Dr. Ira L. Shannon, Veterans Administration Hospital, Houston, reported in Sugars in Breakfast Cereals, *Chicago Tribune* (October 30, 1977), sec. 1, p. 4.

43. That is, $44.67 - 0.77 \times 34.44 = 18.15$. According to the 1972 *Census of Manufactures*, vol. 2, p. 20D-8, materials costs averaged 38 percent of sales for the cereals industry as a whole in 1970.

44. See also Adams and Yellen [2], [3].

45. See note 18.

46. On this facet of the cereal makers' conduct, see the author's testimony at TR 27,819–820, 27,828–829, 27,915–918 and 28,495–504.

47. See Scherer [26, pp. 254, 258, 340] and Adams and Yellen [2], [3].

48. Compare Schmalensee [28].

49. Compare Spence [29, p. 219]. This approach accepts the assumption of well-defined

independent consumer preferences. At least for children's cereals, the assumption is arguable. Thus a General Foods task force concluded that children's advertising should among other things stress "helping join the crowd" (CX-GF-4039Z97). This implies contrived interdependence of preferences, violating a basic assumption of traditional consumer choice theory.

50. The demand function in figure 8.4 satisfies the equation $P = 1 - 0.001\ Q^3$, where Q is denoted in millions of pounds per year. With the assumed marginal cost of 32 cents/lb, the profit-maximizing price-cost relationships appear representative of 1970 experience for relatively new RTE products.

51. CX-K-1090Z21.

52. CX-GF-485Z6.

53. The thirteen-year-old son of a referee for this paper is apparently one such exception. Ignoring such exceptions leads to mismeasurement, but the error is probably offset by the neglect of surplus-decreasing price effects and the fixed investment necessitated by new product launchings.

54. Testimony of Kellogg executive R. F. Nicholls at TR 12,547 and 12,613.

55. See the testimony of General Mills executive Robert Bodeau at TR 16,609 along with CX-GM-278 and CX-GM-280. See also General Foods new product pricing analyses CX-GF-137M and CX-GF-1412J.

56. Note that this surplus rate is fairly high in comparison to the four leading cereal producers' before tax profit return on sales, which was approximately 15 percent in 1964. See National Commission on Food Marketing [21, p. 206]. The rate is low compared to gross margins (averaging about 50 percent) and the price minus variable manufacturing cost margin (averaging about 62 percent).

57. Note that launching costs are not incurred precisely at time $t = 0$. Of the estimated $4.4 million, $922,000 is incurred over several years prior to $t = 0$ and the remainder in the 14 months following $t = 0$. Any error introduced by centering the cost estimate on $t = 0$ is undoubtedly small. First year sales were discounted at midyear (i.e., with $t = 0.5$, with annual incrementing from that value for subsequent years).

58. CX-434.

59. Many products were withdrawn from the market before year 20, in which case market shares subsequent to withdrawal were uniformly zero.

60. See CX-Q-188B and CX-K-9020B.

61. Since the market share data are denominated in pounds, the sales figures have been inflated by 23 percent relative to total industry values to reflect the higher average price per pound of newer cereals. Taking sales benchmarks for years later than 1967 would not materially change the results because all the brands at the margin of satisfying inequality (1) had rapidly declining market shares over time, and all but one were introduced by 1963.

62. They are Cocoa Crispies, Product 19, Bran Buds, Froot Loops, Apple Jacks, Cocoa Puffs, Frosty Os, Lucky Charms, Total, Post Oat Flakes (including Fortified Oat Flakes), Crispy Critters, Honeycombs, Alpha Bits, Life, Quisp/Quake (launched jointly), regular Captain Crunch, and Corn Chex.

63. The five are OKs, All Stars, Twinkles, Country Corn Flakes, and Team. Although the data for brands achieving relatively small market shares are less complete, increasing the value of a market share point by as much as 50 percent would appear to add at most only a very few brands to the list of new products satisfying the inequality.

64. See Comanor and Wilson [7, pp. 49–53], Lambin [13, pp. 94–8, 127–9], Ackoff and Emshoff [1] and Scherer et al. [27, pp. 249–50].

References

1. Ackoff, Russell L., and Emshoff, James R. Advertising Research at Anheuser-Busch, Inc. (1963–68). *Sloan Management Review* (Winter 1975): 1–15.

2. Adams, W. J., and Yellen, Janet L. Commodity Bundling and the Burden of Monopoly. *Quarterly Journal of Economics* (August 1976): 475–498.

3. Adams, W. J., and Yellen, Janet L. What Makes Advertising Profitable? *Economic Journal* (September 1977): 427–449.

4. Archibald, G. C., and Rosenbluth, Gideon, The "New" Theory of Consumer Demand and Monopolistic Competition. *Quarterly Journal of Economics* (November 1975): 569–590.

5. Buzzell, Robert D., and Nourse, R. E., *Product Innovation, the Product Life Cycle and Competitive Behavior in Selected Food Processing Industries, 1947–64*. Cambridge: Arthur D. Little, Inc., 1966.

6. Chamberlin, Edward H., *The Theory of Monopolistic Competition*. Cambridge: Harvard University Press, 1933.

7. Comanor, William S., and Wilson, Thomas A. *Advertising and Market Power* Cambridge: Harvard University Press, 1974.

8. Dixit, Avinash K., and Stiglitz, Joseph E. Monopolistic Competition and Optimum Product Diversity. *American Economic Review* (June 1977): 297–308.

9. Douglas, George W., and Miller, James C., III, *Economic Regulation of Domestic Air Transport*. Washington, D.C.: Brookings, 1974.

10. Greenhut, Melvin L. *A Theory of the Firm in Economic Space*. New York: Appleton-Century-Crofts, 1970.

11. Hay, D. A. Sequential Entry and Entry-deterring Strategies in Spatial Competition. *Oxford Economic Papers* (July 1976): 240–257.

12. Hotelling, Harold. Stability in Competition. *Economic Journal* (March 1929): 41–57.

13. Lambin, Jean-Jacques. *Advertising, Competition and Market Conduct in Oligopoly over Time*. Amsterdam: North-Holland, 1976.

14. Lancaster, Kelvin. A New Approach to Consumer Theory. *Journal of Political Economy* (April 1966): 132–157.

15. Lancaster, Kelvin. Socially Optimal Product Differentiation. *American Economic Review* (September 1975): 567–585.

16. Lancaster, Kelvin. Monopolistic Competition as a Perfect Market Structure. Processed (October 1977).

17. Leland, Hayne E. Quality Choice and Competition. *American Economic Review* (March 1977): 127–137.

18. Lovell, Michael C. Product Differentiation and Market Structure. *Western Economic Journal* (June 1970): 120–143.

19. Loesch, August. *The Economics of Location*, 2nd ed. Trans. W. H. Woglom. New Haven: Yale University Press, 1956.

20. Meade, J. E. The Optimal Balance between Economies of Scale and Variety of Products. *Economica* (November 1974): 359–367.

21. National Commission on Food Marketing. *Studies of Organization and Competition in Grocery Manufacturing*. Technical Study No. 6. Washington, D.C., June 1966.

22. Noll, Roger G., Peck, M. J., and McGowan, J. J. *Economic Aspects of Television Regulation.* Washington, D.C.: Brookings, 1973.

23. Ornstein, Stanley I. *Industrial Concentration and Advertising Intensity.* Washington, D.C.: American Enterprise Institute, 1977.

24. Robinson, Joan. *The Economics of Imperfect Competition.* London: Macmillan, 1934.

25. Scherer, F. M. Research and Development Resource Allocation under Rivalry. *Quarterly Journal of Economics* (August 1967): 359–394.

26. Scherer, F. M. *Industrial Market Structure and Economic Performance.* Chicago: Rand McNally, 1970.

27. Scherer, F. M., Beckenstein, Alan, Kaufer, Erich, and Murphy, R. D. *The Economics of Multi-plant Operation: An International Comparisons Study.* Cambridge: Harvard University Press, 1975.

28. Schmalensee, Richard. Entry Deterrence in the Ready-to-Eat Breakfast Cereal Industry. *Bell Journal of Economics* (Autumn 1978): 305–327.

29. Spence, Michael. Product Selection, Fixed Costs and Monopolistic Competition. *Review of Economic Studies* (June 1976): 217–235.

30. Spence, Michael. Product Differentiation and Welfare. *American Economic Review* (May 1976): 407–414.

31. Spence, Michael, and Owen, Bruce. Television Programming, Monopolistic Competition and Welfare. *Quarterly Journal of Economics* (February 1977): 103–126.

32. Steiner, Peter O. Program Patterns and Preferences and the Workability of Competition in Radio Broadcasting. *Quarterly Journal of Economics* (May 1952): 194–223.

33. Stern, Nicholas. The Optimal Size of Market Areas. *Journal of Economic Theory* (April 1972): 154–173.

34. Triffin, Robert. *Monopolistic Competition and General Equilibrium Theory.* Cambridge: Harvard University Press, 1960.

35. Usher, Dan. The Welfare Economics of Invention. *Economica* (August 1964): 279–287.

36. Willig, Robert D. Consumer's Surplus without Apology. *American Economic Review* (September 1976): 589–597.

III MARKET STRUCTURE AND INNOVATION: STATISTICAL STUDIES

In economics as in other sciences the proof of the theory is in the empirical testing. A good part of my work on the "Schumpeterian hypothesis" has been devoted to statistical studies. The tradition here is much broader than for the theoretical work of Part II, since Schumpeter's conjectures were both sweeping and vague, and his interpreters necessarily took liberties translating them into testable hypotheses. As the literature evolved, there were three main hypothesis clusters: (1) that monopoly, reflected in a concentrated market structure and/or a pool of funds available for discretionary investment, was a propitious climate for technological innovation; (2) that large corporations could better support and execute ambitious, risky R & D programs than smaller enterprises; and (3) that diversified enterprises could exploit new technical possibilities more fully than narrowly based firms.

As one moves from theory to statistical testing, a sizable chasm must often be hurdled. One problem is that the structural hypotheses of Part II are formulated in terms of individual R & D projects, whereas the available statistical data on R & D at best cover company (or even industry) aggregates, which almost always entail portfolios encompassing many individual projects. The gap can be bridged by invoking Keynesian marginal efficiency of investment (or business school capital budgeting) logic: a firm's decision makers proceed down a list of return-ranked projects until the marginal project has an expected return only slightly greater than the cost of capital. Thus, if under some market structures projects are conducted faster and at higher cost, or if more projects pass payoffs-greater-than-costs tests, more will be spent in the aggregate on R & D, all else equal. But as I hinted in note 7 of chapter 5, if firms set total R & D budgets more or less arbitrarily and then engage in capital rationing, this link may not hold. Despite evidence by Mansfield et al. (1968, 23–31; see also chapter 16 this volume) that firms adjust their R & D budgets in accord with profitability expectations, it is uncertain whether the aggregation assumption holds fully. An alternative theoretical foundation has been proposed by Needham (1975) and extended by Stoneman and Leech (1983). They invoke the Dorfman-Steiner theorem to predict the aggregate R & D/sales ratio of firms, given various market structure and R & D responsiveness parameters.

A different problem arises in studies of R & D incentives as a function of firm size. One neo-Schumpeterian argument is that because of economies of scale or scope, large firms can conduct R & D more efficiently than small firms. This can have two effects. The cost-saving effect per se should lead to lower R & D outlays, all else equal. But with lower costs, firms may approve more projects, increasing outlays. Whether on balance the R & D/sales ratio rises depends on whether the elasticity of project approvals with respect to scale-related cost savings exceeds unity. Thus, as Fisher and Temin (1974) argued and Kohn and Scott (1982) elaborated, studies of R & D spending behavior as a function of firm size may provide only ambiguous support for, or contradiction of, Schumpeterian hypotheses. The obvious solution is to secure data on the *output* of firms' R & D efforts along with data on inputs.

Chapter 9 was the capstone of my first foray into the statistical testing of Schumpeterian hypotheses. On the whole, the conjectures inspired by Schumpeter's *Capitalism, Socialism, and Democracy* fared badly. There was little evidence of disproportionately great R & D input or output associated with the largest corporations, and market concentration showed no significant positive impact on progressiveness. In addition to these substantive results my 1965 paper had several methodological features differentiating it from earlier works in the same vein (e.g., the papers cited as items [7], [8], [11], [12], and [29] in the references section of chapter 9).

First and foremost was a concern for obtaining data better-suited to the task at hand. The National Science Foundation statistics used in early market structure hypothesis tests were in my view far too aggregated to be of much relevance. R & D spending data at the firm level were virtually unavailable to the public at the time, and they, like the employment tallies analyzed by Worley (1961), suffered from a possible cost-saving vs. portfolio-expanding ambiguity. It seemed important therefore to obtain output data that were susceptible to disaggregation and reasonably precise industry classification. Absent data on significant innovations like those collected for three industries by Mansfield (1963) and, despite evident limitations, patent data appeared to be the best solution. A concern for improving the quality of data also motivated my efforts as a bureaucrat at the Federal Trade Commission in developing the line of business program, which helped make chapters 3, 12, 13, 15 and 16 possible.

A second characteristic has been my concern for interindustry differences, especially those associated with differences in the richness of the technological opportunities enjoyed by particular industries. My attempt to account for technology-push differences, among other things minimizing the biases that might come from a correlation between opportunity and the structural variables being tested, is evident in all the papers reprinted here.

Third, most investigators of firm size–R & D relationships (with Mansfield as a notable exception) have estimated equations of the form $RD = \alpha S^{\beta}$, where RD is the cross-sectional variable under study, S is a size variable, and an elasticity β exceeding 1.0 is interpreted as supporting Schumpeterian conjectures. I have normally avoided this approach. Preliminary work (Scherer 1965) revealed that the convention adopted to deal with missing R & D observations (a common occurrence) could dominate the results (e.g., with deletion of the missing observations driving β below 1.0 and insertion of arbitrarily small values driving it above unity). Also elasticity equations estimated in the logarithms place maximum weight on the observations for the typically more numerous smaller firms, whereas the Schumpeterian hypotheses most directly concern the behavior of the largest firms. If β varies with firm size, misleading conclusions can follow. Quadratic and cubic forms are less elegant but better-suited to detecting such anomalies. Numerous other checks against spurious inferences have been made, especially in chapter 9.

Chapter 10 summarizes some of the work done to determine how antitrust-based compulsory licensing decrees affected firms' propensity to patent, which could impart structure-correlated biases when patent counts are used to measure inventive output. It also yields the surprising conclusion that such decrees had little discernible impact on market structure. One set of tests utilized the first comprehensive data on R & D spending available for a broad cross section of U.S. corporations. Among other things, the analysis reveals no significant association between R & D intensity (i.e., R & D/sales ratios) and firm size. This is consistent with the patent-based findings of chapter 9 and contrary to the neo-Schumpeterian hypothesis that large firms are more vigorous R & D supporters.

The availability of finely disaggregated, linked R & D expenditure and patent data—undoubtedly the richest data ever assembled on U.S. R & D activity—brought me back to the firm size question a third time in chapter 11, which is excerpted from a longer paper. Again the case for big business receives at best faint support. The largest corporations as a group perform more company-financed R & D than their share of sales, but they do not contribute disproportionately many inventions or significant innovations. And within the cohort of large corporations, R & D input and output appear most often to rise only proportionately with size.

Chapter 12 carried the analysis of seller concentration's effects on scientific and engineering activity to a new, comprehensive yet relatively disaggregated data set. Contrary to chapter 9, it found that concentration *did* matter in a positive way, although the exact chain of causation was left in doubt.

Chapter 13 took advantage of vastly superior Line of Business R & D data to check others' puzzling finding of a positive association between seller concentration and productivity growth. As anticipated, when well-measured R & D variables are included, the association fades. However, the positive correlation between R & D intensity and concentration found in chapter 12 persists with the new data. It is noteworthy that the correlation is much stronger for product R & D than process R & D—a result consistent with my early theory-building emphasis on new product, as contrasted to process, rivalry models. More remarkable is the fact that, when the industries are grouped into technological opportunity classes, significantly positive R & D/sales–concentration correlations are found only for the traditional and general and mechanical technology groups. This duplicates chapter 12's result at a much higher level of disaggregation. It suggests that high concentration encourages R & D primarily in fields experiencing slow-moving development possibility function shifts. In such fields, theoretical contributions of chapters 5 and 6 tell us, a fairly large share of the market might be required before firms have sufficiently favorable profit expectations to risk their funds on R & D. The "positive expected profits" effect outweighs the stimulating effect of greater competition.

My statistical studies have yielded no definitive answer to the question of how industry structure responds to vigorous R & D rivalry. As noted in chapters 12 and 13, Gibrat's law and the building of strong patent positions might lead to rising and eventually high seller concentration. Without good pooled time series–cross sectional data on R & D, it will be hard to piece together a general answer. I suspect, however, that entry behavior will prove to be the missing link. It is well known that entry can attenuate or even nullify the tendencies predicted by Gibrat's law. When technological opportunity is rich, two opposing forces can operate. As some incumbent firms succeed and others stumble in the stochastic

R & D rivalry game, concentration tends to increase. But rich opportunity and rapid market growth also facilitate new entry, which tends to erode concentration. The net effect must depend on which of the two concentration-changing forces is stronger

References

Fisher, Franklin M., and Peter Temin. Returns to Scale in Research and Development: What Does the Schumpeterian Hypothesis Imply? *Journal of Political Economy* (January–February 1973): 56–70.

Kohn, Meir, and John T. Scott. Scale Economies in Research and Development: The Schumpeterian Hypothesis. *Journal of Industrial Economics* (March 1982): 239–249.

Levin, Richard, and Peter Reiss. Tests of a Schumpeterian Model of R & D and Market Structure. In the National Bureau of Economic Research conference report, *R & D, Patents and Productivity*. Chicago: University of Chicago Press, forthcoming.

Mansfield, Edwin. Size of Firm, Market Structure, and Innovation. *Journal of Political Economy* (December 1963): 556–576.

Mansfield, Edwin. *Industrial Research and Technological Innovation*. New York: Norton, 1968.

Needham, Douglas. Market Structure and Firms' R & D Behavior. *Journal of Industrial Economics* (June 1975): 241–255.

Scherer, F. M. Size of Firm, Oligopoly, and Research: A Comment. *Canadian Journal of Economics and Political Science* (May 1965): 256–266.

Stoneman, Paul, and D. Leech. Product and Process Innovation and the R & D/Market Structure Relationship. *Quarterly Journal of Economics*, in press.

Worley, J. S. Industrial Research and the New Competition. *Journal of Political Economy* (April 1961): 183–186.

9 Firm Size, Market Structure, Opportunity, and the Output of Patented Inventions

During the past three decades hypotheses concerning the most favorable industrial environment for technological progress have proliferated like foliage in the Vietnam jungles.[1] Only recently have we begun to penetrate the rich theoretical growth with empirical insights. This paper contributes to the defoliation program, reporting on a statistical study of the relationships between inventive activity and technological opportunity, firm size, product-line diversification, and monopoly power.

The main sample consisted of 448 firms on *Fortune's* list of the 500 largest U.S. industrial corporations for the base year 1955.[2] Independent variables included three measures of firm size for 1955, profits for 1955 through 1960, liquid assets for 1955, an index of diversification, dummy variables differentiating industry and technology classes, and (for a special sample to be described later) four-firm concentration ratios. The principal dependent variable is the number of U.S. invention patents issued to the sampled firms in 1959 [33]. The year of patent issue is lagged four years from the base year 1955, whose inventive output is to be measured, because on the average nine months pass between the conception of an industrial invention and the filing of a patent application [17, p. 71] and because during the 1950s three and a half years were required for the Patent Office to process an average application to the point of issue.

9.1 Patent Statistics as an Index of Inventive Output

Unfortunately, no completely satisfactory index of inventive output is available to the researcher. A straight count of patents has two well-known limitations: (1) the propensity to patent an invention of given quality may vary from firm to firm and from industry to industry, and (2) the quality of the underlying inventions varies widely from patent to patent.

The most important countermeasure is to recognize the existence of these deficiencies, but other steps are also available. Interindustry differences in the propensity to patent will be analyzed through the use of dummy variables. Within a given major industry or field, interfirm differences in the propensity to patent can be viewed as a random disturbance which, unless correlated with some independent variable, imparts no

Source: *American Economic Review* 55 (December 1965): 1097–1123. Journal of the American Economic Association.

bias to regression estimates of inventive output, only increasing the unexplained variance.

The underlying economic (or technological) significance of any sampled patent can also be interpreted as a random variable with some probability distribution. Here a more serious problem arises, however. Fragmentary data on the profitability of patents—one indicator of economic significance—reveal a distribution highly skewed toward the low private value side, with a very long tail into the high value side [18], [20]. A graphic test suggested the existence of a Pareto-type distribution of profits with an α coefficient of less than 0.5. Asymptotically such a distribution possesses neither a finite mean nor a finite variance, and so one cannot be sure that the mean economic value of any particular sample of patents converges (under the weak law of large numbers) toward the true population mean value if large enough samples are drawn [10]. This forces us to acknowledge that patent statistics are likely to measure run-of-the-mill industrial inventive output much more accurately than they reflect the occasional strategic inventions which open up new markets and new technologies. The latter must probably remain the domain of economic historians.[3]

Given the limitations of patent data, many of the hypotheses explored in this paper were also tested with respect to 1955 research and development employment (including supporting staff members) for a subsample of 352 firms on which data were available. One finding of this double-barreled attack deserves immediate mention. The number of patents received in 1959 by the 352 firms was (by cross-section standards) fairly strongly correlated with the number of 1955 R & D employees, with an r^2 of 0.72.[4] More generally, as we shall see, the results of the analyses were similar whether patents or R & D employment was taken as the index of inventive activity.

9.2 Demand-Pull and Technology-Push Hypotheses

Let us consider now the relationship between patenting and the gross size of the 448 firms. Regression of the ith firm's patents P_i on its 1955 sales S_i (in billions of dollars) gave the equation

$$P_i = 10.65 + 73.81 S_i, \tag{1}$$
$$(4.09)$$

with r^2 of 0.422. (Standard errors of regression coefficients will be given in parentheses.) In comparable regressions the r^2 was 0.431 when 1955 assets were the scale variable and 0.480 with 1955 employment as the scale measure. Although least suitable in terms of a crude goodness-of-fit test, 1955 sales will be used as the scale variable in most of the analyses that follow.[5] This choice is taken for three main reasons. First, the sales variable is most likely to be responsive to short-run changes in demand. Second, the sales variable is essentially neutral with respect to factor proportions—an important attribute, given the fact that more than three-fourths of U.S. industrial research and development is directed toward new products, as opposed to new internal production processes [6]. Third, interview studies show that sales are the principal scale variable considered in company research and development budget decisions.

The correlation between patenting and firm size can be interpreted, along lines suggested by Schmookler and Brownlee [26] and extended by Schmookler and Griliches [27], as reflecting the response of inventive output to the overall pull of demand. Presumably, the greater the sales of a firm in any given market, the more incentive and resources the firm has to generate patentable inventions related to that market.

Nevertheless, systematic differences between industries not related to mere sales volume also affect corporate patenting in an important manner. This can be seen in the effect of estimating separate linear regressions for each of the fourteen two- and three-digit industries covered by my study. The results are summarized in table 9.1 and in the appendix.[6] By letting each industry assume its own best-fitting slope and intercept, we are able to "explain" 84.7 percent of the total variance in corporate patenting about its grand mean. This represents an incremental gain of 42.5 percentage points over the simple regression of patents on sales for 448 firms together.[7] Thus interindustry differences accounted for almost exactly the same amount of variance as interfirm variations in sales volume.

These observed interindustry differences in patenting, holding firm sales constant, can have a number of underlying causes. Perhaps most important is a set of influences best described under the heading "technological opportunity." Technological opportunity in this context could relate partly to industry traditions or to demand conditions not manifested in mere sales volume, but it seems most likely to be associated with dynamic supply conditions dependent in turn on the broad advance of scientific and technological knowledge. Thus the high sales regression

Table 9.1
Linear regressions of patenting on sales, by industry

Industry	Intercept	Regression coefficient	N	R^2	Total patents
Food and tobacco products	−0.4	+18.05 (2.04)	75	0.52	366
Textiles and apparel	2.8	−0.48 (7.00)	25	0.00	70
Paper and allied products	4.5	+7.11 (6.14)	21	0.07	120
General chemicals[a]	8.1	+262.48 (25.68)	41	0.73	3,316
Miscellaneous chemicals[b]	13.0	+19.33 (20.50)	14	0.07	231
Petroleum	4.5	+81.10 (10.50)	30	0.68	2,194
Rubber products	7.3	+52.32 (11.29)	8	0.78	303
Stone, clay, and glass	−12.4	+200.92 (25.03)	19	0.79	434
Primary metals	0.4	+23.21 (2.50)	50	0.64	486
Fabricated metal products and miscellaneous[c]	5.9	+61.86 (16.56)	31	0.32	516
Machinery	6.1	+90.40 (12.58)	46	0.54	967
Electrical equipment and communications	22.5	+311.06 (17.61)	35	0.90	5,036
Transportation equipment, except aircraft	2.7	+59.72 (5.28)	30	0.82	1,685
Aircraft and parts	6.8	+70.38 (22.39)	23	0.32	739
All industries combined	10.7	+73.81 (4.09)	448	0.42	16,463

[a] Includes SIC 281, 282, and 283 (inorganic, organic, and drugs).
[b] Includes SIC 284, 285, 287, and 289 (soap, paints, fertilizer, and misc.).
[c] Includes, in addition to fabricated metal products, ordnance, watches and clocks, optical equipment, and the SIC 39 miscellaneous category.

coefficients for the electrical and general chemicals industries are undoubtedly due mainly to the vigorous scientific climate of those fields,
which has assured a continuous supply of new technical possibilities
exploitable to satisfy existing or latent demands. In effect, science and
technology exert a push on inventive output in these fields. On the
other hand, common observation suggests that the low-coefficient paper,
food products, and conventional textile and clothing industries face a
much more limited (although not empty) barrel of new technological
possibilities.

At least part of the observed interindustry differences in patent output
is nonetheless attributable to a different set of causes: systematic variations in the propensity to patent inventions actually made. It is well
known, for example, that aircraft makers and other defense specialists
seldom seek patent protection on inventions made under government
contract, since they must give their principal customer either exclusive
rights or at least a royalty-free license in any event [24, pp. 80 82].
Conversely, patent attorneys reported in interviews that in such fields
as organic chemicals and petrochemicals, the ease of gaining differentiated
market positions through "manipulated molecule" patents encourages
profuse patenting. A crude indicator of differences in the propensity to
patent is differences in average patent output per unit of engineering
input. As table 9.2 demonstrates, the average number of 1959 patents
received per thousand 1955 research and development employees varied
from a low of 27 in the rubber goods industry to a high of 150 in the
machinery industry.[8]

Further analysis suggests that these differences in the propensity to
patent account for only a minority of all systematic interindustry differences in patenting. To see this, we assume that varying propensities
to patent should show up as differences in patent outputs per unit of
R & D input. As indicated in section 9.1, a simple regression of patent
outputs on R & D employment inputs for 352 firms yielded an r^2 of 0.72.
If slope (not intercept) dummy variables for fourteen industries are
introduced into this regression, permitting each industry to have its own
input-output coefficient, the multiple R^2 rises to 0.84. This 12-percentage
point gain in patenting variance thus explained affords a maximum
estimate of the effect of interindustry differences in the propensity to
patent.[9]

We may consequently partition the overall variance in corporate

Table 9.2
Patents per thousand 1955 R & D employees for 352 firms, by principal industry, 1959

Industry	Mean P/R & D	Number of firms
Machinery	150.0	34
Stone, clay, and glass	134.6	18
Petroleum	119.5	21
Fabricated metal products and miscellaneous	117.9	25
General chemicals	111.1	37
Primary metals	95.6	39
Electrical equipment and communications	84.5	31
Paper and allied products	84.2	18
Textiles and apparel	81.3	17
Transportation equipment, except aircraft	72.1	18
Food and tobacco products	61.8	55
Miscellaneous chemicals	55.1	14
Aircraft and parts	33.4	19
Rubber products	26.6	6
All industries	83.4	352

patenting as follows: 42 percent to interfirm differences in sales; less than 12 percent to interindustry differences in the propensity to patent; more than 30 percent to interindustry differences in technological opportunity, broadly defined; and 16 percent as (thus far) unexplained residual. Even if this 12–30 split of the 42.5 percentage point interindustry component is inaccurate by a wide margin, it is impossible to avoid a conclusion that interindustry differences unrelated to mere sales volume account for a major proportion of the variance in corporate patenting.

9.3 Corporate Bigness and Inventive Output

We have seen that patenting is an increasing function of firm size, with or without technological opportunity taken into account. We turn next to a question more in the Schumpeterian vein: Does patenting increase more than proportionately with firm size, less than proportionately, or is the relationship essentially linear? Disciples of Schumpeter argue that

Table 9.3
Concentration of sales, patents, R & D employment, and total employment in a sample of 352 corporations

Number of firms included, ranked by 1955 sales	Percentage of total for all 352 firms			
	1955 sales	1959 patents	1955 R & D employment	1955 total employment
First 4	19.9	10.4	9.7	16.1
First 8	27.5	16.8	16.4	24.1
First 12	32.8	24.9	25.9	28.3
First 20	41.5	32.9	36.7	35.0
First 30	49.0	42.9	44.7	42.4
First 40	55.0	45.0	50.4	48.8
First 50	59.9	50.8	57.8	55.1
First 75	69.3	64.5	68.1	63.9
First 100	75.9	71.0	71.9	71.9
First 150	84.9	81.3	81.7	81.8
First 200	90.8	89.4	90.0	88.9
First 250	94.9	94.2	94.8	93.5
First 300	97.7	97.6	97.8	97.2
All 352	100.0	100.0	100.0	100.0

inventive output ought to increase more than proportionately with firm size due to the scale economies and more effective incentives associated with bigness. Others have postulated the opposite relationship, pointing mainly to the stultifying effects of bigness on incentives and initiative.

Tests of the neo-Schumpeterian scale hypothesis encounter a number of methodological problems. One is that the results depend to some extent on the choice of a scale variable. For reasons analyzed in [22], the neo-Schumpeterian bigness contention receives greatest support when total employment is chosen as the scale measure and least when assets are chosen. Here the sales variable is emphasized partly because it compromises the extremes, but chiefly because it is considered most frequently in actual R & D budget decisions and because it is neutral with respect to factor proportions.

The relationship between sales and patenting or R & D employment can be studied by computing concentration measures or through non-linear regression methods. The concentration approach is less elegant but more lucid, so let us use it first. Table 9.3 presents cumulative sales, patenting, and R & D employment shares for selected groups from my subsample of 352 firms on which fully comparable data were available. Firms are ranked on the basis of 1955 sales for all cumulations. Two findings stand out. First, sales volume is persistently more concentrated among the largest firms than R & D employment, which in turn tends to be slightly more concentrated than patenting. The top twenty firms by sales, for example, made 41.5 percent of the sales of all 352 firms, but employed only 36.7 percent of the R & D personnel and received only 32.9 percent of the patents. Second, it follows by subtraction that smaller firms were responsible for a higher relative share of inventive activity than sales. The implication is that inventive inputs (R & D employment) and outputs (patents) increase less than proportionately with sales.

The last column of table 9.3 gives cumulative total employment for the 352 companies, again ranked by sales volume. It illustrates the earlier suggestion that a somewhat different result is obtained when employment is taken as the scale variable, R & D employment in particular being more concentrated than total employment for firms ranked below the twelve sales leaders.

Further insight into the role of size can be gained by introducing outside data. The 448 firms in my full sample accounted for 56.9 percent of the sales of all U.S. manufacturing corporations in 1955, as estimated by the Federal Trade Commission. They accounted for 55.1 percent of the 29,888 patents issued to U.S. corporations in 1955.[10] These figures are not quite comparable, since the population of all U.S. corporations includes non-manufacturing corporations. But the latter do very little patenting. It is estimated that nonmanufacturing corporations received no more than 600 patents in 1959.[11] Thus manufacturing corporations excluded from my sample—mostly firms with sales of less than $55 million in 1955—accounted for approximately 43.1 percent of manufacturing sales and 43.9 percent of patents issued to manufacturing corporations.

This interpolation is a bit surprising, in view of National Science Foundation data showing that industrial firms with fewer than 5,000 employees—a population closely analogous to the population of firms excluded from my sample—accounted for a much smaller share of U.S. research and development expenditures (about 14 percent) than their share of sales and employment [32, pp. 23–24].[12] At least three explanations for the disparity between inventive input and output shares among small firms seem relevant. First, government-contract R & D spending, which leads to few patents, is much more concentrated among large firms than private R & D expenditures. Second, small firms apparently obtain a higher proportion of their patented inventions from employees not assigned to formal R & D activities [21]. Finally, there is weak evidence that small firms conduct their R & D with greater cost-consciousness than large firms, and therefore they may tend to generate more inventions per unit of input [2]. In any event the data suggest that smallness is not necessarily an impediment to the creation of patentable inventions and may well be an advantage.

Nonlinear Regression Analyses

For a more detailed analysis of the relationship between patenting and sales, nonlinear regression methods were employed. If, when P_i is regressed nonlinearly on S_i, the second derivative d^2P/dS^2 of the estimated function is positive, P_i is increasing at an increasing rate with S_i, and so patenting must generally be increasing more than proportionately with sales.[13] A negative second derivative implies the opposite relationship. For expositional convenience let us call the positive d^2P/dS^2 case the "increasing returns" case and the negative d^2P/dS^2 case the "diminishing returns" case, taking care not to confuse this use of terms with the somewhat different usage accepted in the standard theory of production.

Considering first all 448 firms together, P_i was estimated as a function of S_i with squared and cubic S_i terms:

$$P_i = -3.79 + (144.42S_i - 23.86S_i^2 + 1.457S_i^3, \atop (14.44) \quad (4.83) \quad (0.316)} \tag{2}$$

with R^2 of 0.454. This is the nonlinear analogue of equation (1). Introduction of the two nonlinear terms permitted a statistically significant incremental variance reduction of 3.22 percentage points (see the appendix). When the second derivative of (2) is taken, we find diminishing returns dominating up to a point of inflection at 1955 sales of $5.5 billion, after which increasing returns set in. Since only three firms in the sample of 448 (General Motors, Standard Oil of New Jersey, and Ford) had 1955 sales greater than $5.5 billion, and since the cubic (increasing returns) coefficient is of doubtful statistical significance, the indication is that patent outputs generally increase less than proportionately with increases in sales among corporations large enough to appear on *Fortune's* 1955 list.[14]

To determine whether this result was influenced by the industry distribution of firms, separate regressions of P_i on S_i with nonlinear terms were estimated for each industry with nineteen or more observations. In ten out of twelve industries, the equations were of the same form as (2), with negative squared-term coefficients and positive cubic-term coefficients. In the two nonconforming cases (paper and aircraft) diminishing returns set in with firms of intermediate size and continued all the way out to the largest firms. However, due to the small number of observations for many industries and the high intercorrelations among S_i, S_i^2, and S_i^3 terms, most of the nonlinear coefficients were not statistically significant by conventional standards.[15] Some regressions with few observations were also dominated by one or two extreme values.

To combat these statistical problems while taking into account differences in technological opportunity, the original list of fourteen industries was consolidated into four groups, depending on the linear regression coefficients reported in table 9.1. The group with coefficients from 0 to 23, including food, textiles, paper, miscellaneous chemicals, and primary metals, will be called the unprogressives. The group with coefficients from 52 to 90 will be called the moderates. Stone, clay, and glass was combined with general chemicals to form a third group, while the electrical industry stood alone in the fourth group. Separate regressions of patents on sales for these four groups explained 83.6 percent of the total variance in patenting about its grand mean, closely approaching the 84.7 percent reduction achieved with the fourteen separate industry regressions of table 9.1. This indicates that the four-group classification was able to allow for the most significant interindustry differences in patenting relative to sales.

Cubic regression equations estimated for the four groups were as follows:

For electrical,

$$P_i = -21.9 + 582.87S_i - 177.41S_i^2$$
$$\quad\quad\quad\quad (98.16) \quad\quad (95.88)$$

$$+ 26.67S_i^3; \quad R^2 = 0.94.$$
$$(22.13)$$

(3)

For chemical,

$$P_i = -23.1 + 432.04S_i - 203.85S_i^2$$
$$\quad\quad (131.45) \quad\ (221.7)$$

$$+ 58.42S_i^3; \quad R^2 = 0.74.$$
$$(85.59)$$

(4)

For the moderates,

$$P_i = 5.7 + 82.85S_i - 10.63S_i^2$$
$$\quad\quad (12.98) \quad\ (3.78)$$

$$+ 0.789S_i^3; \quad R^2 = 0.77.$$
$$(0.235)$$

(5)

For the unprogressives,

$$P_i = 1.9 + 21.04S_i - 10.18S_i^2$$
$$\quad\quad (6.53) \quad\ (5.61)$$

$$+3.00S_i^3; \quad R^2 = 0.55.$$
$$(1.06)$$

(6)

All four equations, plotted in figure 9.1, display the initially diminishing and then increasing returns pattern of equation (2).[16] Despite multicollinearity, three of the four squared (diminishing returns) terms' coefficients are significant at the 0.10 level or higher. In the increasing returns stage dominated by the positive cubic coefficients, the unprogressive group included five large firms, the moderates three, chemicals and stone-clay-glass two, and the electrical industry only one. Thus the indication again is one of diminishing returns except for a few giant firms that led their two-digit industries in sales.

All of the regression equations discussed thus far are dominated to some extent by the observations for large firms. This is not wholly undesirable, since the largest firms account for such a substantial proportion of the full sample's sales and presumably had the market penetration and resources to support a similar lion's share of inventive activity. Still for the sake of accuracy two further analyses were executed which either avoided large firm biases or erred in the opposite direction.

First, along lines suggested by Edwin Mansfield [11], logarithms of the sales variables were taken to compress the large-firm tail of the sales distribution, and then P_i was regressed on $\log S_i$, $(\log S_i)^2$ and $(\log S_i)^3$ for

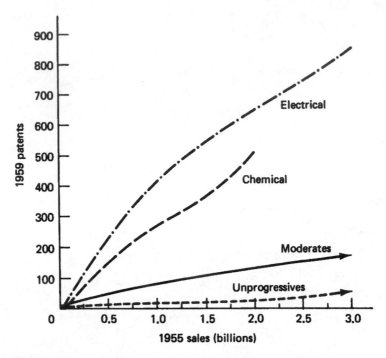

Figure 9.1
Plot of conventional cubic regressions by technology group

each of the four groups. Because the equations are almost impossible to interpret intuitively, the results are presented graphically in figure 9.2.[17] Diminishing returns in patenting are evident for both chemicals and electrical equipment—the most progressive groups. For the unprogressives there is a tendency toward increasing returns up to sales of about $1 billion, and then initially imperceptible diminishing returns set in. This relationship, however, is probably due in part to the greater diversification of the largest firms in unprogressive fields, as discussed in section 9.4.[18] For the moderates slightly increasing returns prevail up to sales of $800 million, at which point a faint diminishing-returns effect begins to dominate.

Second, each group was broken down into from three to five size subgroups, and separate linear regressions were estimated for each subgroup. The results are shown in figure 9.3. Although many of the coefficients were not statistically significant, the diverse pieces splice

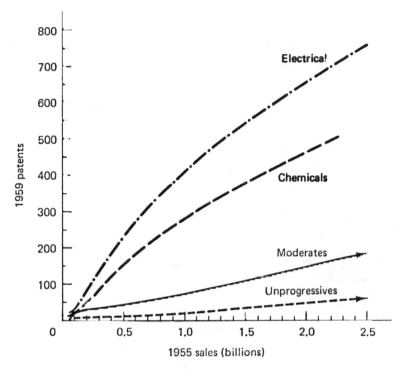

Figure 9.2
Plot of cubic regressions with logarithmic transformations

together well enough to suggest that something more than random phenomena was at work. For both chemicals (with stone, clay, and glass) and electrical equipment, there may be slightly increasing returns up to sales of roughly $500 million, but beyond that point a definite flattening out of the patenting function is evident. For the moderates very slightly decreasing returns appear to prevail continuously. The pattern for the unprogressives is so irregular that no conclusions can be drawn.

By way of synthesis, two possible interpretations can be attached to the full set of regression results, depending on one's attitude toward statistical significance tests generally and the disutility of type I as opposed to type II inferential errors. Where significance is doubtful by traditional standards, one may incline toward the Scotch verdict that corporate patenting has not been shown to increase either more or less than proportionately with sales. But if the regressions are accepted as best estimates

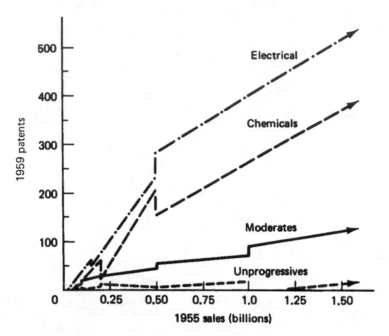

Figure 9.3
Spliced linear size subgroup regressions by technology group

of some true behavioral pattern, it would appear that after a stage of slightly increasing returns extending to 1955 sales of approximately $500 million, corporate patenting tends to increase less than proportionately with sales, except in the case of a few giant firms which lead their two-digit sectors in sales. The least vigorous patent recipients relative to their size appear to be nonleader firms with sales over $500 million.

Conditions Underlying the Observed Relationships

The relevance of these observed relationships might be questioned if one could show that the propensity to patent is inversely correlated with firm size. It is conceivable that large firms receive proportionately fewer patents than smaller firms, not because they generate fewer inventions but because they patent a smaller proportion of what they invent.[19] This could be so, for instance, because their inventive output includes a higher fraction of unpatentable contributions to pure knowledge, or because patents afford less marginal benefit than they do for smaller and more vulnerable firms,

or because government antitrust policies have been hostile to the exploitation of patent power by large firms [24]. But arguments for the opposite
conclusion are also compelling. Notably, restrictive power may grow
more than proportionately with the accumulation of patents, and for
large firms with a staff of in-house patent attorneys the short-run marginal
cost of patenting may be less than for smaller firms dependent on outside
counsel.[20]

It is impossible to choose between these arguments on a priori grounds,
so we must resort to two slender reeds of data. First, an intensive questionnaire survey of more than 500 randomly selected patents issued in
1938, 1948, and 1952 showed no tendency for the proportion of inventions
actually produced or used in production to vary with firm size for firms
with 1949 sales exceeding $55 million [18]. There was, however, evidence
that the percentage of patents in *current* use varied inversely with firm
size.[21] One would expect firms which patent profusely to have a lower
utilization rate than firms which patent only significant inventions, and
so the survey results imply either a constant or (for current utilization) an
increasing propensity to patent as firm size increases. Second, and in
partial conflict with the survey results, the data underlying table 9.3 show
that the forty largest corporations ranked by sales received an average of
74.7 patents per 1,000 R & D employees, compared to the overall average
of 83.4 patents for 352 firms (as in table 9.2). Similar results are found for
the twenty largest, thirty largest, and fifty largest. On the other hand,
industry leaders Swift, New Jersey Standard Oil, U.S. Steel, Pittsburgh
Plate Glass, International Harvester, and General Electric each received
more than 120 patents per 1,000 R & D employees. These findings suggest
that marked differences in the propensity to patent among the largest
firms may in part explain both the relatively poor showing of large firms
which did not lead their two-digit sectors in sales and the increasing
returns associated with leading firms.

Variations in the propensity to patent clearly do not tell the whole
story, however. Nonlinear regressions of R & D employment on sales
presented in [22] generally paralleled those estimated here for patenting
on sales. A global regression analogous to equation (2) had coefficients
with the same signs as (2), but the nonlinearities were more pronounced.
Cubic regressions for seven industries with twenty or more observations
and grouped regressions similar to equations (3) through (6) revealed a
general tendency toward diminishing returns, although the chemicals

industry was an exception with R & D employment increasing more than proportionately with sales.[22] There was somewhat less evidence of an upturn in R & D employment for industry sales leaders (consistent with their high ratio of patents to R & D employment) and somewhat more evidence of increasing returns for firms with sales under $500 million.

Thus one is led to believe that the diminishing returns observed in connection with patenting are related at least in part to similar tendencies in research and development employment, especially for firms with sales exceeding $500 million in 1955. It is not completely clear why this is so. My guess is that a firm's optimal competitive strategy tends to vary systematically but not monotonically with both absolute and relative size. Relatively small firms have strong incentives to do product-differentiating R & D and to patent the results in order to secure their positions against large rivals with economies of scale in promotion, distribution, and perhaps production. Giant firms in positions of industry sales leadership *may* also have effective incentives to support R & D—possibly on prestige grounds, or to guard against the hazard of organizational stagnation and decline, or because they inherited a research orientation which was partly responsible for their growth. At the same time such firms also tend to have a high propensity to patent. Large firms that do not lead their two-digit sectors in sales, on the other hand, appear to be least active relative to their size in both R & D employment and patenting, perhaps because they find it advantageous to focus their main attention on promotional activities and production, counting on rapid imitation or licensing of others' inventions to guard against technological displacement.

Two further observations on the relationship between R & D inputs and patent outputs must be recorded. First, there was no evidence that patenting increased either more or less than proportionately with R & D employment. A regression of P_i on $R\&D_i$ with quadratic and cubic terms was very nearly linear. Second, there was some indication of diminishing returns to R & D input intensity, as suggested in the following regression, where S_i is scaled in billions of dollars and $R\&D_i$ in thousands of employees:

$$\frac{P_i}{S_i} = (14 \text{ constants}) - \underset{(7.92)}{12.54 S_i} + \underset{(7.87)}{61.33 \frac{R\&D_i}{S_i}}$$

$$- \underset{(0.51)}{2.84} \left(\frac{R\&D_i}{S_i}\right)^2,$$

(7)

with R^2 of 0.54. The last two terms are of primary interest here. The more R & D employees per million dollars of sales a firm retained, the more patents per billion dollars of sales it received, but with diminishing returns. The function attains a maximum at 16.7 R & D employees per million dollars of sales—an input intensity exceeded only by the Raytheon Corporation in 1955. It would appear that for firms with sales under $500 million, which tended to have the highest ratios of R & D employees to sales, patenting was damped by the intensity effect of equation (7), and so some of the increasing returns found in R & D employment did not show up in patent outputs. The diminishing returns relationship of equation (7) is in turn probably due to organizational problems associated with high R & D input intensity, although the precise mechanism of this phenomenon is not clear.[23]

In conclusion, the evidence does not support the hypothesis that corporate bigness is especially favorable to high inventive output. If anything the results show that firms below the half-billion dollar sales mark generate more inventions relative to their size than do giant firms. Such a conclusion is not necessarily grounds for a campaign of breaking up large firms, since the observed tendencies are less than completely uniform. It is also possible that large size does confer advantages for the development and integration of complicated "systems"—activities less likely to yield patentable inventions. Small firms at the same time may enjoy a comparative advantage at inventing and developing the more readily patentable component parts for such systems. My results do suggest, however, that a heavy burden of proof must be sustained by firms emphasizing research and development potential as a justification (i.e., in merger cases) for bigness.

9.4 The Role of Diversification

One of the most interesting neo-Schumpeterian hypotheses assigns a potentially important role to diversification as a stimulus to invention. The idea, as formulated by Richard Nelson [15], is as follows: research, and especially basic research, is an uncertain activity, yielding inventions and discoveries in unexpected areas. The firm with interests in a diversity of fields will generally be able to produce and market a higher proportion of these unexpected inventions than a firm whose product line is narrow. Therefore the expected profitability of speculative research is greater for highly diversifed firms, and such firms will tend to support more research.

Even though patentable inventions are undoubtedly not the leading product of basic industrial research, uncertainty is an important component of all research, and so the diversification hypothesis seemed worth testing. The usual list of 447 SIC four-digit manufacturing industries was consolidated into a more technologically meaningful list of roughly 200 industries. A diversification index was compiled for each of the 448 companies sampled by counting the number of consolidated industries in which the company operated.[24] The index varied from 43 (for General Electric) down to 1, with a mean of 5.7.

The results of the global 448-firm analysis were striking. Although the diversification index was correlated with sales, with r^2 of 0.20, it was much more strongly correlated with patents, with r^2 of 0.37. When the index was added to a regression of patents on sales, the variance in patenting was reduced by 13 percentage points. Similar results were obtained when the diversification variable was introduced into regressions of P_i/S_i on sales, $R \& D_i$ on sales, and P_i on $R \& D_i$. In every case the diversification variable permitted a significant reduction in unexplained variance, and the t-ratio of its regression coefficient was on the order of 5.0 or more.

The picture changed considerably when each of the fourteen two- and three-digit industry groups was permitted to assume its own best-fitting sales and diversification coefficients. For all industries summed, inclusion of the diversification variable accounted for an incremental variance reduction of 1.05 percentage points beyond the contribution of the simple linear sales regressions in table 9.1—an increment just significant at the 1 percent point in an F-ratio test.[25] This decline in explanatory power suggests that the diversification index acted partly as a surrogate industry dummy variable and that two- or three-digit industry groups with high patenting tended to be the home base of firms operating in a greater number of narrow fields, as defined in my consolidation procedure.

Within the two-digit groups diversification played an uneven role. For five industries, including the three (electrical, general chemical, and stone, clay, and glass) with the highest patenting per billion dollars of sales (table 9.1), the diversification coefficients were negative but statistically insignificant. For nine industries, patenting was positively correlated with diversification, in most cases with t-ratios exceeding 2.0, and the diversification variable accounted for an appreciable reduction in variance not explained by the simple regressions of table 9.1. These included, with the incremental variance reduction percentage in parentheses, textiles and apparel (33), paper (26), aircraft (26), rubber (12), miscellaneous chemicals (10), petroleum (5), food products (4), machinery (4), and land transportation equipment (1). With the exception of machinery, petroleum, and perhaps aircraft, these were for the most part industries whose members obtained few patents per billion dollars of sales.

A similar result was experienced when the diversification variable was introduced into regressions of R & D employment on sales for seven two-digit industry groups with twenty or more observations. R & D employment did not increase at all with diversification for the general chemicals and electrical groups, which were by far the most R & D oriented of the seven. It increased most for food products, which ran a close second to primary metals in fewness of R & D personnel per million dollars of sales. (The metals diversification coefficient was also positive, but significant at only the 0.20 level.)

The main reason for these relationships becomes clear when one examines in detail the product structure of diversified companies classified in a parent two-digit industry with relatively little private research and development and patenting. The more diversified such a firm is, the higher is the probability that it will operate also in a more progressive industry, that is, one with ample opportunities for profitable private investment in new technology. For instance, of the food-products firms with sales of less than $500 million, the leading patent recipient was National Distillers Products, which manufactured basic chemicals in addition to its more thirst-quenching specialities. Sales leaders in the food products, textiles, paper, and miscellaneous chemicals groups tended to be a good deal more diversified than most of their followers, and despite some collinearity the diversification index for these firms picked up incremental variance in patenting. And for a final example from the government-oriented sector, aircraft makers General Dynamics and North American, which were in 1955 either established in or moving aggressively into electronics, atomic energy, and chemicals, received many more patents than less diversified Douglas and Boeing, which had higher sales at the time. It would appear then that diversification was not per se a structural condition necessarily favorable to patentable invention. Rather, the diversification variable's impressive performance shows chiefly the effect of operation in dynamic industries by firms whose home base is not conducive to patenting and (except for aircraft) research and development.

9.5 Market Power and Patented Inventions

We consider now market power's effect on corporate inventive output. There are two broad hypotheses assigning a favorable role to monopoly. No attempt is made to test the older but still controversial hypothesis that the expectation of a future monopoly position (e.g., through a patent grant) is necessary before risk capital will be committed to invention or development.[26] We will examine only the assertion more original to Schumpeter that monopoly power already attained is a favorable base from which to make advances in modern technology.

Schumpeter's writings on this subject consist of little more than *dicta* demanding further interpretation. One construction is that profitable exploitation of market power is the easiest way to assemble the funds necessary for investment in new technology [28, p. 87]. This can be subdivided into two related hypotheses: that technological output (or input) increases with corporate profitability, or that technological output increases with corporate liquidity. The latter is not explicitly Schumpeterian, but it presupposes the same assumptions.

To test these hypotheses, data on base year 1955 profits and liquid assets were collected for the 448 corporations.[27] None of a variety of tests showed any noteworthy tendency for 1959 patenting or 1955 research and development to increase with either 1955 profitability or liquidity. The r^2 between patents per billion dollars of sales and 1955 profits as a percentage of sales was 0.001. Between P_i/S_i and liquid assets as a percentage of total assets it was 0.003. The 1955 profit rate, measured in relation to both sales and total assets, was included in some twenty-six regressions involving raw and deflated patents, R & D personnel, and an assortment of other variables for both the full sample and particular industries. Although there was a tendency for more of the coefficients to be positive than negative, in only five cases was a t-ratio of more than 1.0 achieved, and there were no profitability t-ratios of 2.0 or more.[28] Similarly negative results appeared when the liquid asset/total asset ratio was included in the same equations.

Rejection of the profitability and liquidity hypotheses does not, however, exhaust the list of proposals ascribing a progressive bias to market power. Schumpeter argued that the temporary security and longer-range perspective afforded by a monopoly position facilitated shooting at the rapidly and jerkily moving targets of new technology [28, pp. 88 and 103]. This implies that technological output should tend to increase with industrial concentration, other things being equal. More recently it has been proposed that oligopolists colluding overtly or tacitly on the price dimension have especially vivid incentives to engage in new product rivalry [4, p. 575]. This implies that technological output should tend to increase with concentration up to a point, but that it may decline if too much of an industry's output becomes concentrated in the hands of a single dominant seller.

Prior attempts to test these hypotheses quantitatively [1], [7], [8] aggregated both the technological progressiveness indexes and the concentration indexes into twenty or fewer two- and three-digit industry categories. While the multitude of sins underlying such a procedure may well cancel out, one never really knows what has been cooked in the stew. Therefore a completely different approach was tried.

The only published source that links firm names with concentration ratios for a large sample of industries is a Federal Trade Commission report covering the base year 1950 [31]. That report lists the four leading firms in four- and five-digit industries, along with industry concentration ratios and sales. From the report's listings a sample of forty-eight industries was drawn based on several selection criteria:[29] (1) The industry definition had to be as meaningful as possible in terms of economic analysis. (2) The Census Bureau's coverage of industry producers had to be at least 75 percent for industries with four-firm concentration ratios below 50 percent and 85 percent for industries with higher concentration ratios. (3) Primary-product sales had to comprise at least 75 percent of reported sales for the industry. (4) The broad parent industry had to be reasonably well suited for making and patenting inventions. On the strength of this criterion the food and tobacco, apparel, conventional textile, lumbering, furniture, and publishing two-digit sectors and all primarily defense-oriented industries were excluded. (5) The industry's technology had to be such that classification of patents was feasible. (6) To the extent that all other criteria could be satisfied, a wide range of technologies, concentration ratios, and industry sizes was sought.

The index of inventive output P_{4i} employed in this analysis was the number of industry-related patents issued in 1954 to the leading four firms in the ith industry. A four-year lag from the 1950 base year was used to approximate the mean lags between invention, patent application, and patent issue. Each patent assigned in 1954 to each of 152 different firms occupying leadership positions in the forty-eight industries was separately examined to determine whether or not it pertained primarily to a sampled industry. Some 5,000 patents were examined in this manner; 2,202 patents were assigned to the sampled industries and the rest were thrown out. This procedure was fairly straightforward for most industries, but in a few cases (especially in those involving by-products and substantial vertical integration) a good deal of judgment had to be applied, and the count was subject to uncertainty.

Independent variables included the value of shipments S_{4i} of the leading four firms in the ith industry in 1950, four-firm concentration ratios M_i for 1950, and slope (not intercept) dummy variables to differentiate industries operating primarily in chemical and electrical technologies from those facing largely mechanical technologies.[30]

The analysis revealed a positive but very modest and statistically insignificant influence on patenting for the market share variable. The simple linear r^2 between patenting and M_i was 0.069, with a t-ratio of 1.85 for the corresponding regression coefficient. In a regression of the logarithms of P_{4i} on the logarithms of M_i, r^2 was 0.051, and the t-ratio 1.57. The t-ratios and partial correlation coefficients for market share declined when additional variables, especially the value of shipments S_{4i}, were introduced.[31] Because one would expect the effects of scale, market share, and technology to be multiplicative rather than additive, and in order to suppress the undesirable effects of heteroscedasticity, the regression model most suitable on theoretical and statistical grounds appeared to be

$$P_{4i} = aS_{4i}^{\alpha}M_i^{\beta}C_i^{\gamma}E_i^{\delta}u_i, \tag{8}$$

where C_i is a chemical technology slope dummy variable, E_i is an electrical technology dummy variable, and u_i is the error term. The fitted regression equation in logarithmic form was

$$\log P_{4i} = 1.51 + 0.680 \log S_{4i} + 0.064 \log M_i + 0.192 \log C_i$$
$$(0.133) \qquad\qquad (0.302) \qquad\qquad (0.181)$$
$$+ 0.498 \log E_i, \tag{9}$$
$$(0.193)$$

with R^2 of 0.47. The partial correlation for market share was 0.032, far lower than any of the other variables' partial r's. If despite the low t-ratio for market share we use (9) as a best estimator, we find that for four industry leaders with total shipments valued at $100 million, an increase in market share from 15 to 90 percent brings an increase of one patent. For four firms with sales of $1 billion, the same market share differential implies a difference of five patents.

It must be noted that, although (9) was deemed most suitable on theoretical and statistical grounds, it assigned a weaker role to market share than the analogous additive (nonlogarithmic) equation (where the M_i coefficient's t-ratio was 1.06). But further analysis showed this difference to be largely the result of patenting and market shares associated with the telephone and telegraph industry (with $M = 92$ percent). When the observations for that industry were deleted, the market share coefficient's t-ratio in the additive regression fell from 1.06 to 0.09.[32]

To test further the sensitivity of my results to potential biasing factors, regressions were run without the observations for eight industries with marked patent classification and assignment uncertainties.[33] The general effect was a distinct but far from statistically significant increase in the t-ratios and partial correlation coefficients associated with M_i. For example, the M_i t-ratio for equation (9) rose from 0.21 with $n = 48$ to 0.67 with $n = 40$. Deletion of telephone industry observations in addition to those of the uncertain industries caused t to fall in this case from 0.67 to 0.51.

Additional additive regression equations were estimated with a quadratic market share term in order to test for nonlinearities. In every such regression a U-shaped relationship was found, with minimum patenting occurring at four-firm concentration ratios between 44 and 71 percent. Since the nonlinear coefficients made little incremental contribution to the reduction of variance and had no t-ratio exceeding 1.46, and since no compelling theoretical rationalization for such a relationship is known, it seems likely that the observed U-shape was the result of chance elements.

In sum, the analysis suggests that if structural market power has a beneficial effect on the output of patented inventions, it is a very modest effect indeed. One highly monopolistic industry—telephone and telegraph equipment—was responsible for much of the observed correlation between market share and patenting, and that industry, dominated as it is by quasi-regulated Western Electric, is clearly a special case.

This conclusion would have to be reconsidered if there were indications that the propensity to patent varied inversely with market power. But although nothing even approximating proof is available, conventional wisdom holds that the opposite is more apt to be true. In many of the most concentrated industries sampled (i.e., gypsum products, razors, synthetic fibers, flat glass, telephones, and aluminum) the market power of the leaders was built partly on a patent base, and this fact could scarcely have been forgotten by company executives anxious to preserve that power.

It is also conceivable that existing monopoly power is a uniquely favorable environment only for investment in basic and the most fundamental applied research, either because these activities carry the highest risks or because their benefits are apt to be largely external to more competitive firms. Since knowledge—presumably an important output of such activities—cannot be patented, patent statistics do not permit a sensitive test of this narrower interpretation.[34]

As a final caveat, it must be pointed out that my data assign a weaker beneficial role to market power than do the studies of two-digit industry R & D spending reported by Hamberg [7] and Horowitz [8]. Still the fact that their analyses were unable to take into account differences in technological opportunity may have permitted the correlations to attribute a spuriously strong influence to market power.

9.6 Conclusions

The principal conclusions of this study are as follows: (1) Inventive output increases with firm sales, but generally at a less than proportional rate. (2) Differences in technological opportunity (e.g., differences in technical investment possibilities unrelated to the mere volume of sales and typically opened up by the broad advance of knowledge) are a major factor responsible for interindustry differences in inventive output. (3) Inventive output does not appear to be systematically related to variations in market power, prior profitability, liquidity, or (when participation in fields with high technological opportunity is accounted for) degree of product line diversification.

These findings among other things raise doubts whether the big, monopolistic, conglomerate corporation is as efficient an engine of technological change as disciples of Schumpeter (including myself) have supposed it to be. Perhaps a bevy of fact-mechanics can still rescue the Schumpeterian engine from disgrace, but at present the outlook seems pessimistic.

Appendix: Incremental Analysis of Covariance, 448-Firm Patenting

Step	Description		Sum of squared deviations	SSD as percent of A-1 SSD	Degrees of Freedom	F-ratio
A-1	No independent variables		3,928,423	100.00	1	
A-2	Global regression of P_i on S_i (eq. 1)	Reduction from A-1 / Residual	1,657,710 / 2,270,713	42.20 / 57.80	1 / 446	326
A-3	Global regression on S_i and diversification	Reduction from A-2 / Residual	498,012 / 1,772,701	12.68 / 45.12	1 / 445	125
A-4	Global regression on S_i and S_i^2	Reduction from A-2 / Residual	23,440 / 2,247,273	0.60 / 57.20	1 / 445	4.64**
A-5	Global regression on S_i, S_i^2, and S_i^3	Reduction from A-4 / Residual	102,985 / 2,144,288	2.62 / 54.58	1 / 444	21.32
A-6	Global regression on S_i, S_i^2, S_i^3, and diversification	Reduction from A-5 / Residual	400,700 / 1,743,588	10.20 / 44.38	1 / 443	102
A-7	14 Industry regressions on S_i (table 9.1)	Reduction from A-2 / Residual	1,667,626 / 603,087	42.45 / 15.35	26 / 420	44.66
A-8	14 Industry regressions on S_i and diversification	Reduction from A-7 / Residual	41,314 / 561,773	1.05 / 14.30	14 / 406	2.13*
A-9	14 Industry regressions on S_i and 12 S_i^2	Reduction from A-7 / Residual	170,788 / 432,299	4.35 / 11.00	12 / 408	13.43
A-10	14 Industry regressions on S_i, 12 S_i^2, and 12 S_i^3	Reduction from A-9 / Residual	30,494 / 401,805	0.77 / 10.23	12 / 396	2.50*
A-11	14 Industry regressions on S_i, 12 S_i^2, 12 S_i^3, and diversification	Reduction from A-10 / Residual	48,700 / 353,105	1.24 / 8.99	14 / 382	3.76*
A-12	4 Technology group regressions on S_i	Surplus over A-7 / Residual	42,211 / 645,298	1.08 / 16.43	−20 / 440	1.44***
A-13	4 Technology group regressions on S_i, S_i^2, and S_i^3 (eqs. 3–6)	Reduction from A-12 / Residual	94,471 / 550,827	2.41 / 14.02	8 / 432	9.26

Appendix (continued)

Step	Description		Sum of squared deviations	SSD as percent of A-1 SSD	Degrees of Freedom	F-ratio
A-14	Global regression of P_i on R & D_i ($n = 352$)	Original variance	3,784,738	100.00	1	
		Reduction	2,732,927	72.21	1	909
		Residual	1,051,811	27.79	350	
A-15	Regression of P_i on 14 R & D slope dummies	Reduction from A-14	458,905	12.12	13	20.03
		Residual	592,906	15.67	337	

*** Significant at the 10 percent point, ** at the 5 percent point, * at the 1 percent point. F-ratios with no asterisk are significant at well above the 1 percent point.

Notes

The research was supported by a grant from the Inter-University Committee on the Micro-economics of Technological Change, sponsored in turn by the Ford Foundation. Use was also made of computer facilities supported in part by National Science Foundation Grant NSF-GP 579. I am indebted to Jacob Schmookler and to numerous participants in the Princeton seminar on economic research in progress, and especially to Jesse Markham, for critical comments; to Roald Buhler and Insley Pyne for computer-programming assistance; to E. C. Taylor for advice on the classification of organic chemical patents; and to Mrs. Dorothy Register, Mrs. Noah Meltz, and my wife for help in collecting data.

1. For surveys of the literature, see [7], [11], [13], [14].

2. Fifteen firms on *Fortune's* 1955 list merged with other surviving firms between 1955 and 1959. Their data were consolidated, and so the sample includes 463 firms independent in 1955. Twelve firms were excluded because they were not primarily engaged in manufacturing; sixteen because they could not be fitted into industries with sufficient observations; two because of inadequate data; two because they were liquidated by 1959; four because their merger records were too complex to unscramble; and one inadvertently.

3. In accepting this limitation, we in effect cut off the most valuable tail of the invention value distribution, eliminating the cause of the infinite mean and variance problem. This is analogous to limiting the number of plays in defining the value of a St. Petersburg game. See [3, pp. 228–237].

4. An even higher r^2 of 0.89 was obtained in a correlation with patents and R & D employment of the 352 firms aggregated into fourteen two- and three-digit industry groups. This gain in explained variance is undoubtedly due to the canceling out of special, perhaps transitory, factors influencing individual firm patenting. When the ratio of government R & D support for the various industries in 1956 was added as a second independent variable, R^2 increased to 0.94 in this aggregated correlation. The more government support an industry received, the less patenting it did relative to R & D employment, no doubt because exclusive rights cannot be retained for patents received in connection with government contracts. Both regression coefficients were statistically significant at the 0.01 level.

5. The reasons why different scale variables give different results and a more complete argument for using sales are presented in [22]. The differences in correlation coefficients are due to peculiarities in the industry distribution of firms. Notably, when each industry assumes its own best-fitting slope and intercept, the overall fit is closer with sales than with employment.

   Ideally we should like to use value added rather than sales to eliminate any biases due to differences in vertical integration, but value-added data for a large sample of firms are not available.

6. A further implication of table 9.1 is worth noting. The slopes of the industry regression equations are correlated positively with the r^2 for those equations, with a rank correlation coefficient of 0.69. The higher an industry's average patent output per sales dollar is, the less variable patenting tends to be relative to size. My interpretation of this result is that in technically progressive fields like electrical equipment and general chemicals, technological competition forces firms to match each others' inventive efforts. But in unprogressive fields like textiles, food products, paper, fertilizers, soap, and cosmetics, invention is only a business strategy option.

7. See A-7 of the appendix, which provides a step-by-step analysis of covariance. Actually, as appendix step A-12 shows, most of the patenting variance can be explained with even fewer variables, and twenty of the slope and intercept terms allowed to vary in table 9.1 contribute little incremental variance reduction.

8. The extremes of this distribution deserve further comment. If we delete the 3,919 R & D employees of Goodyear Aircraft Company, a subsidiary specializing in defense work which accounted for 34 percent of all rubber industry R & D personnel, the industry's $P/R\&D$ ratio rises to 40.5. Other rubber companies were also deeply involved in defense work. At the other extreme, I suspect that the craft-oriented machinery industry obtained many patented inventions from employees not in formal R & D organizations.

9. It is a maximum estimate because other factors such as the type of R & D done also affect patenting per R & D employment input. For instance, the auto industry's preoccupation with styling change may lead to a low output of patentable inventions per engineering man-year.

10. This figure was provided by P. J. Federico, examiner-in-chief, U.S. Patent Office.

11. Total patents issued in 1959 to the 150 corporations on *Fortune's* 1955 lists of leading retailers, transportation firms, and public utilities amounted to 55. The sampled firms accounted for about one-fifth of all nonmanufacturing corporate sales, suggesting an estimate of 300 patents for all such corporations. A count based upon several published lists indicated that 153 additional patents were issued to universities, nonprofit research institutions, and nonprofit patent management corporations. Doubling this last figure and adding the two estimates leads to the overall estimate of roughly 600 patents issued to all nonmanufacturing corporations. This is consistent with National Science Foundation data showing that nonmanufacturing firms do 2 percent of all industrial R & D [32, p. 19].

12. Out of the 448 firms sampled, 341 had 5,000 or more employees in 1955, and only three had fewer than 1,000 employees. The firms with 5,000 or more employees had 95.8 percent of all sample employees and 97.0 percent of all sample patents.

13. The last statement is strictly true only when the intercept term is equal to zero. In fact all the intercept terms for regressions discussed in this section were insignificantly different from zero. The two statements are also not strictly consistent in the neighborhood of inflection points.

14. The standard error estimates in equations (1) and (2) are biased downward because of heteroscedasticity. When equation (2) was recomputed, letting each centered observation be weighted by the inverse of the standard error of estimate for firms of its size, the squared term's coefficient was significant in a two-tail test at the 0.09 level and the cubic coefficient at only the 0.25 level. The heteroscedasticity problem was not nearly as severe for the individual industry regressions, since standard errors of estimate were typically smaller and less correlated with firm size.

15. Intercorrelation coefficients among the three sales variables ran from 0.930 to 0.995, causing the standard errors of all coefficients to explode. For example, the unsquared sales term's t-ratios fell by an average of 70 percent from the values obtained for the regressions in table 9.1. This is a common result of multicollinearity which cannot be avoided without getting into even more serious specification problems discussed in [22]. However, as appendix steps A-9 and A-10 show, the introduction of the twelve squared and twelve cubic sales variables led to variance reductions, each significant in F-ratio tests at the 1 percent point.

16. An alternative way of interpreting the figures is to sweep a straight line from the origin to points on the plotted curves. The slope of the line intersecting any point shows estimated patenting per billion dollars of sales. It is readily seen that P/S generally attains a maximum at sales levels below \$500 million and a minimum at higher sales levels.

The upward bending part of the moderates' curve, including only General Motors, Jersey Standard, and Ford, is excluded from figure 9.1 to maintain a larger drafting scale.

17. For the unprogressive and moderate groups, all three regression coefficients were statistically significant at the 0.01 level. None of the chemical and electrical regression

coefficients was significant at even the 0.20 level, even though the three coefficients together permitted reductions in variance significant in F-ratio tests at well beyond the 1 percent point. The latter result was again due to extreme collinearity among the three independent variables, with intercorrelation coefficients running between 0.980 and 0.996. Also, because of the logarithmic transformations, the more concavely nonlinear the functions appear when plotted on arithmetic grids, the more the regressions are likely to be linear on semilog grids.

18. Notably, in a regression of unprogressive group patents on S_i, S_i^2, S_i^3, and a diversification index, the diversification variable had by far the highest t-ratio and (positive) partial correlation coefficient and raised R^2 to 0.594 from the value of 0.545 for equation (6).

19. It is also possible that large firms tackle more complex problems than small firms, and so their patents reflect greater inventive input. The former statement is probably valid, but the latter is doubtful. Complex "system inventions" are usually broken down into many elementary parts for purposes of patenting, and I see no reason to expect the quality of these elementary inventions to vary with firm size. For example, RCA has well over a thousand patents on color television transmitting and receiving devices.

20. Patents assigned in 1959 to the 448 firms in my sample were correlated with an incomplete count of in-house patent attorneys derived from the Martindale and Hubbell 1955 law directory, with a resultant r^2 of 0.78. Although 365 of the 448 firms received patents in 1959, only 161 were found to employ in-house patent attorneys.

21. This may be the more relevant result due to lower response error and the survey's closer proximity in time to my sample. The survey also showed that the largest corporations had a somewhat shorter mean duration of utilization for their patents.

22. Recognition of this exception brings my results into full agreement with Mansfield's findings concerning major inventions, major innovations, and R&D spending in the petroleum, steel, chemicals, and glass industries [11], [12].

23. Also involved are some peculiarities in the distribution of propensities to patent. The six firms with the highest $R\&D/S$ ratios in 1955 were all predominately engaged in defense contracting, and so they undoubtedly had low propensities to patent. Ideally, the industry dummy variables should have compensated for this, but five of the six firms were defense specialists from the electrical industry, which on the whole was much less defense oriented. Still when equation (7) was estimated for six separate industries (chemicals, food, petroleum, metals, machinery, and electrical), the diminishing returns phenomenon appeared for all but the chemicals industry.

24. My index is analogous to, but because of consolidation not the same as, one of the indexes developed for a smaller number of companies by M. Gort [5, pp. 155–157]. Our samples overlapped for eighty-eight companies. The r^2, when his indexes were correlated with mine, was 0.71. An industry-by-industry comparison of his indexes with mine yielded an average Spearman rank correlation coefficient of 0.83.

25. See appendix steps A-8 and A-11. When the diversification variables were added to the set of industry regressions with quadratic and cubic sales terms, the incremental variance reduction was 1.24 points. In total, the set of linear and nonlinear sales and diversification variables for fourteen industries accounted for 91 percent of the variance in company patenting about its grand mean.

26. But see [24], which deals with this problem at length.

27. The principal items included in the liquid-assets definition were cash, marketable securities, government securities, foreign currency, and bank acceptances.

28. There *was* a tendency for lagged profits to increase with patenting. This is discussed in [23].

29. The sample includes hard-surface floor coverings; pulp, paper, and paperboard; paperboard boxes; sanitary paper food containers; sanitary paper health products; plastics materials; synthetic fibers; soaps and organic detergents; paints and varnishes; inorganic color pigments; printing ink; dentifrices; carbon black; tires and inner tubes; leather; footwear (excluding house slippers and rubber footwear); flat and laminated glass; glass containers; vitreous plumbing fixtures; porcelain electrical supplies; gypsum products; abrasive products; iron, steel, and rolling mill products; primary, rolled, drawn, and extruded aluminum; tin cans; razors and razor blades; files and rasps; power boilers; wire springs; wheeled tractors and farm machinery; track-laying tractors; machine tools; textile machinery; industrial pumps; conveyors and conveying equipment; household mechanical washing machines; vacuum cleaners; valves and fittings; ball and roller bearings; motors, generators, and steam turbines; transformers; electrical welding apparatus; household radios, television sets, and phonographs; electron tubes and transistors; storage batteries; telephone and telegraph equipment; motor vehicles and parts; and locomotives.

30. Another approach to the interindustry technological opportunity problem, using deviations of actual patenting from what adjusted equations based on those in table 9.1 would predict, gave results essentially the same as those reported here.

31. Since M_i was correlated with S_{4i}, with an r^2 of 0.065 in the linear version and 0.049 in the logarithmic version, it is possible that the higher simple correlations between patenting and market share were partly spurious. Notably, introduction of M_i into regressions of P_{4i} on S_{4i} with the two dummy variables permitted an incremental reduction in unexplained variance of only 1.2 percentage points in the additive version and 0.1 points in the logarithmic version.

32. Because more nearly homoscedastic logarithmic regression (9) assigned much less weight to the telephone industry's deviant patent value, it estimated a weaker role overall for the market share variable.

33. They were plastic materials, synthetic fibers, printing ink, tracklaying tractors, transformers, radios and related products, motor vehicles, and locomotives.

34. And a narrow interpretation it is, since basic research expenditures have comprised only about 4 percent of all industrial R & D outlays in recent years, and since private industry has done only about 30 percent of all U.S. basic research. Patentable inventions may also emerge from basic and certainly from applied research, even though knowledge is the main output. For instance, the early basic transistor patents were one output of Bell Laboratories' fundamental semiconductor research.

References

1. Brozen, Y. R & D Differences among Industries. In Richard Tybout, ed., *The Economics of Research and Development*, Columbus, O., 1965.

2. Cooper, A. C. R & D Is More Efficient in Small Companies. *Harvard Bus. Rev.* 42 (May–June 1964): 75–83; and ibid. (September–October 1964): 44–51.

3. Feller, W. *An Introduction to Probability Theory and Its Applications*. 2nd ed. New York, 1957.

4. Fellner, W. The Influence of Market Structure on Technological Progress. *Quart. Jour. Econ.* 55 (November 1951): 556–577.

5. Gort, M. *Diversification and Integration in American Industry*. Princeton, 1962.

6. Gustafson, W. E. Research and Development, New Products, and Productivity Change. *Am. Econ. Rev., Proc.* 52 (May 1962): 177–185.

7. Hamberg, D. Size of Firm, Oligopoly, and Research: The Evidence. *Can. Jour. Econ.* 30 (February 1964): 62–75.

8. Horowitz, I. Firm Size and Research Activity. *So. Econ. Jour.* 28 (January 1962): 298–301.

9. Kuznets, S. Inventive Activity: Problems of Definition and Measurement. In [16, pp. 19–43].

10. Mandelbrot, B. New Methods in Statistical Economics. *Jour. Pol. Econ.* 71 (October 1963): 421–440.

11. Mansfield, E. Size of Firm, Market Structure, and Innovation. *Jour. Pol. Econ.* 71 (December 1963): 556–576.

12. Mansfield, E. Industrial Research and Development Expenditures. *Jour. Pol. Econ.* 72 (August 1964): 319–340.

13. Markham, J. W. Market Structure, Business Conduct, and Innovation. *Am. Econ. Rev., Proc.* 55 (May 1965): 323–332.

14. Nelson, R. R. The Economics of Invention. *Jour. Bus.* 32 (April 1959): 101–127.

15. Nelson, R. R. The Simple Economics of Basic Scientific Research. *Jour. Pol. Econ.* 67 (June 1959): 297–306.

16. Nelson, R. R. ed. *The Rate and Direction of Inventive Activity.* Nat. Bur. Econ. Research Conference Report. Princeton, 1962.

17. Sanders, B. Some Difficulties in Measuring Inventive Activity. In [16, pp. 53–77].

18. Sanders, B. Patterns of Commercial Exploitation of Patented Inventions by Large and Small Corporations. *Patent, Trademark, and Copyright Jour.* 8 (Spring 1964): 51–93.

19. Sanders, B. Speedy Entry of Patented Inventions into Commercial Use. *Patent, Trademark, and Copyright Jour.* 6 (Spring 1962): 87–116.

20. Sanders, B., J. Rossman, and L. J. Harris. The Economic Impact of Patents. *Patent, Trademark, and Copyright Jour.* 2 (September 1958): 340–363.

21. Sanders, B. Patent Acquisition By Corporations. *Patent, Trademark, and Copyright Jour.* 3 (Fall 1959): 217–261.

22. Scherer, F. M. Size of Firm, Oligopoly, and Research: Comment. *Can. Jour. Econ.* 31 (May 1965): 256–266.

23. Scherer, F. M. Corporate Inventive Output, Profits, and Growth. *Jour. Pol. Econ.* 73 (June 1965): 290–297.

24. Scherer, F. M., S. E. Herzstein Jr., A. W. Dreyfoos, W. G. Whitney, O. J. Bachmann, C. P. Pesek, C. J. Scott, T. G. Kelly, and J. J. Galvin. *Patents and the Corporation.* 2nd ed. Boston, 1959.

25. Schmookler, J. Changes in Industry and in the State of Knowledge as Determinants of Industrial Invention. In [16, pp. 195–232].

26. Schmookler, J., and O. Brownlee. Determinants of Inventive Activity. *Am. Econ. Rev., Proc.* 52 (May 1962): 165–176.

27. Schmookler, J., and Z. Griliches. Inventing and Maximizing. *Am. Econ. Rev.* 53 (September 1963): 725–729.

28. Schumpeter, J. A. *Capitalism, Socialism, and Democracy.* 3rd ed. New York, 1950.

29. Worley, J. S. Industrial Research and the New Competition. *Jour. Pol. Econ.* 69 (April 1961): 183–186.

30. National Academy of Sciences, National Research Council. *Industrial Research Laboratories of the United States.* 10th ed. Washington, D.C., 1956.

31. U.S. Federal Trade Commission. *Report on Industrial Concentration and Product Diversification in the 1,000 Largest Manufacturing Companies: 1950.* Washington, D.C., 1957.

32. U.S. National Science Foundation. *Research and Development in Industry: 1961.* Washington, D.C., 1964.

33. U.S. Patent Office. *Index of Patents* (annually).

10 Statistical Evidence on Antitrust Decree Effects

Further perspective on the effects of mandatory patent licensing under antitrust decrees can be obtained through three statistical analyses—one done nearly two decades ago and the others executed in conjunction with the research underlying this monograph.

10.1 The Impact on Patenting

The first effort to shed some quantitative light on the issues was by my colleagues and me at the Harvard Business School.[1] We compared changes in patenting activity between two periods: a base period spanning 1939 to 1955 and a potential impact period consisting of the three years 1954 to 1956. Given the choice of time periods, which was dictated by data limitations, an attempt was made to select companies subjected to mandatory licensing decrees whose scope and timing were such that an impact on research and patenting might plausibly be expected during the 1954 to 1956 period. Thirty-eight corporations were so identified and included in the "compulsory licensing sample." The selections were made without the benefit of the Hollabaugh-Wright compendium, the Frost et al. case studies, and diverse statistical sources that now enrich economists' lives, so I suspect the list would be at least marginally different if reformulated now. But in statistical analysis, integrity is best assured when there is no ex post facto tampering with samples, so I present the results as they originally appeared.

Relative to the patenting of all corporations (adjusted to reflect the size composition of the compulsory licensing sample), patenting of companies in the compulsory licensing sample declined by 15 percent if a simple average is taken or 21 percent if a patent-weighted average is taken. This difference was highly significant statistically. Taking into account published materials and interview evidence on decree timing, the proportion of company patents affected, royalty payment provisions, coverage of future patents, and retention of judicial oversight, the thirty-eight company sample was then subdivided into three categories reflecting subjective judgments as to how severe the patent-licensing decrees were. For the

Source: This paper is excerpted from the monograph, *The Economic Effects of Compulsory Patent Licensing*, Monograph Series 1977-2 in Finance and Economics, New York University Graduate School of Business Administration, 1977. Notes have been renumbered to match the material reprinted.

eleven companies having experienced decrees of "little impact," average 1954 to 1956 patenting rose by 1.5 percent relative to the 1939 to 1955 base period. For the ten "moderate impact" companies it fell by 24.3 percent, and for the sixteen "great impact" companies it fell by 22.4 percent. The sharpest decline of all—33.3 percent—was observed for six companies required to license future patents to be acquired during the 1954 to 1956 period.

These results provide strong support for the hypothesis that the patenting of companies impacted by mandatory licensing decrees declined. The only alternative explanation I have been able to adduce since the analysis was published nineteen years ago is that the observed phenomena may have exhibited Galton's "law of regression." [2] That is, it is conceivable that the companies singled out for patent-oriented antitrust action were among the most active patent acquirers in American industry during the 1940s and early 1950s. If so, there could be a tendency for their patenting to regress toward the mean of all U.S. industry as time passed and other corporations took up vigorous R & D and patenting efforts. This regression toward the mean would show up as a decline in relative patenting rates between the base and comparison periods. However, the decline in patenting for compulsory licensing companies holds up for firms in diverse size and base period patenting activity categories. In view of this and the "little" versus "moderate" versus "great" decree impact results, I am inclined to believe still that the observed fall in compulsory licensing sample patenting was more than a statistical fluke.

10.2 The Impact on R & D Expenditures

The question remains, Was it the result of decreased research and development effort by decree-impacted corporations or decreased patenting of a given flow of R & D results? Complementary interview and questionnaire evidence led us to conclude that "the effect thus far has been greater reliance upon secrecy rather than diminished investment in research and development." [3] It would be desirable, however, to have more objective quantitative evidence in support or contradiction. Recent changes in corporate financial reporting practice have made it possible for the first time to analyze R & D expenditure patterns for a broad cross section of industrial firms whose securities are publicly traded. These new R & D spending data have been utilized to test for compulsory licensing effects.[4]

The point of departure was a *Business Week* compilation of privately financed 1975 R & D expenditures for some 730 U.S. corporations.[5] From this list fifty-three companies in the publishing, restaurant, and services industry categories were omitted because those industries are generally not research-oriented and because comparable companies are absent from our compulsory licensing group. An effort was then made to identify all corporations on the *Business Week* list subjected to mandatory patent licensing of appreciable scope under antitrust decrees and to pinpoint further the timing and severity of the decrees. Four explicit impact variables were quantified:

DECREE = a dummy variable with a value of 1 if the company was subjected to one or more compulsory licensing decrees of appreciable scope and zero otherwise,

IMPACT = a dummy variable with a value of 1 if the company was subjected to one or more compulsory licensing decrees of substantial impact and zero otherwise,

LAG = 1975 minus the last year for which new patents were required to be licensed by the company,

MULTIPLE = the number of independent antitrust cases leading to compulsory licensing decrees affecting the company.

Relevant information on the forty-four companies for which DECREE was assigned a value of 1 is presented in table 10.1. In determining which companies to exclude from the list because their decrees were not of appreciable scope and which decrees were of substantial impact, subjective judgments had to be made. Generally, companies were excluded if their decrees involved product lines with combined sales less than 20 percent of company sales in 1950, if (like Automatic Sprinkler) the companies had changed the industry composition of their operations radically since the time of the decree or were acquired by a much larger parent, or if only a very few patents or a small part of the company's patent portfolio were affected.[6] Doubtful cases were resolved in favor of including companies on the DECREE list. Companies with litigated antitrust cases pending in which patent licensing was sought were also included.[7] In judging whether one or more decrees were of substantial impact for

Table 10.1
Sample companies with compulsory licensing decrees of appreciable scope

Company	Number of ML cases	Fields or products affected	Major impact?	Future patents?	Last year affected
Airco	1	Carbon dioxide products	No	Yes	1962
American Air Filter	1	Air filters	No	No	1946
American Can	1	Can-closing machinery	Yes	Yes	1955
American Cyanamid	1	Aureomycin	No	No	1967
American Motors	1	Pollution-control devices	No	Yes	1975
AT & T	1	Telephone equipment and components	Yes	Yes	1975
Ball Brothers	1	Glass bottle-making machinery	No	No	1947
Bausch & Lomb	1	Opthalmic goods	Yes	Yes	1958
Bendix	3	Aircraft instruments, air brakes, hydraulic brakes	Yes	Yes	1958
Bristol-Myers	1	Ampicillin case pending	No	Yes	1975
Carrier Corp.	2	Air-conditioning equipment, cooling coils	Yes	No	1945
Chrysler	1	Pollution control devices	No	Yes	1975
Cincinnati Milacron	1	Milling machines	No	No	1954
Corning Glass Works	3	Light bulbs, flat glass, glass containers	Yes	No	1947
A.B. Dick	1	Duplicating machines	Yes	Yes	1958
du Pont	2	Titanium pigments; nylon and other chemicals	Yes	No	1952
Eastman Kodak	2	Motion picture film; Kodachrome	Yes	No	1954
Emhart (Hartford-Empire)	1	Glass bottle-making machinery	Yes	Yes	1975
Exxon	1	Synthetic rubber	No	No	1942
Ford Motor Co.	1	Pollution control devices	No	Yes	1975
General Cable	1	Fluid-filled cables	No	No	1948

General Electric	6	Incandescent lamps, light bulbs, fluid-filled cables, switches, fluorescent lamps, electrical equipment	Yes	Yes	1958
General Motors	2	Busses, pollution control devices	No	Yes	1975
Hughes Tool	1	Oil well equipment	No	No	1958
IBM	1	Tabulating machines and tab cards	Yes	Yes	1961
Kearney & Trecker	1	Milling machines	No	No	1954
Merck	1	Drug patents of German affiliate	No	No	1945
Minnesota Mining	2	Abrasives, Scotch and magnetic tape	Yes	Yes	1974
NCR	1	Cash registers	No	No	1947
NL Industries	1	Titanium pigments	Yes	Yes	1950
Owens-Corning	1	Fiberglass	Yes	Yes	1954
Owens-Illinois	2	Glass bottles and closing, bottle machinery	Yes	No	1947
Pfizer	1	Tetracycline	No	No	1967
Phelps-Dodge	1	Fluid-filled cables	No	No	1948
Pitney-Bowes	1	Postage meters	Yes	Yes	1964
PPG Industries	1	Flat glass	Yes	Yes	1953
RCA	1	Television	Yes	Yes	1968
Robertshaw Controls	1	Temperature controls	No	Yes	1962
Rohm & Haas	1	Plexiglass and related acrylics	Yes	No	1948
Singer	1	Sewing machines	No	No	1964
Syntex	1	Synthetic steroids	Yes	No	1958
U.S. Gypsum	1	Gypsum board	Yes	No	1951
Westinghouse Electric	4	Incandescent lamps, switches, fluorescent lamps, electrical equipment	Yes	Yes	1954
Xerox	1	Copying machines	Yes	Yes	1975

the IMPACT variable, the number of patents affected, the strategic significance of the affected product line to the company, and such special features as future patent licensing and royalty-free provisions were assessed.
Emphasis was on the severity of the patent relief per se and not on its
economic consequences (e.g., as revealed in subsequent interviews, industry studies, or the Hollabaugh-Wright survey of actual licensing histories).
Twenty-four companies were counted as having experienced high-impact
decrees by these criteria. The time lag variable was computed by subtract-
ing from 1975, the year for which R & D expenditures were measured,
the date of the last new licensing order pertaining to the company or,
when decrees included provisions for future patent licensing (most commonly for five years), the date of the decree plus the future licensing
extension period. Measuring the MULTIPLE variable involved a simple
count of unrelated cases requiring licensing (e.g., for General Electric,
the all-time champion, six).

There are at least three ways 1975 R & D behavior might plausibly be
affected by antitrust-connected patent-licensing decrees. First, if an order
required future licensing of patents issuing from 1975 R & D, or if a
pending antitrust suit threatened that result, an especially direct behavioral impact might be expected. There were few companies in this situation—only seven with future licensing orders still in force during 1975
and one with a major patent-oriented suit pending.[8] To test for such a
causal link, heavy weight should be given those instances. Second, company executives might view past orders as connoting a risk of similar
future actions, either in the same product line or in others. This expectation
might be stronger, the more licensing orders there were imposed in the
past, the more sweeping their scope, and the more recent their incidence.
Third, compulsory licensing orders might have a generalized trauma effect
on R & D decision makers, leading them to assign less weight to patent
protection as a barrier to imitation. One would expect this effect to
attenuate as time passes, so again the LAG variable becomes relevant.

The dependent variable, or the variable hypothesized to be affected
by mandatory licensing, is the ratio of 1975 company-financed R & D
expenditures to sales. Naturally, the R & D-to-sales ratio is also influenced
by other factors. Perhaps the most important is "technological opportunity," or the richness of the science and engineering base confronting
an industry.[9] This can be taken into account by using industry dummy
variables, that is, by letting a firm in any given industry be related to its

home base industry average R & D/sales ratio rather than to the ratio for all companies. The *Business Week* compilation provided such industry breakdowns, which we have generally followed except in correcting some obvious misclassifications, especially into the "miscellaneous manufacturing" category. Also there is reason to believe that R & D/sales ratios might vary systematically with firm size, but not necessarily in the same way for every industry. This can be taken into account by including as a separate independent variable the logarithm of company sales. Logarithms are used to reflect probable diminishing marginal returns in the size to R & D relationship.

The simple zero-order correlation between the R & D/sales ratios and the four main compulsory licensing effect variables was $+0.075$ for DECREE, $+0.088$ for IMPACT, $+0.070$ for MULTIPLE $\times$ DECREE and $+0.053$ for the time lag variable, which was used in the form $1/\log_{10}$ LAG to reflect the probable decaying impact over time of older decrees.[10] In each case the correlation has a sign the opposite of what one would expect if forced licensing had an adverse impact on R & D, but only the IMPACT correlation passes a 95 percent statistical significance test. Between R & D/sales and $\log_{10}$ SALES there was a modest but highly significant correlation of -0.221, suggesting that larger corporations tend to spend less on R & D per sales dollar than smaller listed corporations (which tend to be of medium size relative to the entire manufacturing corporation population).

In multiple regressions with industry dummy variables, the "general machinery" category, with fifty-seven company observations and an average R & D/sales ratio close to the *Business Week* total sample average, was taken as the base industry. There were then twenty-five additional zero-one intercept dummy variables to permit average R & D/sales levels to vary for the other industry categories enumerated by *Business Week*. There were also twenty-five sales slope dummy variables of the general form $DUMMY_j \times \log_{10} SALES_i$ for firm i in the jth industry category. Owing to this profusion of industry dummy variables, the multiple regression results are quite complex, and no attempt will be made to present them in their entirety for all model specifications. Their general character is illustrated by the following condensed regression equation, with DECREE as the mandatory licensing variable and with the R & D/sales variable scaled in ratio (as distinguished from percentage) form:

$$\frac{R\&D}{SALES} = 0.056 + [25 \text{ intercept dummies}] - 0.0162 \log_{10} SALES$$
$$\phantom{\frac{R\&D}{SALES} = } (0.014) \qquad\qquad \Delta R^2 \cong 0.283 \qquad (0.0059)$$

$$+ [25 \text{ slope dummies}] + 0.00785 \text{ DECREE};$$
$$\Delta R^2 \cong 0.047 \qquad (0.00362)$$

$R^2 = 0.386,$

$N = 679.$

Standard errors of individual coefficients are given in parentheses. The coefficient for the DECREE variable is positive and statistically significant at the 95 percent level. The DECREE coefficient value of 0.00785 means that corporations having experienced one or more compulsory licensing decrees of appreciable scope had on average an R & D/sales ratio 0.00785 higher than other firms of comparable size classified in their industries. Since the simple average R & D/sales ratio was 0.0219, this means that decree-impacted companies had R & D/sales ratios 36 percent *higher* than the average for all industries, other things (e.g., industry base and firm size) being held equal. This of course is inconsistent with the hypothesis that compulsory licensing had an adverse impact on R & D.

Both the intercept and slope dummy variable clusters contribute incremental reductions in unexplained variance statistically significant (in an *F*-ratio test) at the 99 percent level. Because the dummy variable coefficients have some interest in their own right, complete results for the above regression are reproduced in table 10.2. As one might expect, aerospace, computers and office equipment, electrical equipment, and instruments had positive intercept dummy variable values connoting above-average R & D intensity, all else equal. Given the inclusion of twenty-five SALES slope dummies, the negative coefficient for $\log_{10}$ SALES reflects only relationships in the general machinery industry, which was taken as the base. Many industries had slope dummy variable coefficients positive and larger in absolute value than the $\log_{10}$ SALES coefficient, suggesting that R & D intensity increased rather than decreased with firm size in those industries. None, however, was large enough to reject at the 95 percent confidence level a null hypothesis that the effect of firm size was zero or negative.

Turning to the results for the other compulsory licensing variables, the

Table 10.2
Complete regression equation: effect of compulsory licensing on R & D

$$\frac{R \& D}{SALES} = \frac{0.0564}{(0.0140)} - \frac{0.0162}{(0.0059)} \log_{10} SALES \text{ (millions)} + \frac{0.00785}{(0.00362)} DECREE$$

Intercept dummy	SALES slope dummy	Industry
+0.0810 (0.0231)	−0.0200 (0.0087)	Aerospace
−0.0179 (0.0376)	+0.0063 (0.0142)	Appliances
−0.0364 (0.0203)	+0.0151 (0.0078)	Automotive
−0.0564 (0.1141)	+0.0171 (0.0377)	Beverages
−0.0330 (0.0225)	+0.0114 (0.0092)	Building materials
−0.0291 (0.0181)	+0.0140 (0.0073)	Chemicals
−0.0633 (0.0392)	+0.0224 (0.0130)	Conglomerates
−0.0489 (0.0403)	+0.0154 (0.0154)	Containers
−0.0132 (0.0226)	+0.0168 (0.0089)	Drugs
+0.0121 (0.0165)	+0.0025 (0.0071)	Electrical and electronics
−0.0528 (0.0240)	+0.0166 (0.0089)	Food
+0.0021 (0.0184)	+0.0077 (0.0082)	Instruments
−0.0432 (0.0321)	+0.0175 (0.0140)	Leisure time
−0.0254 (0.0226)	+0.0090 (0.0089)	Metals, mining, and steel
−0.0555 (0.0230)	+0.0208 (0.0102)	Miscellaneous manufacturing
−0.0589 (0.0224)	+0.0178 (0.0078)	Natural resources/fuel
+0.0173 (0.0188)	+0.0039 (0.0079)	Office equipment and computers
−0.0682 (0.0303)	+0.0250 (0.0119)	Oil service and supply
−0.0580 (0.0290)	+0.0193 (0.0112)	Paper
−0.0440 (0.0324)	+0.0169 (0.0121)	Personal care products
−0.0615 (0.0339)	+0.0249 (0.0124)	Special machinery
−0.0360 (0.0225)	+0.0111 (0.0099)	Textiles and apparel
−0.0545 (0.0252)	+0.0217 (0.0099)	Rubber
−0.0561 (0.0601)	+0.0177 (0.0221)	Tobacco
+0.0043 (0.0395)	+0.0037 (0.0126)	Telecommunications

$R^2 = 0.3864$; $N = 679$

Note: The base industry is general machinery. Standard errors of the regression coefficients are given in parentheses.

partial regression coefficients (given the sales, sales dummy, and intercept dummy variable relationships) and their standard errors (in parentheses) were as follows:

$$\text{IMPACT} \quad +0.0146,$$
$$(0.0048)$$

$$\text{MULTIPLE} \times \text{DECREE} \quad +0.00551,$$
$$(0.00209)$$

$$\frac{1}{\log_{10} \text{LAG}} \quad +0.00224.$$
$$(0.00142)$$

In every case the coefficient signs are positive—the opposite of what one would expect if mandatory licensing adversely affected firms' R & D incentives. And for all but the LAG relationship, the coefficients are statistically significant in a two-tail test at the 95 percent level. The only shred of support for the negative effect hypothesis is that the compulsory licensing coefficient value is smallest relative to its standard error for the $1/\log_{10}$ LAG variable, for which one might expect any adverse effects of forced licensing to show up most strongly.[11] On the other hand, the largest coefficient/standard error ratio is for the high-impact decree variable IMPACT, for which one might also anticipate a relatively strong disincentive effect.

To sum up, the analysis of 1975 R & D-spending patterns provides no significant indication that forty-four companies subjected to compulsory patent licensing under antitrust decrees sustained less intense R & D efforts than other firms of comparable size and industry origin. If anything, the opposite tendency is revealed. One is led by the results to speculate whether the chain of causation might have run in a direction opposite to what was postulated—that firms singled out for compulsory patent licensing decrees were relatively more research oriented than nondecree companies, all else equal. If this were the case, the analysis conducted here, being focused on only a single year, could not detect whether any retrogression from even higher prior R & D intensities occurred. Still it is clear that, if such a link did exist, the companies forced to license their patents did not relax their efforts so much that they fell below the norms for nonimpacted enterprises of comparable size and industry origin.

10.3 The Impact on Market Structure

A third essentially quantitative question of substantial interest is whether compulsory patent-licensing decrees, by reducing barriers to imitation and new entry, led to significantly less monopolistic industry structures. A clear-cut statistical test here is even more difficult than for patenting or R & D expenditures for two main reasons. First, it is harder to obtain usable data. The main source of data on industry structure is the quinquennial Census of Manufactures. It is sometimes hard to match Census industry or product line definitions to the product lines covered in antitrust decrees; the Census industry classifications have been revised several times, making intertemporal comparisons difficult; and concentration data at the five-digit product class level are not available for all years. Second, changes in market structure may occur for a variety of reasons unrelated to patent licensing—for example, because of other entry barrier reducing provisions in the same antitrust decree, market growth, changes in technology, or the choice of pricing policies by industry leaders that either strengthen or undermine their market positions. Despite these substantial obstacles, a crude quantitative analysis was attempted.

The dependent variable was the four-firm concentration ratio CONC, that is, the combined share of industry sales accounted for by the leading four suppliers in an industry. From the research through which we determined compulsory licensing decrees of appreciable scope with respect to individual companies, *industries* experiencing decrees of appreciable scope were identified. A few not covered by the table 10.1 listing are included here—notably, when the principal companies affected were too small or too much transformed by merger to appear in *Business Week's* R & D-spending compilation, or when narrowly defined industry statistics were available for activities that represented only a small part of individual company operations. This list of industries was then matched with Census industry structure statistics, and decree-impacted industries for which there were no data on market structure at approximately the time of the decree as well as for 1972 had to be excluded from the analysis. The nineteen surviving industries are listed in table 10.3. Also presented in the table are the principal compulsory licensing order dates, four-firm concentration ratios for the Census year nearest the most important of those dates (with the relevant Census year indicated in subscripted paren-

Table 10.3
Concentration changes in industries with compulsory licensing

Industry	SIC code	Decree date	Initial concentration	1972 concentration	Concentration change	Predicted concentration change
Stockings (full-fashioned)	2251	50,54	19(54)	34	+15	+5.8
Carbon dioxide and dry ice	28133	52	80(54)	75	−5	−3.5
Titanium pigments	28161	45	100(47)	80	−20	−13.1
Synthetic rubber	2822	42	92(47)	62	−30	−11.5
Synthetic fibers (noncellulosic)	2824	52	100(52)	73	−27	−8.7
Flat glass	3211	46,53	90(54)	92	+2	−5.6
Glass bottles	3221	46	63(47)	55	−8	−6.5
Fiberglass	32293	49	96(58)	95	−1	−6.2
Gypsum board	3275	51	85(47)	80	−5	−9.7
Sand paper & other coated abrasives	32913	50,54	73(58)	82	+9	−3.1
Metal cans	3411	50	79(50)	66	−13	−5.5
Gear cutting machines	35413	56	73(58)	79	+6	−3.0
Milling machines	35416	40,54	65(54)	62	−3	−1.7
Electric lamps	3641	53,54	93(54)	87	−6	−3.7
Television receivers	36512	58	55(58)	66	+11	+0.6
Telephone equipment	3661	56	90(54)	93	+3	−7.8
Opthalmic goods	3851	48	58(47)	54(70)	−4	−6.4
Photographic film and plates	38615	48,54	96(54)	96	0	+3.1
Matches	39993	46	83(47)	73	−10	−7.7

theses), the most nearly comparable 1972 concentration ratio, and the percentage point increase or decrease in industry concentration.[12]

On the average, concentration in the nineteen industries fell by 4.53 percentage points between the approximate time of the principal compulsory licensing decree(s) and 1972. There is considerable variability among industries, however; the standard deviation of the changes in concentration is 11.93 percentage points. The observed average concentration change is significantly different from zero in a one-tail test at the 90 percent confidence level.

Knowing that concentration fell on average in the decree-impacted industries does not necessarily permit us to conclude that compulsory licensing or other antitrust remedies were the cause. The sample of decree-impacted industries is clearly atypical, with much higher average initial four-firm concentration (i.e., a mean of 78) than manufacturing industry generally. Partly because of the statistical tendency for unusually high observation values to regress toward the mean and partly because firms with market power may pursue pricing policies that encourage new entry, one might expect industries with above-average concentration to exhibit declining concentration over time, with or without government intervention. Also many of the industries listed in table 10.3 grew rapidly in the postdecree period, and growth has a well-known concentration-eroding effect. To take these and other influences into account, regression equations originally estimated by Mueller and Hamm for a much larger number of manufacturing industries were used to predict the expected change in concentration from information on initial concentration, value added or sales growth, ultimate industry size, and the extent of product differentiation.[13] To illustrate, the prediction equation used for industries whose initial concentration was measured as of 1947 was as follows:

$$\Delta CONC = 9.94 - 0.21\ INITCR - 0.004\ GROWTH - 0.001\ SIZE$$
$$+\ 16.54\ HIGHDIF + 5.35\ MODDIF - 2.27\ LOWDIF,$$

where $\Delta CONC$ is the predicted change in concentration from 1947 to 1972; INITCR the 1947 four-firm concentration ratio; GROWTH the percentage growth in value added or sales from 1947 to 1972; SIZE is 1972 value added; HIGHDIF a zero-one dummy variable singling out consumer goods industries of high product differentiation as measured by the Mueller-Hamm method; MODDIF a dummy variable for moderate product differentiation industries; and LOWDIF a dummy variable for low differentiation industries. The concentration changes predicted in this way are presented in the last column of table 10.3. The average predicted change in concentration is a decline of 4.96 percentage points— somewhat more than the actually observed drop of 4.53 points. The differences, however, are not statistically significant.[14] We are led to the negative conclusion that, in addition to having no discernible adverse effect on R & D-spending incentives, compulsory licensing under antitrust decrees had no significant observed impact in reducing concentration relative to the changes that might have been expected in any event, given the initial market structure, subsequent market growth, and the panoply of public policies (including antitrust actions) affecting manufacturing industry structures.

Notes

1. F. M. Scherer, S. E. Herzstein, A. W. Dreyfoos, W. G. Whitney, O. J. Bachman, C. P. Pesek, C. J. Scott, T. G. Kelly, and J. J. Galvin, *Patents and the Corporation* (rev. ed.; Boston: privately published, 1959), pp. 137–146.

2. Francis Galton, *Natural Inheritance* (London: Macmillan, 1889).

3. *PATC*, p. 153.

4. I am indebted to Paul Burik and Levent Ormancioglu for assistance in compiling and analyzing the data.

5. Where Private Industry Puts Its Research Money, *Business Week* (June 28, 1976): 64–84. One possible source of bias should be noted immediately. SEC regulations require that R & D expenditures be publicly reported only when they are "material." Consequently data are still unavailable for some companies with R & D outlays of less than 1 percent of sales. This means that R & D/sales ratios for companies that do report their expenditures tend to be higher than for a completely representative cross section of listed corporations.

Some indication of the degree of bias can be gleaned by observing that a National Science Foundation survey showed company-financed R & D to be 2.0 percent of sales for all surveyed corporations conducting R & D in 1973. U.S. National Science Foundation, *Research and Development in Industry: 1973* (Washington, D.C.: NSF 75-315), p. 52. For the *Business Week* sample, the weighted average R & D/sales ratio was 1.85 percent, and for our subsample thereof (deleting some companies doing little research) the weighted average was 1.89 percent and the simple (unweighted) average 2.19 percent. The *Business Week* figures include all R & D and sales of U.S.-based multinational corporations, both domestically and abroad, whereas the NSF data cover domestic expenditures and sales only. It is impossible to make an exact comparison, but it would appear that the *Business Week* data are biased only slightly on the high side relative to the population of all research-performing corporations.

6. Used for this facet of the analysis was the Federal Trade Commission staff statistical report, *Value of Shipments Data by Product Class for the 1,000 Largest Manufacturing Corporations of 1950* (Washington, D.C.: 1972).

7. However, the aircraft manufacturers were excluded, in part because a pending suit involved most members on which R & D data were available and partly because of the special defense-R & D-oriented character of the industry.

8. Four of the future licensing orders involved automobile companies. Paragraph VI(B) of the September 1969 *Automobile Manufacturers Association* decree is ambiguous, but a Justice Department representative said that the paragraph does require reasonable royalty licensing to at least some competitors, including other auto manufacturers.

9. See F. M. Scherer, Firm Size, Market Structure, Opportunity, and the Output of Patented Inventions, *American Economic Review* (December 1965): 1097–1114; and Jacob Schmookler, *Invention and Economic Growth* (Cambridge: Harvard University Press, 1966), ch. 8.

10. When a company had no decree of appreciable scope, the value of this variable was set equal to zero. Companies with pending cases or decrees whose future licensing impact extended into 1975 were assigned the arbitrary minimum LAG value of 1.5 to avoid infinite value problems. Thus the values of $1/\log_{10}$ LAG ranged from zero to 5.68, with a five-year-old decree having a value of 1.43 and a ten-year-old decree a value of 1.00.

11. The LAG coefficient value can be interpreted as follows: for decrees with the most current impact (LAG = 1.5 years), the R & D/sales ratio averages about 58 percent higher than the all-company simple average; for decrees five years old, 15 percent higher; and for decrees 20 years old, 8 percent higher.

12. Because of a significant change in opthalmic goods industry coverage for 1972, the 1970 concentration ratio is substituted.

13. Willard F. Mueller and Larry G. Hamm, Trends in Industrial Market Concentration, 1947 to 1970, *Review of Economics and Statistics* (November 1974): 516, table 5. Only their equations (1) and (3) were used. Downward adjustments were made in the GROWTH coefficients to account for the use of 1972 rather than 1970 as the terminal year. For industries examined at the five-digit level of detail, value of shipments figures were converted to a value-added basis for the SIZE variable, assuming the same ratio of value added to value of shipments as for the covering four-digit industry.

14. After this analysis was completed, Professor Mueller supplied details on an updating of his regression equations to 1972, with the industry size effect specified in logarithmic rather than absolute terms. The average predicted decline in concentration for our sample of industries with the new Mueller equations is 6.70 percentage points. Again the difference between the predicted and actual average changes is not statistically significant.

11 Corporate Size, Diversification, and Innovative Activity

Approximately 98 percent of the nation's industrial R & D is performed by industrial (i.e., manufacturing and mining) corporations. Along with changes in managerial orientation, there have been palpable changes in the structure of the largest industrial corporations. They have become larger, they have become more diversified, and, although the phenomenon is more difficult to measure, their managerial structures have almost surely become more complex. Because of productivity increases, the most modest size growth occurred on the employment dimension. The number of employees in the company ranked 100th (by employment) on *Fortune's* 500 list for 1955 was 19,548; its 1980 counterpart had 43,799 employees. Between 1953 and 1978 production workers dropped from 81 to 74 percent of total manufacturing employees. Between 1954 and 1972 the number of employees occupied in the central offices, auxiliary units, and sales branches of manufacturing enterprises rose from 6.3 to 9.2 percent.[1] In 1950, thirty-eight of the 200 largest manufacturing corporations were diversified enough to operate in more than twenty different four-digit industries. By 1968—the last year for which comparable statistics have been published—seventy-six of the top 200 satisfied that threshold criterion.[2]

Changes in the size and managerial complexity of the largest corporations lead us to reexamine what has come to be called "the Schumpeterian hypothesis." In an influential 1942 book economist Joseph A. Schumpeter argued that large corporations possessing monopoly power were ideal vehicles for advancing industrial technology (e.g., as later interpreters clarified, because of their superior access to capital, ability to pool risks, and economies of scale in the maintenance of research and development laboratories).[3] Critics of the Schumpeterian view have argued to the contrary that greater size stultifies technological dynamism because of more bureaucratic decision making (a phenomenon Schumpeter also feared) and longer chains of command between the person with a good idea and the manager able to provide the definitive go-ahead. A fierce debate, theoretical and empirical, has raged over the relative validity of these contending theses.

Diversification has also found a role in the debate. The early view,

This paper is excerpted from a longer paper, Technological Change and the Modern Corporation, to be published in *The Modern Corporation*, Betty Bock, Harvey J. Goldschmid, Ira Millstein, and F. M. Scherer, eds. (New York: Columbia University Press), 1984. Notes have been reorganized to match the material remaining.

advanced by Richard R. Nelson, was that diversification was unambiguously favorable, especially to basic industrial research, because the more diversified a company was, the better poised it was to derive commerical advantage from possibly serendipitous technical advances.[4] However, diversification might also have negative effects if it means more complex decision-making channels. And in the Hayes-Abernathy view a managerial preoccupation with diversification, especially through merger, diverts attention from the painstaking work required to take full advantage of new technological opportunities in one's home-base industries.[5] It is at least intriguing, even though quite possibly coincidental, that the sharp slowdown in U.S. industrial R & D growth began only a year after the peak of the conglomerate merger wave of the 1960s.

These issues have since the early 1960s been thoroughly researched, surveyed, debated, and resurveyed. To add still another survey here would be the height of redundance.[6] Instead, I shall try to advance the state of knowledge by analyzing some new data, including one data set of unprecedented scope and richness.

11.1 The Gelman Research Associates Results

Having promised no survey, I immediately renege. A recent study by the Gelman Research Associates firm has been cited repeatedly in the debate over big vs. small and the vigor of technological innovation, and yet, as nearly as I can tell, the study itself has not been widely available, reposing in the aloof reaches of National Technical Information Service microfiche.[7] My curiosity was aroused, so I invested $4 and a case of eyestrain in the microfiche original.

The results actually reported turned out to be consistent with the interpretations given them in public citations. Out of a larger initial cross section, 500 technological innovations first introduced into the market between 1953 and 1973 were selected for analysis as most important in terms of technological, social, economic, and political criteria. These were traced to their innovating (not always synonymous with inventing) organizations, in all cases business enterprises, and the companies were classified according to size at the time when the innovations were first marketed. For the 319 sample innovations contributed by U.S. enterprises, the shares originated by firms in diverse employment size classes were as listed in table 11.1.[8]

Table 11.1
Innovation shares of U.S. firms by size class

Company employment	Percent of all U.S. innovations
Less than 100	23.5
100–1,000	23.8
1,001–5,000	13.2
5,001–10,000	5.0
Greater than 10,000	34.5

Companies with fewer than 1,000 employees originated 47.3 percent of the important innovations—a fraction higher than their 41.2 percent share of all manufacturing and mining company employment in 1963—the midpoint and median year of the innovation sample. Conversely, companies with more than 10,000 employees accounted for 34.5 percent of the innovations but 36 percent of 1963 employment.[9] The implication seems clear: smaller firms are disproportionately prolific contributors to the generation of important technological innovations. Large corporations barely pull their own weight.

The validity of this conclusion depends on the representativeness of the innovation sample analyzed by the Gelman research group. On this point it is difficult to reach an informed judgment, since details of the innovations, including the names of the companies credited with introducing them, were kept confidential. The most that can be said is that the list of innovations, identified individually in brief qualitative terms, is impressive in its coverage; and the expert panel procedure used to winnow out the 500 most important innovations from a broader initial list of 1,310 (augmented with 150 contributions suggested by panelists) shows no obvious signs of bias toward small as compared to large organizations. In the absence of contrary evidence, one is inclined to impute credence to the findings from an unusually ambitious data-gathering job.

One further conclusion deserves mention. The disproportionate contribution of smaller enterprises was especially marked for innovations first entering the market in the United States. Smaller businesses did less well abroad and particularly in Japan, as the innovation shares for firms with dollar-equivalent sales less than $50 million in table 11.2 show.[10]

This finding is consistent with work by scholars at Britain's Science Policy Research Unit at Sussex University, who discovered from a compi-

Table 11.2
Small firm innovation shares in five nations

Nation	Percent of innovations in companies with sales less than $50 million
United States	50
France	57
West Germany	37
United Kingdom	33
Japan	20

lation of 2,293 significant innovations introduced into the U.K. between 1945 and 1980 that only 25 percent originated in companies with fewer than 1,000 employees and that, contrary to U.S. patterns, the most prolific innovators per thousand employees were companies with 10,000 or more employees.[11] It is also readily reconciled with what we know about the Japanese economy: that the universities' best and brightest graduates go preponderantly to large corporations, and that the small-business sector is the refuge of less-educated workers and those who have received a "golden handshake" from their employers at age fifty-five. Evidently, the smaller-company sector in the United States is nearly unique. This almost surely has something to do with the ease with which new technology-oriented firms can obtain venture capital here. Less certainly, it may also support the assertion by Hayes and Abernathy that large European corporations are run by executives with more intimate knowledge of their home industry's technology and a longer decision-making horizon than their U.S. counterparts, and hence with greater receptiveness to innovation proposals from their technical staffs.[12]

11.2 A New Survey: The IR Competition Winners

Since 1963 the magazine *Industrial Research & Development* (previously *Industrial Research*) has conducted an annual competition to name the hundred most significant technical advances of the year. The annual lists, published in the journal's October issue, have long seemed to me an interesting untapped resource for examining the relative roles of small and large enterprises. Preparing this paper provided an opportunity to exploit the resource.

Further probing dampened my enthusiasm. The annual "sample" of winners is decidedly nonrandom. Entrants are self-nominated and must pay an entry fee ($40 for 1981). The entries are judged by a distinguished and reasonably well-balanced panel of large corporation research directors and academicians, but the roster of winners is visibly skewed toward instrumentation and laboratory gadgets—the sort of thing with a special appeal to research directors. Conspicuously absent or underrepresented on the lists were pharmaceutical entities, weapon systems, space systems, and communications systems, where there has been much technical progress, and consumer products (only a dozen clear cases among 498). There are also company anomalies: for instance, Union Carbide's Oak Ridge government contract laboratories had twenty and a half winners in five years (the half shared with another organization) while other more extensive parts of Union Carbide's R & D operation had none. IBM was also absent from the list over the five years (1976 to 1980) for which an analysis was carried out. Since the data had to be assembled before most of these problems became evident, the analysis was completed and is reported for whatever worth it may have.

Of the 498 technical advances tallied, 357, or 72 percent, came from U.S. profit-seeking corporations. The remainder were attributed to U.S. government laboratories (12.9 percent), foreign corporations (10.7 percent), academic institutions (2.4 percent), and other not-for-profit entities (2.3 percent). To determine the role of large vs. small companies in the domestic profit-seeking subset, a simple dichotomy was imposed. "Large" corporations were defined as those included in the Federal Trade Commission's 1974 line of business (LB) survey, which included the 250 largest manufacturing corporations ranked by domestic sales and other companies of almost uniformly substantial size. "Small" corporations were those not included, which, with at most twenty-two IR list-entering exceptions, were indeed small by any standard. Other research to be described shortly revealed that the "large" LB corporations accounted in 1974 for 73 percent of both company-financed and contract (typically federal contract) U.S. industrial R & D expenditures, as determined from a parallel National Science Foundation survey, along with roughly 55 to 60 percent of manufacturing sector sales and value added.[13] They originated 197.5, or 55 percent, of the 357 IR award-winning technical advances credited to U.S. corporations. Thus the large corporations' share of award-winning technical advances was roughly commensurate with, or perhaps slightly less than, their share of industrial corporation sales and value added and substantially less than their share of total U.S. industrial R&D expenditures. In view of possible selection biases, the most that can be said is that this result provides no support for the Schumpeterian hypothesis that large corporations are disproportionately fecund sources of significant technological advances.

11.3 Size and Inventive Output in the FTC's LB Sample

A new data source provides the opportunity for a much richer analysis without the possible sampling biases of the Gelman research and *Industrial Research & Development* data. It begins with data collected from 443 characteristically large manufacturing corporations by the Federal Trade Commission for the year 1974. Among the variables reported was company-financed expenditure on R&D in 1974. As noted earlier, the LB sample companies together conducted 73 percent of all such domestic U.S. research and development in that year—much more than their 55 to 60 percent share of manufacturing sales and value added. Clearly, corporate size appears conducive to the conduct of R&D. Two important questions remain. First, is the advantage of size continuous so that the few very largest entities are even more intensive supporters of R&D than their more numerous medium-sized counterparts, or do the advantages of size peter out at some intermediate scale, or does size make little difference once a certain threshold has been attained? Second, can further light be shed on the technical productivity of large enterprises' R&D programs? In particular, do large firms generate more, fewer, or roughly the same number of inventions per million dollars of R&D outlays than smaller companies?

The variable used here to illuminate this second question is a count of invention patents. Such a count has advantages and limitations. Its main advantage is comprehensiveness. The count exhaustively covers all issued patents and is not governed by a panel susceptible to possible sample biases. The main limitation is that bias may creep in more subtly at an earlier stage, such as in intercompany or interindustry differences in the propensity to seek patent protection on inventions of given quality. The limitation is an important one, but it can be controlled for and subjected to a variety of tests.[14] I shall therefore assume provisionally, subject to qualifications at appropriate points, that a count of issued patents provides an acceptably homogeneous index of inventive output.

On the average, various studies indicate that nine months elapse between the conception of a patentable invention (e.g., through research or development) and application for a patent. In the mid-1970s the lag between application and issuance was nineteen months. The sample of patents linked to LB sample company 1974 R & D expenditures therefore covered the ten-month period of June 1976 through March 1977, centered on mid-1974 with a twenty-eight-month lag. Each patent obtained by each of 443 LB sample companies was individually inspected by a team of technically trained Northwestern University students to screen out inventions of overseas origin and to link the patents not only to the responsible companies but to the specific lines of business within those companies giving rise to the inventions. This was done because the FTC survey, unlike any previously conducted, required companies to report their R & D broken down into some 276 standardized industry categories (later reduced for purposes of my analysis to 249 categories). On average a sample company reported its activities in 9.65 categories, so there were 4,274 individual LB reports altogether. Again, the patents were traced to the individual LBs in which they originated, with allowance being made for multiple LBs of origin in the case of joint (e.g., central research laboratory) inventions.

Altogether, the LB sample companies obtained 15,112 U.S. invention patents in the period covered. This was approximately 61 percent of patents issued during the same period to all U.S. industrial corporations. Thus the characteristically large LB sample companies originated a slightly higher share of patented inventions than their 55 to 60 percent share of manufacturing corporation sales and value added. In this sense the largest corporations' performance comes off more favorably than with the Gelman research tally of significant innovations. The difference between the LB companies' patent share (61 percent) and their share of *Industrial Research & Development* competition winners (55 percent) is in the same direction, but not large.

From another perspective the LB companies' performance is less favorable. They accounted for 73 percent of U.S. industrial R & D expenditures but generated only 61 percent of the patented inventions. Evidently, their yield of inventions per million dollars of R & D was lower than that of the much smaller companies excluded from the LB sample. There are several possible explanations for, and clarifications of, this differential.

For one, both sampled and nonsampled companies make patentable inventions not only in the context of formal R & D programs but also through the activity of operating-unit engineers and others.[15] Of the 1,271 LBs reporting no R & D outlays for 1974, 12.6 percent received patents. It is reasonable to suppose that small companies are particularly likely to sustain activity leading to patentable inventions but not formally organized, or reported to federal statistical agencies, as R & D.

Second, it is possible that the propensity to patent inventions of given quality varies systematically with corporate size. The relationship here could go either way. On one hand, my earlier research showed a decline in the propensity to patent for the characteristically large corporations subjected during the 1940s and 1950s to antitrust compulsory patent licensing decrees.[16] However, the niveau from which their patenting declined could have been a high one. Surveys in both the United States and West Germany reveal that the largest corporations commercially utilize an appreciably smaller fraction of their patented inventions than do relatively small companies.[17] This implies either a lower propensity to patent in smaller corporations, or higher average inventive quality, or both. Either interpretation would be consistent with the observed differences in the Gelman and patent sample size relationships.

But third, there is evidence of at least one relationship between size and "quality" favoring the larger corporations. The patents of larger LBs tend more frequently to cover complex systems and subsystems entailing high R & D outlays per invention. The relationship is a weak one. Holding field of technology constant, an increase in LB sales from $100 million to $1 billion was found to raise the fraction of systems and subsystems inventions by 5 to 6 percent—for instance, in mechanical fields of technology, from 51.0 to 53.8 percent.[18]

Leaving a final interpretation to the concluding section, we move on to the question of how size affects R & D support and patented invention output once a corporation has become large enough to be graced by inclusion in the FTC's LB sample. In other words, once some substantial size threshold has been reached, do *further* scale increases lead to more or less than proportional increases in innovative effort and output?

The method used to address this question is nonlinear regression analysis. The dependent variable is the count of patents received by a line of business or the amount of company-financed R & D (in millions of dollars) performed by a line of business. The size of an LB (i.e., the independent variable) is measured by its 1974 sales (in millions of dollars). To take into account the fact that some industries enjoy richer opportunities to perform R & D and make patentable inventions than others, each industry category (of 249) with five or more nonzero observations on the dependent variable was allowed to have its own best-fitting regression equation. With R & D as the dependent variable, 196 of the 249 industry categories satisfied this five-or-more criterion; with patents, 124 industries did. Observations for the industries that failed to satisfy the criterion were consigned to a common pool for which a single regression was computed.

Our basic concern is with the existence and nature of nonlinearities in the relationship between size (i.e., LB sales) and innovative activity (R & D or patents). There is a substantial literature on the theory and measurement of such relationships.[19] The theoretical literature has paid little attention to problems of measurement, so a brief expository integration may be helpful both to economists and the uninitiated. The newest theoretical works focus on the question of elasticity (denoted as E): does innovative activity or output increase exactly proportionately with size ($E = 1$), more than proportionately with size ($E > 1$), or less than proportionately with size ($E < 1$)? These may with only slight imprecision be referred to as the constant returns, increasing returns, and diminishing

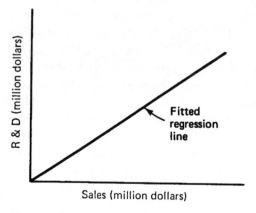

Figure 11.1
Simple regression with constant returns, $E = 1$

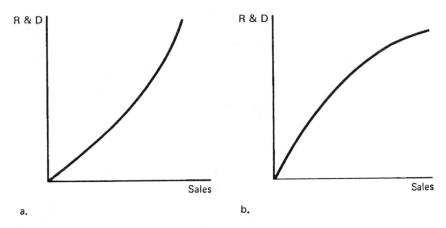

Figure 11.2
Nonlinear regression plots: (a) increasing returns, $E > 1$; (b) diminishing returns, $E < 1$

returns cases, respectively. To the extent that size offers compelling advantages, one might expect the increasing returns case ($E > 1$) to predominate.

For compelling measurement reasons discussed elsewhere, we proceed here by computing quadratic regression equations—those in which the independent (size) variable enters in squared as well as unsquared (linear) form.[20] The translation from quadratic coefficient values to elasticity values is often, but not always, simple. If the quadratic (i.e., squared) variable's coefficient is insignificantly different from zero and if in addition the regression equation's vertical axis intercept is zero, as illustrated in figure 11.1, constant returns prevail, and $E = 1$. Large units (LBs) are no more or less innovative relative to their size than small units, all else equal. If the intercept coefficient is zero and the quadratic coefficient is significantly positive, as in figure 11.2a, the increasing returns case holds unambiguously. As one can see, the support of R & D rises more than proportionately with size. If the intercept coefficient is zero and the quadratic coefficient is significantly negative, the relationship will be like that shown in figure 11.2b, and diminishing returns prevail unambiguously.

Matters become more complex when the fitted regression line does not intersect the vertical and horizontal axes where they in turn intersect, that is, when the intercept coefficient is significantly different from zero.

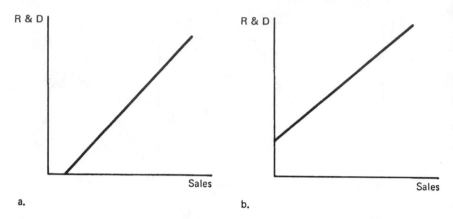

Figure 11.3
Regressions with nonzero intercepts: (a) increasing returns, $E > 1$; (b) diminishing returns, $E < 1$

If it is negative and the fitted line is linear, as in figure 11.3a, $E > 1$ continuously despite the lack of a significantly positive quadratic coefficient. In effect, this says that there are increasing returns because a certain size threshold must be reached before any R & D takes place. With a positive intercept, as in figure 11.3b, $E < 1$ continuously. Under certain conditions elasticity transitions can occur. When the intercept is negative and the quadratic coefficient is significantly negative too, the relationship is elastic at low sales levels but, at sufficiently high sales values, turns inelastic. With positive intercepts and quadratic terms, the relationship goes from inelastic to elastic.

Our null hypothesis (i.e., the hypothesis to be contradicted) is that the relationship is linear with zero intercept, as in figure 11.1. If either the Schumpeterians or the anti-Schumpeterians are right, they should have to bear the burden of proving departures from linearity or (almost equivalent) constant returns. Because we do not want to infer departures from constant returns when they do not truly exist but occur only by chance, we impose a conventional 95 percent statistical confidence criterion on our tests for nonzero values of the estimated quadratic coefficients and intercept values. It is also useful to know the "goodness of fit" of the fitted regression line. The statistic used for this purpose is R^2, or the square of the correlation coefficient. It measures the fraction of the dependent variable's variation from its mean "explained" by the fitted regression line. An R^2 value of 1.0 reveals that all of the individual LB observations lie exactly on the fitted regression line; there are no departures. An R^2 value of 0 means that the actual observations lie in random disarray, conforming to no systematic curve or line. R^2s for most real-world cross-sectional relationships lie somewhere in between.

We proceed now to the results, considering first LB sample companies' incentive to conduct R & D as a function of the size of the lines. The linear regression of R & D on LB sales, with each of 196 industries having its own best-fitting parameter values, has an R^2 value of 0.959. This is a remarkably high degree of explanatory power. With nearly 96 percent of the variation in R & D spending depending linearly on LB sales and industry characteristics, there is not much left to be explained by other variables. Adding 196 quadratic sales coefficients to test for nonlinearities raises R^2 by 0.0098 to 0.969. The increment is small but statistically significant at the 99 percent confidence level. One hundred four of the fitted quadratic coefficients were positive (suggesting but not proving increasing returns), and 92 were negative. Of the smaller number that passed a 95 percent statistical significance test, forty were positive and sixteen were negative. Thus the tests for nonlinearity provide mild support for a Schumpeterian increasing returns hypothesis in the performance of R & D.

This conclusion must be checked for possible complications from non-zero intercept coefficients. In fact, the intercept problem was minor. Only eleven regression intercept coefficients were significantly different from zero—slightly more than twice as many as one would expect to appear significant purely by chance. All eleven were positive, and all eleven coincided with significantly positive quadratic coefficients. Thus a pos-

Table 11.3
Results of the nonlinear R & D on sales regressions

	Number of industries	Percent
No significant departure from constant returns	140	71.4
Increasing returns ($E > 1$)		
Throughout	29 ⎱	20.4
At higher sales levels	11 ⎰	
Diminishing returns ($E < 1$) throughout	16	8.2

Table 11.4
Results of the nonlinear patenting on sales regressions

	Number of industries	Percent
No significant departure from constant returns	91	73.4
Increasing returns ($E > 1$)		
Throughout	9 ⎫	
At higher sales levels	5 ⎭	11.3
Diminishing returns ($E < 1$)		
Throughout	18 ⎫	
At higher sales levels	1 ⎭	15.3

sible transition from an inelastic relationship at low sales levels to an elastic relationship at high sales levels could occur. The transition took place at a sales level 40 percent or less than the sales of the leading LB in all but three cases, and in those three, the transition had occurred at two-thirds the largest seller's sales. We therefore summarize our R & D-sales findings for the 196 industries in table 11.3. The results again tilt on the side of supporting the Schumpeterian hypothesis that size is conducive to the vigorous conduct of R & D.

We turn now to our measure of inventive output, the patent counts. There were 124 industries in which five or more LBs had nonzero patenting. When the linear regression of patenting on sales for these 124 industries individually plus a residual pooled group is computed, the R^2 value is 0.841. Introducing 124 quadratic coefficients raises R^2 by 0.026 to 0.867, an increment statistically significant at the 99 percent confidence level. The overall nonlinear effect, although still quite small compared to the linear effect, is somewhat larger than in the R & D-sales analysis. However, the pattern of nonlinearities is different. Altogether, there were seventy negative quadratic coefficients (suggesting diminishing returns) and fifty-four positive ones. Of those that passed a 95 percent significance test, seventeen were negative and fourteen positive.

Intercept complications must also be checked. Only eight intercept coefficients were significantly different from zero, seven of them positive and one negative. One significantly negative coefficient coincided with a significantly negative quadratic term, but the transition from elastic to inelastic occurred at 22 percent of the largest LB's sales. There were five

Table 11.5
Results of the nonlinear patenting on R & D regressions

	Number of industries	Percent
No significant departure from constant returns	74	59.7
Increasing returns $(E > 1)$		
Throughout	16 ⎫	
At higher R & D levels	3 ⎭	15.3
Diminishing returns $(E < 1)$		
Throughout	30 ⎫	
At higher R & D levels	1 ⎭	25.0

significant positive intercept, positive quadratic term cases, all with a transition at 55 percent or less of the largest LB's sales. Moving the two positive intercept, insignificant quadratic term cases into the $E < 1$ category, we recapitulate in table 11.4.

There is again a clear preponderance of constant returns cases. Among the exceptions the evidence leans weakly against the Schumpeterian conjecture that the largest sellers are especially fecund sources of patented inventions.

The weak disparity between the R & D-sales and patenting-sales results is easily reconciled. When patents are regressed linearly on R & D (i.e., in an analysis of input-output relationships), there is a bias toward diminishing returns, as we see from table 11.5.[21] Thus the tendency toward increasing returns in the R & D-size relationship is counteracted by a tendency toward diminishing returns in the patents-R & D relationship to yield in the net a slight tendency toward diminishing returns in the patented invention output-size relationship.

11.4 Diversification, R & D, and Inventive Output

To readers who may have overlooked the point, the preceding analysis is absolutely unique. Never before have scholars been able to test the Schumpeterian innovation-size hypotheses at the level of individual lines of business. The analysis was made possible by the Federal Trade Commission's line of business program. Still there are other dimensions of size that might also affect innovative activity. In particular, business enterprises may be large not only by virtue of substantial sales in specific lines of business but by operating in numerous lines of business, that is, by being more diversified. The LB data also permit a test of that hypothesis.

The index of diversification used here is the inverse Herfindahl numbers equivalent, defined as $1/\Sigma_{i=1}^{N} S_i^2$, where S_i is the share of total company unregulated domestic sales contributed by the ith line of business (among N lines of business in total). If the company operates in only one line, the index has a value of 1.0. The index rises with an increase in the number of lines, but less so when the sizes of the various lines are highly unequal. Its value can be interpreted as indicating the equivalent number of lines in which the company operates, assuming (contrary to normal fact) each to be of equal size. For the 443 sample companies, the computed values ranged from 1.0 to an average of 19.8 for the five most diversified companies. The median value was approximately 3.0.

To ascertain the role of diversification, the residual error values from the linear regressions of R & D on sales and patents on sales, industry by industry, were correlated with our index of diversification.[22] If, say, LBs from diversified companies were more vigorous R & D performers than their sales in an industry category and industry conditions alone dictated, their residuals would tend to be positive, and those of undiversified companies would be negative, so a positive correlation between the residuals and the diversification index would emerge. In fact, the resulting (unsquared) correlations were minute and statistically insignificant: −0.023 for residuals of the R & D on sales regressions and +0.018 for residuals of the patents on sales regressions. There was, however, a weak but statistically significant correlation of +0.040 between diversification and residuals from the patents on R & D regression. More diversified corporations tended to receive more patents per million dollars of R & D than their less diversified counterparts, all else equal, perhaps because they were better able to commercialize, and hence chose to patent, inventions meshing imperfectly with their main lines of endeavor. The observed effect was quite small; it indicates that a unit increase in the numbers equivalent diversification index is accompanied in the average line of business by an increase of 0.056 patents per million dollars of R & D outlay, or 3.2 percent of the mean number of patents (1.70) per million R & D dollars for all sample lines. This implies an elasticity of patenting with respect to diversification of 0.1.

11.5 Conclusion

Three new and in many respects unusually rich sets of data have been analyzed here to reassess the Schumpeterian hypothesis that large corporations are uniquely powerful engines of technological advance. On the whole, the hypothesis fares badly. Its best innings have to do with merely entering the R & D game. As we have long known, the largest industrial corporations conduct a share of formally organized R & D considerably larger than their share of sales, value added, or employment. The LB data add the new insight that in more industries than not, this phenomenon of size continues up to the scale of the largest seller, although in *most* industries, size appears to be neither stimulating nor retarding. What the largest corporations accomplish with their R & D dollars is less impressive. By every measure used, the group of large corporations as a whole contributed fewer significant innovations, contest-winning technical advances, and invention patents per million dollars of R & D than smaller enterprises. Only by the count of patents do the largest corporations contribute a share of inventive output greater than their share of sales or employment. Their advantage on this dimension is at best modest and, in view of possible size group-related differences in the propensity to patent, uncertain. Within the population of large corporations it is clear that greater size does not in general contribute to a disproportionately greater output of patented inventions. Nor does greater diversification help appreciably.

Notes

1. Source: U.S. Bureau of the Census, *Enterprise Statistics*, for 1958 and 1972.

2. F. M. Scherer, *Industrial Market Structure and Economic Performance*, 2nd ed. (Boston: Houghton Mifflin, 1980), p. 76, citing two Federal Trade Commission studies.

3. Joseph A. Schumpeter, *Capitalism, Socialism, and Democracy* (New York: Harper, 1942).

4. Richard R. Nelson, The Simple Economics of Basic Scientific Research, *Journal of Political Economy* (June 1959): 297–306.

5. Robert H. Hayes and William J. Abernathy, Managing Our Way to Economic Decline, *Harvard Business Review* (July–August 1980): 75–76.

6. See e.g. Morton I. Kamien and Nancy L. Schwartz, Market Structure and Innovation: A Survey, *Journal of Economic Literature* (March 1975): 1–37; updated and expanded in the book, *Market Structure and Innovation* (Cambridge University Press, 1982).

7. Stephen Feinman and William Fuentevilla, *Indicators of International Trends in Technolog-*

ical Innovation, Final Report to the National Science Foundation (Jenkintown, Pa.: Gelman Research Associates, April 1976), NTIS document PB-263-738.

8. Ibid., table 3-8. There is a possible ambiguity in the size classifications, since Feinman and Fuentevilla did not always consolidate self-standing and/or partly owned subsidiaries of large corporations. It is known from studies of aggregate concentration that the employment data to which I make a comparison are also not fully consolidated. Although the size of the bias is probably small, its direction is unclear.

9. U.S. Bureau of the Census, *1963 Enterprise Statistics*, Part 1, General Report on Industrial Organization (Washington: USGPO, 1968), table 8. Not surprisingly, the employment share of corporations with 10,000 or more employees was rising during the sample period. It was 32.7 percent (less than the share of innovations) in 1958 and 44.7 percent in 1972. Data for 1954 are not available.

10. Feinman and Fuentevilla, table 3-32. These figures are for a 352 innovation subset of the 500 innovation sample, with possible nonresponse biases. The number of sampled innovations for nations other than the United States is also small, running from sixteen for France to thirty-four for the United Kingdom.

11. Keith Pavitt, Some Characteristics of Innovative Activities in British Industry, draft, University of Sussex, January 1982. See also C. Freeman, *The Role of Small Firms in Innovation in the United Kingdom Since 1945*, Research Report No. 6, Committee of Inquiry on Small Firms (London: HMSO, 1971).

12. Managing Our Way to Economic Decline, pp. 73, 76.

13. On the difficulties in making an exact sales or value added comparison, see the Federal Trade Commission's *Statistical Report: Annual Line of Business Report, 1976* (Washington: May 1982), pp. 52-75.

14. See F. M. Scherer, The Propensity To Patent, *International Journal of Industrial Organization* 1 (March 1983): 107-124.

15. Indeed, one invention in our sample was made by Harold Geneen, chairman of ITT.

16. F. M. Scherer et al., *Patents and the Corporation* (2nd ed.; Boston: privately published, 1959), pp. 137-146.

17. For an evaluation of the U.S. evidence, see Jacob Schmookler, *Invention and Economic Growth* (Harvard University Press, 1966), pp. 47-55. On Germany, see Klaus Grefermann, Karl Heinrich Oppenländer, Elfried Peffgen, Karl Christian Röthlingshöfer, and Lothar Scholz, *Patentwesen und technischer Fortschritt* (Göttingen: Schwartz, 1974), appendix table 57. The differences in utilization rates between the largest and smallest size classes tabulated in both nations are on the order of 20 percentage points.

18. Scherer, The Propensity To Patent, pp. 124-125.

19. On the theory, see Franklin M. Fisher and Peter Temin, Returns to Scale in Research and Development: What Does the Schumpeterian Hypothesis Imply? *Journal of Political Economy* (January-February 1973): 56-70; and Meir Kohn and John T. Scott, Scale Economies in Research and Development: The Schumpeterian Hypothesis, *Journal of Industrial Economics* (March 1982): 239-250.

20. See e.g. my The Propensity To Patent; and my Size of Firm, Oligopoly, and Research: A Comment, *Canadian Journal of Economics and Political Science* (May 1965): 256-266.

21. Details are added in Scherer, The Propensity To Patent, pp. 113-116.

22. This is equivalent to computing the partial correlation of the dependent variable with diversification, given sales and industry effects.

12 Market Structure and the Employment of Scientists and Engineers

In the December 1965 *American Economic Review*, I reported results unfavorable to Professor Schumpeter's conjectures regarding the relationship between monopoly power and technological innovation [4, pp. 1117–1121]. An analysis of forty-eight narrowly defined manufacturing industries revealed no significant tendency for the output of the industry leaders' 1954 patented inventions to increase with the industries' 1950 four-firm concentration ratios, *ceteris paribus*. Here I shall extend the analysis, utilizing data from a new and more comprehensive sample.

12.1 The Data

The hypothesis tested is that industrial inventive and innovative effort, measured by the employment of technical engineers and scientists, increases with the concentration of market power, other relevant variables such as total industry employment, technological opportunity, and product characteristics being held constant. Three dependent variables were used. One is the number of technical engineers E_i plus natural scientists S_i employed in fifty-six manufacturing industry groups during 1960. The second is the number of natural scientists S_i only (averaging 14 percent of total technical employment $E_i + S_i$). Estimates of both E_i and S_i were obtained from a 5 percent sample of the 1960 Census of Population [6].[1]

The third dependent variable requires more explanation. Although production engineers, quality control mathematicians, and similar personnel are undoubtedly responsible for some inventions and innovations [1], [5], the prime source of new industrial technology is presumably the formally organized research and development laboratory. But only 45 percent of U.S. manufacturing industry's scientific and engineering employees during 1960 were engaged in formal R&D work [8, p. 25]. Furthermore only 57 percent of (nonaircraft) industry's R&D effort was supported with private funds, and hence subject to the market incentives to which Schumpeter's market structure hypotheses are solely applicable [7, p. 65]. Consequently, a third estimated private research and development employment variable $RD_i = (F_i)(P_i)(E_i + S_i)$ was defined, where F_i is the proportion of the ith industry's scientific and engineering work

Source: *American Economic Review* 57 (June 1967): 524–531. Journal of the American Economic Association.

force engaged in formal R & D and P_i is the fraction of the industry's
R & D financed privately.[2]

The definitions of the fifty-six industry groups sampled (covering nearly
all of U.S. manufacturing industry for 1960) were governed by the availability of data. Classification problems forced the Census Bureau to use
a heterogeneous system in aggregating the occupational data by industry.
The industry groups ranged from narrow clusters of one or a few four-
digit SIC industries (i.e., synthetic fibers) to quite broad two-digit sectors
(i.e., electrical machinery, equipment, and supplies), although most were
at the three-digit level of aggregation. It was therefore necessary to use a
weighted average index of concentration as the independent variable of
primary relevance to the hypothesis tested. The concentration index C_i
of the ith industry group is the average (weighted by value of shipments)
of the 1958 four-firm concentration ratios for all four-digit SIC industries
included in that group [9, pp. 11–42].

To take into account interindustry differences in scientific and technological opportunity, dummy variables are defined for four broad classes:
general and mechanical (G & M), electrical, chemical, and traditional.
Each industry group was assigned to one of these classes after analysis
of the group's product technology characteristics.[3] Choices involving the
electrical and chemical classifications were straightforward, but it was
difficult to avoid some arbitrary judgments in distinguishing between
industries with G & M as opposed to traditional product technologies.
In borderline cases the G & M classification (used as the intercept class
in all regressions) was favored.

Three additional dummy variables were used to distinguish durable
from nondurable goods industries, consumer from producer goods industries, and industries characterized by local or regional markets from those
essentially nationwide in scope.

12.2 The Model and Tests

If Schumpeter's conjectures are correct, one would expect the absolute
differences in technical employment associated with concentration to be
greater for large industries than for small. Past experience with similar
data has shown that the error terms of untransformed linear regressions
on the industry size variable are heteroscedastic and that observations
from extremely large industries can dominate the regression estimates.

These theoretical and statistical considerations call for either a multiplicative or ratio specification of the model. In my 1965 article a multiplicative model was chosen to test the concentration hypothesis. With the present sample variables, the model can be written

$$(E_i + S_i) = aN_i^\alpha C_i^\beta \left(\prod_j 10^{\delta_j D_{ij}} \right) u_i, \tag{1}$$

where N_i is total 1960 employment of the ith industry (scaled in thousands), D_{ij} is a dummy variable with the value of 1 if the ith industry is in the jth technology or product characteristic class and zero otherwise, and u_i is the error term. The dummy variables in this model relate to the slope of the regression hyperplane with respect to both industry size N_i and concentration C_i. This specification implies that as C_i tends to zero, $(E_i + S_i)$ also tends to zero, no matter how high δ_j and N_i are—that is, no matter how large the industry is and how favorable the technological opportunities confronting the industry are. But it seems more reasonable that, in a field as enriched as, say, the electronics industries are with opportunities opened up by the advance of science, many scientists and engineers would be employed even if the industry structure were atomistic. While the specification of equation (1) might serve adequately over the range of concentration values actually observed (the lowest was 10 percent), the use of an alternative ratio model appears preferable on a priori grounds:

$$\frac{(E_i + S_i)}{N_i} = c + \sum_j d_j D_{ij} + gC_i + v_i. \tag{2}$$

In this form the influence of interindustry differences operates independently of the concentration level. Even when the industry is atomistic $(C_i \rightarrow 0)$, it can have a significant fraction of its work force assigned to scientific and engineering tasks.

Because it appears more consistent with a priori knowledge, I am inclined to favor model (2) over model (1). But since the case for model (2) is not ironclad, and since the conclusions depend to some extent on the choice of models, I shall first summarize the tests of model (1). Regressions were run in logarithmic form for the three dependent variables on N_i alone; on N_i with C_i; and on N_i with all dummy variables, with and without C_i. When the concentration variable was introduced into regressions of $\log (E_i + S_i)$, $\log S_i$, and $\log RD_i$ on $\log N_i$ without dummy variables, its regression coefficients were in all cases positive and highly significant, and it made an incremental contribution to the percentage of variance explained (100 R^2) of 25.5, 15.9, and 22.4 percentage points, respectively.

The concentration regression coefficients remained positive and significant when all dummy variables (and also subgroups of the dummies) were introduced, as shown in the following equations, where $Elec_i$ is the electrical class dummy, $Chem_i$ the chemical class dummy, $Trad_i$ the traditional product technology class dummy, Reg_i the regional market dummy, Dur_i the durable goods dummy, and $Cons_i$ the consumer goods dummy. Standard errors are given in parentheses under the coefficients.

$$\log(E_i + S_i) = -0.03 + 0.95 \log N_i + 0.94 \log C_i + 0.30 \, Elec_i$$
$$ (0.11) (0.24) (0.24)$$

$$+ 0.44 \, Chem_i - 0.47 \, Trad_i - 0.05 \, Reg_i + 0.05 \, Dur_i$$
$$(0.17) (0.11) (0.13) (0.10) \qquad (3)$$

$$- 0.14 \, Cons_i;$$
$$(0.09)$$

$$R^2 = 0.830.$$

$$\log S_i = 1.09 + 0.95 \log N_i + 1.34 \log C_i + 0.10 \, Elec_i$$
$$(0.22) (0.48) (0.49)$$

$$+ 0.63 \, Chem_i - 0.54 \, Trad_i + 0.14 \, Reg_i - 0.67 \, Dur_i$$
$$(0.34) (0.22) (0.26) (0.21) \qquad (4)$$

$$- 0.37 \, Cons_i;$$
$$(0.18)$$

$$R^2 = 0.600.$$

$$\log RD_i = -0.36 + 0.93 \log N_i + 0.80 \log C_i + 0.27 \, Elec_i$$
$$(0.11) (0.24) (0.24)$$

$$+ 0.51 \, Chem_i - 0.41 \, Trad_i - 0.01 \, Reg_i + 0.10 \, Dur_i$$
$$(0.17) (0.11) (0.13) (0.10) \qquad (5)$$

$$- 0.09 \, Cons_i;$$
$$(0.09)$$

$$R^2 = 0.805.$$

When equations (3) through (5) were computed with the concentration variable deleted, the amount of variance explained ($100\ R^2$) fell by 5.5, 6.6, and 4.5 percentage points, respectively. Thus the incremental explanatory power of concentration is much less when dummy variables are included than when the concentration variable is used with industry employment N_i alone. Still all of the incremental variance gains due to including C_i in equations (3) through (5) are significant in F-ratio tests at the 1 percent level. These results therefore tend to support Schumpeter's hypothesis that inventive and innovative activity increases with market concentration.

Turning now to the ratio model, the simple correlations involving only technical employment, total employment, and concentration also supported the hypothesis, although not as consistently. The r^2's were 0.21 between $(E_i + S_i)/N_i$ and C_i; 0.19 between RD_i/N_i and C_i; but only 0.027 between S_i/N_i and C_i. Introduction of the six dummy variables led to much sharper declines in the explanatory power of concentration than in the multiplicative model. The equations were as follows (with the dependent variables scaled in technical personnel per 1,000 total employees):

$$\frac{E_i + S_i}{N_i} = 16.4 + 0.155C_i + 38.1\ Elec_i + 35.7\ Chem_i - 14.3\ Trad_i$$
$$\qquad\qquad (0.109) \qquad (9.0) \qquad\quad (6.6) \qquad\qquad (4.1)$$

$$\qquad - 4.6\ Reg_i + 4.9\ Dur_i - 1.3\ Cons_i; \qquad\qquad\qquad (6)$$
$$\qquad\quad (5.0) \qquad\quad (4.0) \qquad\quad (3.5)$$

$R^2 = 0.728.$

$$\frac{S_i}{N_i} = 5.0 + 0.01C_i + 0.36\ Elec_i + 25.4\ Chem_i - 2.2\ Trad_i$$
$$\qquad\quad (0.05) \quad (4.16) \qquad\quad (3.0) \qquad\qquad (1.9)$$

$$\qquad - 1.0\ Reg_i - 2.3\ Dur_i - 0.45\ Cons_i; \qquad\qquad\qquad (7)$$
$$\qquad\quad (2.3) \qquad\quad (1.8) \qquad\quad (1.61)$$

$R^2 = 0.715.$

$$\frac{RD_i}{N_i} = 4.3 + 0.054C_i + 8.4\ Elec_i + 11.9\ Chem_i - 4.0\ Trad_i$$
$$\qquad\qquad (0.036) \quad (3.0) \qquad\quad (2.2) \qquad\qquad (1.4)$$

$$\qquad - 1.1\ Reg_i + 1.5\ Dur_i + 0.3\ Cons_i; \qquad\qquad\qquad (8)$$
$$\qquad\quad (1.7) \qquad\quad (1.3) \qquad\quad (1.2)$$

$R^2 = 0.669$

In equations (6) and (8) the concentration coefficient is barely significant at the 10 percent level in a one-tail test; in equation (7) it is clearly not significant. Deletion of the concentration variable from equations (6) and (8) causes reductions in the amount of variance explained of 1.1 and 1.6 percentage points, respectively—increments significant only at the 20 percent level in F-ratio tests.

To determine whether the regression relationship between intensity of technical employment and concentration was consistent within individual technology classes, separate linear regressions (omitting product charac-teristic dummy variables) were computed for the classes on which a reasonably large number of observations was available. For the twenty-five industries classified in the traditional product technology category, the fitted equations were

$$\frac{E_i + S_i}{N_i} = 1.20 + 0.176C_i;$$
$$\phantom{\frac{E_i + S_i}{N_i} =} (2.17) \quad (0.063)$$
$$\tag{9}$$
$$r^2 = 0.223.$$

$$\frac{S_i}{N_i} = -0.18 + 0.079C_i;$$
$$\phantom{\frac{S_i}{N_i} =} (1.33) \quad (0.042)$$
$$\tag{10}$$
$$r^2 = 0.134.$$

For the twenty-four industries classified as having general and mechanical product technologies, the following estimates resulted:

$$\frac{E_i + S_i}{N_i} = 13.36 + 0.291C_i;$$
$$\phantom{\frac{E_i + S_i}{N_i} =} (8.68) \quad (0.197)$$
$$\tag{11}$$
$$r^2 = 0.091.$$

$$\frac{S_i}{N_i} = 0.71 + 0.070C_i;$$
$$\phantom{\frac{S_i}{N_i} =} (2.07) \quad (0.047)$$
$$\tag{12}$$
$$r^2 = 0.091.$$

In all four cases the concentration coefficients are positive. All pass statistical significance tests at the 10 percent level or higher, with the traditional group showing a somewhat more consistent tendency for the intensity of technical employment to increase with concentration.[4]

12.3 Interpretation

We find then divergent results. Using one specification of the model, Schumpeter's hypothesis is sustained with flying colors. Using the alternative and theoretically preferred specification, the support is weaker but not entirely absent. Differences in the role of the dummy variables, and especially the technology class dummies, underlie this divergence. Still one important result is common to both models. When the dummy variables are introduced, the incremental explanatory power of concentration falls sharply.

Further analysis shows that the technology class dummies compete with concentration for explanatory power because they are positively correlated. The technically vigorous electrical and chemical groups had average and minimum concentration indexes well above the full sample means. Average concentration in the electrical subsample (with only two observations) was 58, with a minimum value of 48. For the five chemical observations the average was 44, with a minimum of 31. The G & M group had an average C_i index of 41, with a range of from 18 to 70. In distinct contrast, the least progressive traditional class had an average of 29, with a minimum of 10 and only one observation (tobacco products) exceeding 50. Two alternative causal chains are compatible with this interdependence. The electrical and chemical classes might be more progressive on the average because they are more concentrated, or they may be more concentrated because in the past they have been more progressive.

Neither possibility can be rejected conclusively. It is clear, however, that the greater apparent progressiveness of the chemical and electrical groups is not due solely to higher concentration, for science has obviously been exceptionally generous to these groups during the past century. More support can be mustered for the contention that technological innovation associated with opportunity has led to concentration.[5] The high concentration of market power in such fields as synthetic fibers, plastics materials, electric lamps, telephone equipment, and computing equipment was built at least partly on patent and know-how barriers to entry and (in an earlier era) restrictive patent cross-licensing agreements. The successful exploitation of favorable opportunities may also have permitted especially rapid market share growth for innovating firms, contributing to above-average concentration. On the other hand, the undramatic pace of technological advance in such product areas as sawmill products, furniture, bakery products, shoes, and canned vegetables afforded little opportunity for the erection of strong patent and know-how entry barriers. It seems reasonable to conclude tentatively that the electrical and chemical technology class dummy variables have not captured explanatory power more appropriately attributable causally to concentration, although the possibility of a reverse flow from past opportunity to present concentration cannot be excluded.

Once interindustry opportunity differences are taken into account, the tendency for technical employment to increase with concentration is most persistent for the traditional industries, which are least concentrated on the average. This suggests a possible threshold effect: increases in concentration are conducive to technical vigor only in relatively atomistic industries, becoming an unimportant stimulus once a certain broad threshold is crossed [2]. To explore this possibility, an additional variable C_i^2 was introduced into regressions otherwise identical to equations (9) through (12). This test for nonlinearities yielded modest support for the hypothesis. In all four regressions, a relationship concave to the concentration axis was found, although only in the nonlinear analogue of equation (9) was the squared term's (negative) coefficient significant at the 5 percent level. In all four cases technological employment per 1,000 employees reached a predicted maximum at concentration levels between 50 and 55 percent— values exceeded only by the tobacco products industry in the traditional class, but by five to eight industries in the G & M class. The four regression equations predicted a zero ratio of technical to total employment at concentration levels between 10 and 14 percent, suggesting that the threshold lies somewhere above this low range.

These results appear consistent with the neo-Schumpeterian hypothesis that oligopolists display a special affinity toward nonprice competition. Some degree of concentration is required before firms eschew price-cutting and grapple for market position through more complex innovative strategies. But in industries with high concentration—such as when the four-firm ratio exceeds 55 percent—pricing interdependence is fully recognized, and group discipline may even be sufficiently strong to permit a "live and let live" attitude toward technological innovation.

12.4 Conclusion

Three tentative conclusions emerge. First, the relationship between industrial inventive and innovative effort and concentration is a complex one, since high concentration and rich technological opportunity tend to coincide. Naive tests of the Schumpeterian market power hypotheses are not apt to add much to our understanding. Second, even after interindustry differences in technological opportunity are taken into account crudely, there remains evidence of a modest positive correlation between the employment of scientists and engineers and concentration. This correlation is stronger than the results of my 1965 analysis suggested, undoubtedly because industries with traditional product technologies were deliberately excluded from the sample. And third, technological vigor appears to increase with concentration mainly at relatively low levels of concentration. When the four-firm concentration ratio exceeds 50 or 55 percent, additional market power is probably not conducive to more vigorous technological efforts and may be downright stultifying.

Notes

1. The engineering employment variable excludes sales engineers, while the scientific employment variable includes mathematicians. Three "not specified" catchall groups were excluded from the sample. In addition, the aircraft and shipbuilding industries were left out because their technical activities lie for the most part outside the private market sector, and newspaper publishing was excluded because of its peculiar product and market characteristics.

2. Data on F_i and P_i were obtained for thirteen and nineteen broader industry groups, respectively, from [8] and [7]. These ratios were applied, after a few adjustments based on supplemental knowledge, to the fifty-six narrower industry groups. The resulting estimates are crude, although there is no reason to suppose that the estimation errors are systematic.

3. The classifications conform closely to those found significant in [4, pp. 1103, 1107]. A table giving the industry classifications and other raw data used in the study is available upon request from the author.

4. For the $(E_i + S_i)/N_i$ regressions, a test of the hypothesis that the traditional class intercept is greater than or equal to the G & M class intercept was rejected at the 10 percent level, but a similar hypothesis regarding the slopes can be rejected only at the 35 percent level. This lends support for regression model (2), which assumes different intercepts but equal slopes, over model (1), which assumes identical (zero) intercepts but unequal slopes. For the S_i/N_i regressions, there is no indication of significant differences in either the slopes or intercepts.

Simple linear regressions for industries in the chemical technology class revealed a *negative* correlation between both $(E_i + S_i)/N_i$ and S_i/N_i and concentration. However, the regression coefficients had t-ratios of only 0.61 and 1.24, respectively, and only five observations were involved.

5. See also Almarin Phillips' analysis [3], which stresses this possibility.

References

1. S. Hollander. *The Sources of Increased Efficiency: A Study of du Pont Rayon Plants.* Cambridge, Ma., 1965.

2. J. W. Markham. Market Structure, Business Conduct, and Innovation. *Am. Econ. Rev., Proc.* 55 (May 1965): 323–332.

3. Almarin Phillips. Patents, Potential Competition, and Technical Progress. *Am. Econ. Rev., Proc.* 56 (May 1966): 301–310.

4. F. M. Scherer. Firm Size, Market Structure, Opportunity, and the Output of Patented Inventions. *Am. Econ. Rev.* 55 (December 1965): 1097–1125.

5. J. Schmookler. Inventors Past and Present. *Rev. Econ. Stat. 39* (August 1957): 321–333.

6. U.S. Department of Commerce, Bureau of the Census. *Census of Population: 1960.* Occupation by Industry. PC(2) 7C. Washington, D.C., 1963.

7. U.S. National Science Foundation. *Research and Development in Industry: 1961.* Washington, D.C., 1964.

8. U.S. National Science Foundation. *Scientific and Technical Personnel in Industry: 1960.* Washington, D.C., 1961.

9. U.S. Senate, Committee on the Judiciary, Subcommittee on Antitrust and Monopoly. *Concentration Ratios in Manufacturing Industry: 1958.* Washington, D.C., 1962.

13 Concentration, R & D, and Productivity Change

Using new and unusually rich data, this note reexamines how industrial productivity growth is affected by seller concentration in conjunction with industrial R & D. The data are based upon the Federal Trade Commission's line of business (LB) survey [11], covering 443 U.S. corporations originating 73 percent of 1974 company-financed industrial R & D outlays. Linked to those data were 15,112 of the corporations' invention patents, which in turn were classified as to process vs. product orientation, industries of origin and utilization, and in diverse other ways.[1] Thus the R & D data could be disaggregated and recast so as to shed precise light on their interaction with concentration.

13.1 Background

In an earlier analysis Greer and Rhoades [1] found that seller concentration had a positive and statistically significant impact on labor productivity growth for three different samples of varying time span and industry coverage. A more recent study of estimated total factor productivity growth by Sveikauskas and Sveikauskas (S & S) [8] reported concentration effects positive in durable goods but negative in nondurables. As I wrote in the second edition of my industrial organization text, the Greer and Rhoades results were puzzling:

Why concentration should make this sort of difference is somewhat perplexing.... [L]ess than 20 percent of U.S. enterprises' R & D is directed toward improving internal production processes; most is devoted to new or improved *products*. There is also extensive specialization by certain industries in supplying machines or raw and intermediate materials to other industries. To the extent that process technology is imported from other industries, productivity growth shortfalls over such long periods as 1919–40 or even 17 years, if indeed causally linked to concentration, would have to reflect producers' unwillingness to cooperate with process improvement specialists or reluctance to replace worn-out equipment with the best new techniques available on the market. While pathological cases of refusal to accept what is practically a free lunch may exist, it seems improbable that this is what the Greer-Rhoades results reveal. More plausibly, there may be a tendency for concentrated industries to enjoy richer opportunities to improve productivity—e.g., because labor-saving technical change is biased in favor of industries for which minimum optimal scales are large in relation to market size [4, pp. 433–434].

Source: *Southern Economic Journal* 50 (July 1983): 221–225.

My new data reveal this critique to be wrong in at least one important respect. It is true that most industrial R & D is product oriented. For the LB **company** sample, process R & D was 24.6 percent of total 1974 **company-financed** R & D. It is not true, however, that *manufacturing* enterprises, which were the focus of the Greer-Rhoades and S & S analyses, rely heavily on other specialist suppliers for their process technology. Of the patented inventions used within the manufacturing sector, excluding what manufacturers "exported" to nonmanufacturing industries and consumers, more than half were developed *within* the industry of use. Furthermore, if one singles out the specialized capital goods inventions used by particular manufacturing industries (as distinguished from general-purpose capital goods such as electric motors and forklift trucks), one finds that three-fourths originated internally. That is, the inventions were made and developed by the companies who would use them to improve their own production processes [6, p. 233]. Manufacturers not only have comparative advantage in originating new technology, but they are also remarkably self-reliant for the development of their own specialized internal process improvements.

In view of this new evidence a theoretical case for a positive relationship between concentration and productivity growth emerges. The more concentrated an industry is, the larger will be the market shares of its representative sellers. And the larger a seller's market share is, the larger will be the share of cost savings from process innovations it can appropriate, assuming that licensing the process to competitors is either unattractive or entails high transaction costs.[2] The firm able to appropriate a larger share of benefits should in turn have a stronger incentive to perform process R & D, all else (e.g., technological opportunity and competitive stimulus) held equal. And this in turn could lead to more rapid productivity growth.

13.2 The New Results

To reexamine the Greer-Rhoades findings in the light of these new insights and data, weighted average four-firm 1972 seller concentration ratios, CR4, were compiled for eighty-seven industry groups on which matching R & D and labor productivity growth data were available. The sample covers nearly all of manufacturing, disaggregated into eighty-one groups at roughly the three-digit SIC level, plus six nonmanufacturing groups—

agriculture, crude oil and gas production, railroads, air transport, tele-communications, and the combined electric-gas-sanitary utilities sector. Concentration ratios were initially estimated for product lines defined as meaningfully as possible, sometimes at the five-digit level or narrower, and then aggregated with value-added weights (or, for the nonmanufacturing groups, asset weights) to the eighty-seven group level.[3] No attempt was made to correct for regional markets or imports, since the concentration ratio had to serve as an index of process benefit appropriability, and the R & D conduct incentives of, say, a ready-mix concrete producer with 40 percent of its local market but only 0.5 percent of national output would be proxied better by its national than its local market share.

The productivity indexes ΔLP used as dependent variables came from a new Bureau of Labor Statistics series [10] using input-output industry definitions. They estimate the average annual percentage change in real output (i.e., output value deflated by price indexes) per employee hour over the relevant time period. Two periods are analyzed. Given data limitations, the best approximation to a correct lag between productivity growth and 1972 concentration or 1974 R & D was for the business cycle peak-to-peak period 1973 to 1978. However, because work reported elsewhere [5] revealed considerable "noise" in productivity relationships for a period as short as five years, an alternate variable measures annual labor productivity growth over the fourteen-year 1964 to 1978 interval.[4] Since both concentration and R & D/sales ratios tend to be quite stable over time, their explanatory power might be expected to remain strong even though no backward causation is implied. For each of the two productivity variables ΔLP_{73-78} and ΔLP_{64-78}, complementary variables ΔGK were defined. They measure the annual percentage change in gross (i.e., undepreciated) plant and equipment stock (in constant 1972 dollars) per worker hour over the same intervals.[5]

With capital stock growth and concentration as the only explanatory variables, the regression for 1973 to 1978 productivity growth was as follows:

$$\Delta LP_{73-78} = -0.02 + 0.302^{**}\ \Delta GK_{73-78} + 0.023\ CR4;$$
$$\qquad\qquad\quad (2.74) \qquad\qquad\qquad (1.57) \qquad\qquad\qquad (1)$$

$$R^2 = 0.123, \quad N = 87;$$

with t-ratios given in subscripted parentheses, one asterisk denoting significance at the 0.05 level in a one-tail test, and two asterisks denoting significance at the 0.01 level. For the longer fourteen-year period, the corresponding regression is

$$\Delta LP_{64-78} = 0.53 + 0.466^{**}\ \Delta GK_{64-78} + 0.017^*\ CR4;$$
$$\qquad\qquad\quad (4.27) \qquad\qquad\qquad (1.94) \qquad\qquad\qquad\qquad (2)$$

$$R^2 = 0.220, \quad N = 87.$$

The concentration variables are significant at the 0.07 and 0.03 levels, respectively. The concentration coefficient in equation (2) is identical to the value found by Greer and Rhoades in their most closely corresponding ($N = 80$, 1954 to 1971) regressions, implying a 1 percentage point increase in annual labor productivity growth as the four-firm concentration ratio rises from 20 to 80.

The picture changes when we introduce two research and development variables—*PRODRD*, measuring 1974 product R & D as a percentage of sales, and *PROCRD*, measuring 1974 internal process-oriented R & D as a percentage of sales:

$$\Delta LP_{73-78} = 0.03 + 0.320^{**}\ \Delta GK_{73-78} + 0.0074\ CR4 + 0.277^*\ PRODRD$$
$$\qquad\qquad\quad (2.91) \qquad\qquad\qquad (0.46) \qquad\qquad (1.67)$$

$$\qquad + 0.450\ PROCRD; \qquad\qquad\qquad\qquad\qquad\qquad (3)$$
$$\qquad\quad (0.88)$$

$$R^2 = 0.168;$$

$$\Delta LP_{64-78} = 0.59 + 0.466^{**}\ \Delta GK_{64-78} + 0.0053\ CR4 + 0.200^*\ PRODRD$$
$$\qquad\qquad\quad (4.35) \qquad\qquad\qquad (0.55) \qquad\qquad (2.02)$$

$$\qquad + 0.476\ PROCRD; \qquad\qquad\qquad\qquad\qquad\qquad (4)$$
$$\qquad\quad (1.54)$$

$$R^2 = 0.292.$$

In both cases, unlike the Greer-Rhoades results, the concentration variables are far from significant.[6] Splitting the two samples into durable and nondurable goods subsets provided no reinforcement for the findings of Sveikauskas and Sveikauskas.[7] For both subsets, concentration had positive coefficients in all regressions, but had less explanatory power and was never significant when R & D was also taken into account. If anything, the positive effect was stronger for nondurables than for durables.

13.3 Interpretation

Underlying our results is a complex set of relationships between R & D and concentration. For $CR4$ and product R & D as a percentage of sales, the zero-order correlation is $+0.451$; between $CR4$ and $PROCRD$, it is $+0.207$. Both correlations are significantly different from zero at the 0.05 level in a one-tail test.[8] It would appear that concentration leads to greater R & D intensity, which in turn leads to faster measured productivity growth.

What remains to be clarified is whether the tendency for concentrated industries to do relatively more R & D is the result of greater appropriability, richer technological opportunity, or some third factor. Insight into this question is provided by an analysis of LB sample R & D spending in 236 manufacturing industry categories, usually defined at the four- or three-digit level. The concentration ratios $CR4$ are identically measured, except less aggregated than in the previous analysis. The dependent R & D variable TRD is total company-financed R & D (i.e., product plus process) as a percentage of performing business units' sales. The simple correlation between these variables is $+0.347$ ($t = 5.65$), that is, within the range of the more aggregated product and process R & D-$CR4$ correlations. When dummy variables associated with seven specified "technological opportunity" classes are added (for electronics, other electrical technologies, organic chemicals, other chemicals, metallurgical, mechanical, and "traditional" industries), the resulting multiple regression is

$$TRD = [7 \text{ intercept terms}] + 0.018^{**} \ CR4;$$
$$(4.34) \tag{5}$$

$$R^2 = 0.441, \quad N = 236.$$

Inclusion of the technological opportunity dummies raises R^2 from 0.120 to 0.441, with $F = 21.8$. The concentration variable continues to be positive and highly significant, suggesting that greater appropriability of payoffs does lead to more intensive R & D effort.

A final complication is the possible presence of simultaneity bias. Because interindustry differences in technological opportunity tend to be fairly stable over time, industries with high R & D/sales ratios in 1974 tended to have high R & D/sales ratios also in earlier years. Intensive prior R & D, and especially product R & D, may in turn have led to relatively high 1972 seller concentration by cementing strong patent positions or, under some variant of Gibrat's law [4, pp. 148–149], increasing the variability of market shares.[9] If this were true, one might expect to see stronger correlations between concentration and R & D/sales ratios in the industry clusters enjoying the richest technological opportunity. Yet when regression (5) is reestimated for each opportunity class separately, positive and significant TRD-concentration correlations emerge only in the traditional and mechanical groups, which are characterized by below-average concentration, R & D/sales ratios either below the all-industry average or (for the mechanical technology industries) only slightly above it, and less absolute variability of R & D/sales ratios than the rich-opportunity groups. Thus, although one cannot be certain, it appears that the advantages a high market share confers in appropriating R & D benefits provide the most likely explanation of the observed R & D-concentration associations.

Notes

This research was supported under National Science Foundation grant PRA-7826526. Use is made of data collected under the FTC's line of business program. FTC staff have determined that individual company data are not disclosed. The conclusions are the author's and not necessarily those of the Commission. The author is grateful to Bruce Meyer and Kevin Bespolka for research assistance.

1. For details of the linking and other procedures, see [7].

2. On the difficulty of appropriating benefits through licensing, see McGee [3].

3. The measurements here generally followed, but were not in all cases identical to, those of Weiss [9].

4. Greer and Rhoades analyzed the seventeen-year 1954 to 1971 interval with manufacturing industry data at a similar level of aggregation.

5. ΔGK here performs roughly the same functions as the industry growth and (static) capital/output variables used by Greer and Rhoades but is more consistent with production function theory. Including it on the right-hand side is an alternative to the total factor productivity approach taken by S & S.

6. As elaborated in [5], the R & D results are somewhat different when a subset of fifty-one industry groups with particularly comprehensive output value price deflators is analyzed. Then $PRODRD$ turns insignificant and $PROCRD$ becomes significant ($t = 1.78$) in the 1973 to 1978 analysis. For that subset, $CR4$ is even less powerful, with $t = 0.24$.

7. The S & S research and development data were drawn from the 1971 Survey of Occupational Employment, with appreciable sampling errors for individual industry categories, especially in the smaller industries. The Greer-Rhoades R & D data were extrapolated from two-digit spending data to more narrowly defined industries, introducing other measurement error problems. The LB data are uniquely well suited for studying differences between narrowly defined industries.

8. Consistent with the earlier quotation from [4], a variable measuring used R & D embodied in capital goods and materials purchased from other industries as a percentage of using industry sales was uncorrelated with concentration: $r = +0.031$. Thus unconcentrated industries draw technology "off the shelf" as readily as concentrated industries.

9. See, e.g., Levin and Reiss [2].

References

1. Greer, Douglas F., and Stephen A. Rhoades. Concentration and Productivity Changes in the Long and Short Run. *Southern Economic Journal* (October 1976): 1031–1044.

2. Levin, Richard C., and Peter C. Reiss. Tests of a Schumpeterian Model of R & D and Market Structure. Paper presented at a National Bureau of Economic Research conference on R & D, Patents, and Productivity, October 1981.

3. McGee, John S. Patent Exploitation: Some Economic and Legal Problems. *Journal of Law and Economics* (October 1966): 135–162.

4. Scherer, F. M. *Industrial Market Structure and Economic Performance.* 2nd ed. Boston: Houghton Mifflin, 1980.

5. Scherer, F. M. Inter-Industry Technology Flows and Productivity Growth. *Review of Economics and Statistics* (November 1982): 626–634.

6. Scherer, F. M. Demand-Pull and Technological Invention: Schmookler Revisited. *Journal of Industrial Economics* (March 1982): 225–238.

7. Scherer, F. M. Using Linked Patent and R & D Data to Measure Inter-Industry Technology Flows. Paper presented at a National Bureau of Economic Research conference on R & D, Patents, and Productivity, October 1981.

8. Sveikauskas, Catherine D., and Leo Sveikauskas. Industry Characteristics and Productivity Growth. *Southern Economic Journal* (January 1982): 769–774.

9. Weiss, Leonard W. Corrected Concentration Ratios in Manufacturing—1972. Manuscript, Federal Trade Commission, 1981.

10. U.S. Bureau of Labor Statistics. Bulletin 2018. *Time Series Data for Input Output Industries.* Washington, D.C., March 1979.

11. U.S. Federal Trade Commission. *Statistical Report: Annual Line of Business Survey, 1974.* Washington, D.C., September 1981.

IV THE PROBLEM OF DECLINING PRODUCTIVITY GROWTH

When I first became interested in Schumpeter's conjectures and during the first decade of my academic career, technological innovation was a booming field. Industrial R & D activity was growing briskly, and so, barring occasional recessions, was productivity. Schumpeter knew there was a link, but his views penetrated the main stream of economics only slowly. The shot marking the emergence of a wider revolution was Robert Solow's 1957 article showing that only about 12.5 percent of the great increase in output per worker hour between 1909 and 1949 was attributable to more intense use of capital, conventionally measured. Most of the increase, he concluded, was due to "technical change." Economists began in increasing numbers to study technical change and one of its presumed prime movers, research and development, to understand better how our material prosperity had grown so much.

The 1970s saw a sea change. First slowly and then at a distressing rate, the growth of productivity declined both in the United States and abroad. What went wrong? Economists were not short on explanations: the 1973 oil shock, demographic shifts, government regulation, stop-and-go economic policies, and much else. All no doubt played a part. What interested me particularly, however, was the Schumpeterian factor. From the base created by our Harvard case studies during the late 1950s, I continued to follow developments in many industries closely, and I was beginning to discern a distinct slowdown in the pace of technological advance for an appreciable subset. Also, in 1970 the growth of real company-financed R & D abruptly stopped, resuming its growth later only at a slower rate. Even more strikingly, the number of patents issued to U.S. corporations, which had been growing at a 4.3 percent annual rate in the 1950s and 1960s, peaked in 1971 and then dropped 27 percent by 1978. Were we entering one of the long technological stagnation periods hypothesized by Schumpeter in his 1939 book on business cycles? An invitation by Northwestern's Arts and Sciences college dean to contribute an article for a new alumni magazine allowed me to speculate on these questions. The result is the selection appearing as chapter 14, stripped somewhat of its pictorial adornment.

The growth of R & D had slowed; so had productivity growth. Was there a connection, and if so, how large? It seems a straightforward question, but economists had no fully satisfactory answers. The problem was, much of the time we are forced to content ourselves with the scraps of data thrown to us by government statistical agencies, company financial reports, and the like. And for exploring the R & D-productivity growth nexus, the data simply weren't right. We had long known that three-fourths of industrial R & D was devoted to developing or improving products sold to others; only about a fourth was internal process (i.e., cost-reducing) R & D. There was reason to believe that much of the benefit from product R & D was captured not by the industry performing the R & D but by the industry(ies) buying the improved product. Enter Jacob Schmookler's notion (1966, ch. 8) of a matrix tracing inventions from industries of origin to industries of use. The idea had from the beginning intrigued me, but it seemed too difficult to implement. The availability of R & D data finely segmented by origin lines of business eased the difficulty somewhat, and the remaining effort began to look worth while, given the need for good data on R & D traced to industries of use if we were to estimate accurately how R & D affects productivity growth.

Chapter 15 represents the culmination of that effort. It suggests that R & D is very important indeed to productivity growth. Moving from one standard deviation below the mean in terms of used R & D to one standard deviation above the mean is found to raise an industry's annual growth in output per work hour by one to two percentage points, depending on the data sample analyzed. Chapter 16 uses these estimates to address the question of how the slowdown in R & D spending affected the U.S. economy's productivity growth during the late 1970s. My estimate, subject of course to both statistical and conceptual measurement inaccuracies, lies in the range of 0.2 to 0.4 percentage points per annum.

My work does not resolve whether the slowdown in R & D growth resulted from a depletion of technological opportunities or some other cause (such as declining R & D profitability stemming from intensified imitative competition either at home or from abroad). As the geometric analysis in chapter 16 shows, one can have a stagnation of opportunities but observe (as in chapter 15's "wrong lag" test) no decline in the measured *marginal* social return on R & D investment.

Despite the sparse evidence, I am persuaded that we have run into a period of diminished technological opportunity, at least in many fields. I am also optimistic, from observing recent scientific advances, that the situation will reverse some time during the 1980s. But for the longer run, my optimism fades. Consider the implications of equation (4) from chapter 15, abridged here:

$$\Delta LP = \lambda + \left(\frac{\partial Q}{\partial R}\right)\left(\frac{RE}{Q}\right) + \cdots.$$

ΔLP is the annual rate of labor productivity growth, $\partial Q/\partial R$ is the marginal return on R & D capital, and RE is undepreciated annual research effort. Price's work (1963, ch. 1) indicates that for nearly three centuries, scientific and engineering effort (approximated by RE) has been increasing at an average rate of roughly 4 to 5 percent per year. Labor productivity ΔLP has been rising at a long-term rate of less than 2 percent per year. Is there a law of nature embedded in equation (4), or some formulation accounting for average as well as marginal effects, that says we must increase R & D effort at 4 to 5 percent per annum to continue raising output per work hour at 2 percent? If there is, we are in trouble, for as Price warned (1963, p. 19), with a continuation of historical growth trends over another century, "we should have two scientists for every man, woman, child, and dog in the population." If progress is to continue as it has in the past, we shall have to change the formula, that is, by finding ways to increase the productivity of R & D in generating productivity growth. Among the prospects on which economists have some specialized knowledge, the most likely option for improvement entails increasing the international division of R & D labor. It is hard on the national ego to accept that one cannot be at the forefront of every major technology, but acceptance may be necessary—soon. For the longer run, if we are to sustain the rate of progress, breakthroughs enhancing the productivity of R & D will have to come from science itself.

References

Price, Derek J. de Solla. *Little Science, Big Science.* New York: Columbia University Press, 1963.

Schmookler, Jacob. *Invention and Economic Growth.* Cambridge: Harvard University Press, 1966.

Schumpeter, Joseph A. *Business Cycles.* New York: McGraw-Hill, 1939.

Solow, Robert. Technical Change and the Aggregate Production Function. *Review of Economics and Statistics* (August 1957): 312–320.

14 Technological Maturity and Waning Economic Growth

America in recent years has experienced an unusual spate of economic woes. Price inflation approaching double-digit rates and nagging unemployment are the prime visible manifestations. Much of our inflation ailment, it is widely recognized, reflects an overabundance of money chasing a limited supply of goods and services. Yet the problem, contrary to what you might hear in the more southerly precincts of Chicago, is not just a matter of money. Real disposable income per capita—a measure of the goods and services people can consume—has grown unusually slowly during the 1970s. The inflationary process comes in part from a struggle among diverse groups for a bigger share of the goods-and-services pie. When the pie is growing rapidly, people tend to be relatively content with their lot, but when it grows slowly, they struggle more vigorously to increase their share. If the money-income gains they achieve are not matched by an expanded supply of goods and services, inflation follows.

How large the supply of goods and services is depends on how many people are working and on productivity, that is, on output per worker. Thanks to technological advances, the use of more capital equipment, and better education of the work force, real output per hour of work in the United States has increased by somewhere between 1.5 and 2.0 percent per year from 1909 to 1976. Productivity growth at this rate means that the average worker's output of goods and services doubles every forty years, with average hours of work being held constant. Some of these gains are taken in the form of increased leisure. Yet when this process continues, as it apparently has for two centuries in the so-called industrialized nations, it leads to repeated doubling and redoubling of output. The result has been a radical upgrading of living standards.

Here, however, my plot thickens. Something strange has been happening during the past decade. From 1950 to 1968, real output per hour of work in the private nonfarm economy rose fairly steadily at about 2.6 percent per year. Since 1968 the rate of increase has dropped to 1.4 percent (figure 14.1). The deviation from the trend is both striking and, at least in recent history, unprecedented. If it continues, Americans' demands for a larger goods-and-services pie will be increasingly difficult to satisfy and, among other things, an important source of inflationary pressure will persist.

The reasons for this decline have been the subject of considerable

Source: *Arts and Sciences* 1 (Fall 1978): 7–11.

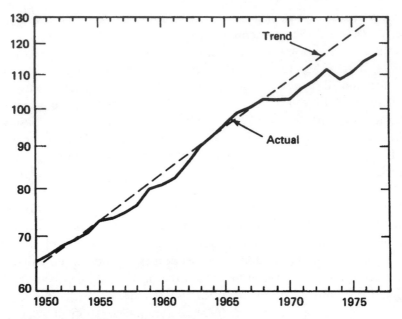

Figure 14.1
Productivity in the private nonfarm business economy

inquiry. Last January's annual report of the President's Council of Economic Advisers listed several possibilities: depressed business conditions, the discouraging effect of economic instability and high energy costs on productive investment, a gradual movement toward a younger and less experienced work force, and the cost of complying with expanding government regulations concerning pollution, health, and safety. All undoubtedly have some relevance. The council paid no explicit attention to what historically has been the most important single wellspring of productivity growth: the rate of technological innovation. This omission may not be surprising, for economists are reluctant to confront phenomena they understand poorly and can't readily measure. Yet the implications of a substantial change in the rate of technological innovation are so important that I am going to rush in where my wiser brethren fear to tread.

Technological innovation affects productivity (i.e., output per worker) both directly and indirectly. The most direct effects come from *process innovations:* new and improved production methods and equipment, cheaper or more easily worked raw materials, more efficient methods of transportation and communication, and the like. Process innovations permit *more* of any given output to be produced by the average worker. *Product innovations*—television, for example, or jet travel, or convenience foods, or polio vaccines—change the total mix of goods and services produced, simply because they are new. They transform the output component of our output-per-worker indexes. Actually measuring *how* output is increased by the appearance of new and improved consumer goods is very difficult. In consequence, existing indexes of productivity tend to underestimate the real growth of economic well-being when technological innovation occurs.

Even more difficult to measure are the indirect effects. Only recently, for example, has it become clear that the United States' greatest success as an exporter of manufactured products has come in just those product lines in which U.S. enterprises have been vigorous technological innovators. Lagging innovation therefore means fewer and less attractive exports, a relative decline in the dollar's value, and a commensurately larger sacrifice of domestic goods and services to buy oil, coffee, tourist services, and Datsuns from other lands.

Joseph A. Schumpeter, the late Harvard economist, argued that fifty- to sixty-year-long cycles in business activity (first observed by Russian statistician N. D. Kondratieff) occurred because major technological innovations tend to appear in clusters. These clustered innovations—so Schumpeter said— stimulate waves of primary and secondary investment and then a stream of follow-on innovations with further investment that drive the economy toward peaks of business prosperity. Then, as the pace of improvement innovation slackens, the growth of economic activity peters out until another cluster of major innovations materializes and triggers a new long cycle. Writing in the 1930s, Schumpeter identified three long cycles in the history of modern industrialized nations—one beginning in the 1780s associated with the Industrial Revolution; one beginning in the 1840s linked to improvements in transportation, especially the railroad; and one beginning in the 1890s propelled by the spread of electrical power, telephony, and the automobile.

Whether or not cyclical movements of the Kondratieff-Schumpeter sort actually occurred is much debated by economists. That need not detain us; my argument does not require the assumption that history repeats itself in regular cycles. What I propose is merely this: that from the 1940s into the late 1960s there was a distinct surge of economic activity very much *like* a Kondratieff-Schumpeter upswing (and perhaps even the first true one ever!). Thereafter, although the evidence is far from complete, the United States entered a period that has all the earmarks of a Kondratieff-Schumpeter downswing.

World War II was followed in the United States by an extraordinary burst of technological innovation. At least three significant phenomena help explain the clustering that took place. First, although depressed business conditions discouraged bold innovative ventures during the 1930s, the stock of basic scientific knowledge continued to accumulate. Second, wartime savings poured into the postwar market to satisfy pent-up demands for consumer goods, creating, among other things, a propitious environment for the sale of new products and for investments in new production processes. Third and perhaps most important, the wartime success of air power, electronics, military medicine, and the atomic-bomb effort demonstrated strikingly how scientific knowledge could be harnessed on a broad front to solve practical problems. Formally organized programs of research and development, once the province of a relatively few business enterprises, proliferated. By 1958, 350 of the 378 manufacturing corporations with 5,000 or more employees supported organized research and development. The result was an outpouring of industrial innovations for a wide array of postwar defense and civilian applications.

Major innovations usually lead to a period of rapidly growing sales attended by heavy investment in plant and equipment. Improvement work follows. Products are made more attractive, effective, and easier to produce; the bugs are worked out of production processes. These improvements may prolong the period of sales growth and investment, but sooner or later the most attractive technological possibilities have been thoroughly worked over, the innovation's benefits are widely diffused, growth slackens, and a stage of relative maturity commences. In short, the surge of economic activity accompanying technological innovation does not last indefinitely.

From two decades as an observer of research and development economics, I have the distinct impression that most of the industries leading the postwar technological boom have entered a maturity phase. It is, of course, very difficult to be confident about such generalizations. Table 14.1 provides a selective supporting overview. It classifies major industries that exhibited marked postwar technological virtuosity into three categories of maturity. For some of these classifications there is solid support.

Table 14.1
Industry Maturity: A Tentative Classification

Technologically Mature or Approaching Maturity

Hybrid seeds	Jet-propelled aircraft
Chemical herbicides and pesticides	Rocket-propelled, inertially guided military and space vehicles
Pharmaceuticals	
Plastic resins	Nuclear power
Synthetic organic fibers	Numerically controlled machine tools
Synthetic fertilizers	Automatic mining equipment
Instant photography	Coaxial and microwave message transmission
Electrostatic copying machines	
Television	Digital electronic computers
High-fidelity sound systems	
Radar detection and ranging	

Still Rapidly Evolving

Semiconductors, integrated circuits, and derivative products, including solar converters	Methods of medical diagnosis
	Electronic typewriters and typesetters

Potential Breakthrough Areas

Molecularly engineered pharmaceuticals	Energy from thermonuclear fusion
Hormonal insecticides	Optical-fiber message transmission
Asexual plant reproduction	

Beginning in the late 1950s, there was a definite decline in the number of new pharmaceutical-chemical entities introduced both in the United States and abroad. A falling rate of productivity growth in many areas of agriculture has been documented by a National Academy of Sciences committee, which concluded that "no major scientific breakthrough comparable with hybrid corn or DDT can reasonably be predicted for the next one or two decades."

Disagreement about other classifications might readily be forthcoming. For example, should the computer industry—which is only now introducing machines based preponderantly on large-scale integrated microcircuits, and which surely has two or three more generations of significant technical advances in the offing—be consigned to the "approaching maturity" stage? In virtually all of the industries improvements continue to be made. President Carter would no doubt affirm that there are buyers—the Saudi Arabians, among others—who consider the F-15 (a fifth-generation jet fighter) appreciably better than the same manufacturer's F-4. It is also true that achieving the extra increments of technological performance that differentiate the F-15 from the F-4, or the Trinitron color-television tube from earlier models, can devour vast amounts of R & D money, often as much as the cost of the original basic innovation.

Yet my central premise remains: the F-4 was a much bigger leap relative to the subsonic F-85 or F-86 than the F-15 was relative to the F-4; the first RCA dot-sequential color-television tube was a much bigger advance relative to black-and-white technology than the Trinitron was relative to sixties-vintage color tubes. And more generally, it appears to me that many more industries belong in the "mature or approaching maturity" category than those whose technologies are still in the phases of early dynamic evolution.

These judgments are qualitative and impressionistic, but they are consistent with indirect quantitative evidence. Between 1957 and 1968 the number of scientists and engineers employed by American industry in R & D grew each year by an average of 4.5 percent. From 1968 to 1975 there was a *decline* averaging 0.9 percent per year. Much of this decline was associated with cutbacks in government-sponsored R & D programs, but until 1977 (when a resurgence apparently took place) real growth of R & D expenditures in the private sector also stagnated.

From the early 1950s to the late 1960s, the number of U.S. invention patents issued to domestic corporations rose by about 4.3 percent per year. With a lag of about three years between invention and the issuance of a patent, the series peaked in 1971 and declined 20 percent by 1976. In 1966, 45 percent of industrial corporations' expenditures for R & D went for *new* products (as contrasted to the improvement of existing products or the development of production processes). The comparable McGraw-Hill survey for 1978 shows only 33 percent of such funds going to new product development. And erstwhile technological pioneers like RCA and DuPont have openly announced that they have made sharp cuts in breakthrough-oriented R & D because the prospective payoffs are too small and speculative.

If I infer correctly that the surge of postwar innovation has entered a phase of maturity, what are the broader economic implications? It doesn't necessarily follow that productivity and real economic growth should stagnate, for as I have said, abundant opportunities for improvement innovations remain. We are a considerable distance from utilizing fully the technology already in hand. Average productivity in agriculture is well below what is technically feasible; the manufacturing industries have not yet taken full advantage of numerically controlled machine tools and computerized process control; and only 61 percent of U.S. households had color-television sets in 1974.

Nevertheless, three pessimistic observations are warranted. First, the last increments in the improvement and diffusion of an innovation seem to come with much greater difficulty than the early increments. If so, one cannot expect the productivity benefits from further diffusion of innovations to be as large as they were in the initial, highly dynamic stages. Second, the United States has been nearer the technological frontier in most industrial fields than other nations. Thus it may experience greater difficulty in sustaining continued productivity growth through improvements and diffusion than other nations do—nations like Japan, France, Korea, and Brazil which began postwar development from a position of inferiority. Third, as Schumpeter argued, new capital investment may be stimulated and entrepreneurial verve instilled much more intensely in a period of rapid widespread pioneering technological innovation than during phases of approaching or actual maturity. About this last potential link, economists know very little. Yet it could be extremely important, explaining at least in part (along with capital market problems) the recent stagnation of capital investment in the United States.

You will be pleased to know that there is an appreciable probability I am wrong in this gloomy perspective. But what if I am not? What might be done about the maturity problem? My medicine bag, I must confess, is not well stocked. Perhaps the most important thing is to work toward understanding the phenomenon better, for otherwise we are apt to take ill-conceived actions. If there is any validity to my analysis, the makers of our macroeconomic policies may be prescribing cures for the wrong diseases.

Acceptance of the maturity hypothesis would mean, among other things, that short-run income stabilization and other policies of the government should assume an environment in which rapid real economic growth will be difficult to sustain. The government would then have to lower its expectations, and it would somehow have to persuade private claimants in the struggle over income distribution to do the same. Obviously, there should also be a search for policies that restore technological dynamism. One's natural inclination is to advocate government tax credits and subsidies in order to stimulate industrial R & D. These might work in selected instances, but across-the-board success is unlikely. When the well is drying up, investing in high-speed buckets is not apt to provide a lasting solution. Rather, restoring the stock of attractive new basic scientific and technological concepts is much more important.

On that matter, we in the United States appear to be doing precisely the wrong things. Industrial outlays for basic research barely increased in current dollar terms between 1968 and 1974; in inflation-adjusted terms, they *decreased* by about a fourth. The growth of university enrollments is gradually ceasing, and that, in combination with the clogging of faculties by middle-aged tenured members, means relatively few promising openings for scientists in the age bracket that has historically yielded a disproportionate fraction of significant new ideas. A generation of America's best and brightest is being diverted from science into law, medicine, management, and public administration—careers that, for all their virtues, do little to replenish the stock of technological possibilities. In these days of taxpayer revolt, one is loath to suggest additional government spending. But a generous program of multiyear research fellowships for promising young physical and biological scientists seems critically needed.

The question remains, will the cycle reverse, leading to a renewed Kondratieff-Schumpeter upturn? Here our ability to understand and forecast is even more meager. I see no fundamental reason why there cannot be a reversal during the next decade or two. But on the more distant horizon further dark clouds loom. As I indicated earlier, real output per hour of work in industrialized nations has grown by something like 1.5 to 2.0 percent per year for at least a century. The scientific and technological knowledge that in large measure propelled those increases has been generated through sustained growth of roughly 4.5 percent per year in the number of scientists and engineers. The latter growth rate cannot continue, for as Derek de Solla Price pointed out in 1963 (five years before the decline in R & D set in), if that rate were to continue for another century, we would have "two scientists for every man, woman, child, and dog in the population."

Is it possible that there is a law of nature requiring a considerably higher technological-effort rate of growth to sustain a given rate of growth in productivity? One can concoct persuasive theoretical rationales for such a link, and the historical record is suggestive, though far from conclusive. The verdict is not in, but it is at least high time to summon an able jury. Should such a law exist, the golden age of growing material prosperity that followed the Industrial Revolution may turn out to be shortlived.

A conceivable escape might come from innovations that greatly enhance the creativity and productivity of the R & D workers who in turn produce further innovations—for example, as a result of inevitable advances in our understanding of the physiology and chemistry of human thought processes. That cannot be ruled out. The only thing of which I am certain is that the future holds important surprises for those who study the relationships between technology and economic growth.

Notes

Before joining the CAS Economics Department in 1976, Professor Scherer was Chief Economist at the Federal Trade Commission. His major interest is industrial economics. Among his books are *Industrial Market Structure and Economic Performance* [1970] *and The Economics of Multi-Plant Operation: An International Comparisons Study* [1975].

15 Interindustry Technology Flows and Productivity Growth

This paper exploits a new, uniquely rich data source to analyze the relationships between research and development (R & D) and productivity growth. It was motivated by recognition (confirmed through new data) that three-fourths of all U.S. industrial R & D is concerned with creating new or improved externally sold products, as distinguished from the development of production processes used internally by the R & D-performing enterprise. Internal process work performed in industry i should lead directly to measured productivity growth in that industry. But for product R & D, the linkage is more complex. Under imperfectly monopolistic pricing and, a fortiori, vigorous competition, much of the benefit from industry i's superior new products will be passed on to buyers (e.g., in industry j). This tendency is likely to be mirrored in the distribution of measured productivity growth as price deflators systematically underestimate the hedonic value of new products and hence undervalue the inputs used by an innovating industry's customers.[1]

15.1 The R & D Flow and Productivity Data

To trace R & D from the industries where it was performed to the industries where its main productivity impacts occur, a novel data set was created. The starting point was the Federal Trade Commission's 1974 line of business (LB) survey, which obtained from 443 large U.S. corporations data on company-financed and contract (mostly federal) R & D expenditures broken down into 262 manufacturing and fourteen nonmanufacturing LBs.[2] Linked to the R & D outlays were 15,112 appropriately lagged U.S. invention patents. Each patent was individually examined to determine the industry of origin (on the basis of which the R & D link was effected), the industry(ies) where use was anticipated, and whether the invention involved an internal process or externally sold product, among other things. The linked R & D, inflated by origin industry sampling ratios, was then distributed through a "technology flows" matrix from industries of origin to as many as 287 industries of use (including personal consumption).[3] R & D dollars for inventions of widespread use were allocated in proportion to sales of the origin industry to using industries, as ascertained

Source: Reprinted from *The Review of Economics and Statistics* 64 (November 1982): 627–634. Published for Harvard University by the North-Holland Publishing Company. Copyright, 1982, by the President and Fellows of Harvard College.

from 1972 U.S. input-output tables (modified, among other things, to integrate current and capital accounts transactions). Row sums for the technology flows matrix measured R & D by industry of origin, column sums R & D by industry of use, and diagonal elements corresponded to pure process R & D.

To minimize the danger of spurious inferences despite well-known measurement difficulties, three quite differently compiled productivity data sets were analyzed. One, used in several earlier R & D studies, is the set of two-digit manufacturing industry productivity indexes originally compiled by John Kendrick and updated by Kendrick and Grossman.[4] A second is the Bureau of Labor Statistics series published annually under the title, *Productivity Indexes for Selected Industries.* Its indexes of output per labor hour are based primarily on physical output quantities with fixed period (usually employment) weights. As such, the series (hereafter BLSPQ) is limited in coverage but is believed to be of particularly high quality. Matching productivity, R & D, and capital stock indexes were available for thirty-seven manufacturing industries originating 29 percent of total 1974 manufacturing value added.[5] The third data set comes from a new Bureau of Labor Statistics series organized according to input-output industry definitions (for which reason it will be called the BLSIO series).[6] It includes eighty-one manufacturing branches originating 94 percent of 1973 manufacturing sector output plus six nonmanufacturing observations—agriculture, crude oil and gas production, air transport, communications, and the combined electric-gas-sanitary utilities sector. Other sectors were excluded because of inadequate data matches or patently deficient productivity measurements. The BLSIO productivity indexes are compiled by taking total industry output value, deflating it by the most closely corresponding industry price indexes, and dividing the resulting real output estimates by total employee hours.

15.2 Model Structure

The theory underlying the analysis is conventional. We assume a production function of the Cobb-Douglas variety:

$$Q_{it} = \phi e^{\lambda t} R_{it}^{\delta} K_{it}^{\alpha} L_{it}^{\beta} M_{it}^{\gamma} \varepsilon_{it}, \tag{1}$$

where Q_{it} is the output of the ith industry in period t, R measures the

R & D capital stock, K is the plant and equipment capital stock, L is labor input, M is materials usage, λ is an exogenous shift variable, and ε is an error term. Since most of the productivity data are in terms of output per unit of labor, we can, assuming that $\alpha + \beta + \gamma = 1$ and suppressing subscripts, write

$$\left(\frac{Q}{L}\right) = \phi e^{\lambda t} R^{\delta} \left(\frac{K}{L}\right)^{\alpha} \left(\frac{M}{L}\right)^{\gamma} \varepsilon. \tag{2}$$

Taking logarithms and differentiating with respect to time, we obtain

$$\Delta LP = \lambda + \delta \Delta R + \alpha \Delta \left(\frac{K}{L}\right) + \gamma \Delta \left(\frac{M}{L}\right) + \ln \varepsilon, \tag{3}$$

where ΔR is the percentage change in the R & D stock (i.e., $100(\dot{R}/R)$), ΔLP is the percentage change in labor productivity, and the other Δ variables are similarly defined. For the R & D variable, we have no stock data, but only 1974 expenditures. Noting that $\delta = (\partial Q/\partial R)(R/Q)$, Terleckyj (1974) has shown that the R & D term can be rewritten $(\partial Q/\partial R)$ $(\dot{R}/Q)$, where the first ratio is the marginal product of R & D, which can be estimated as a regression coefficient. On the further assumption that the social value of the R & D stock depreciates only slowly, $\dot{R}$ is approximated by the *flow* of R & D in a given time period (e.g., a single year) as in our data set.[7] Thus $\dot{R}/Q$ becomes the ratio of 1974 R & D expenditures RE to 1974 dollar output (or value added for the Kendrick and BLSPQ regressions). We therefore wish to estimate

$$\Delta LP = \lambda + \left(\frac{\partial Q}{\partial R}\right)\left(\frac{RE}{Q}\right) + \alpha \Delta \left(\frac{K}{L}\right) + \gamma \Delta \left(\frac{M}{L}\right) + \ln \varepsilon. \tag{4}$$

Since reliable data on $\Delta(M/L)$ are not available, γ could not be estimated, causing an omitted variable problem.

The availability of cross-sectional R & D data for only a single year poses a further challenge. We wish to estimate the impact of R & D on productivity growth and also to test whether the decline in productivity growth during the 1970s might have come in part from a decrease in the fecundity of R & D, for instance because the stock of promising technical opportunities became depleted or because new technologies of the early 1970s were less than optimally suited to the altered economic environment of the late 1970s. The impact of 1974 R & D on productivity can be expected to occur with a lag of at least several years.[8] Given data constraints and the need to minimize the effect of business cycle disturbances, the best approximation attainable to a correct lag was to measure productivity changes between 1973 and 1978, both business cycle peak years.[9] Thus annual labor productivity growth ΔLP is measured as $(100/5)$ $[\ln(Q/L)_{78} - \ln(Q/L)_{73}]$.

To test whether the marginal productivity of R & D declined, we employ what can be called a "wrong lag" hypothesis. The intensity of R & D performance by industries of origin has been quite stable over time. For fifteen broadly defined manufacturing industry groups on which comparable National Science Foundation data are available, the simple correlation between company-financed R & D/sales ratios is 0.98 for the years 1973 and 1963 and 0.90 for 1973 and 1958. Assuming without direct quantitative evidence that there has also been gross stability of R & D *use* patterns over time, the wrong lag hypothesis predicts that one will also observe a positive association between 1974 R & D flows and productivity growth during the 1960s. To be sure, there will be more mismeasurement of these wrong lag relationships, so the associations should be weaker than for a correctly specified lag relationship. Stronger associations in wrong lag regressions than in "correct lag" regressions can be interpreted as evidence of a breakdown in the ability of industrial R & D to drive productivity growth.

With this in mind, the principal wrong lag period was defined as 1964 to 1969. This five-year interval terminates with an end-of-the-year business cycle peak, maximizing comparability with the correct lag period.[10]

15.3 Two-Digit Manufacturing Group Results

The relationship between R & D and productivity growth in two-digit manufacturing industry groups, as measured by Kendrick and Grossman, has been examined by a number of scholars.[11] Table 15.1 presents a comparable analysis. Equations 1.1 through 1.4 take total factor productivity growth (ΔTFP) as the dependent variable. Two results stand out. First, for the long wrong lag period 1948 to 1966 emphasized in most prior studies, R & D variables have significant explanatory power. Of the two, R & D flowed through to industries of use (*USERD*) is more powerful than R & D classified by industry of origin (*ORGRD*). In a multiple regression with both variables (not shown), R^2 rises to 0.497 and *USERD*

Table 15.1
Two-digit manufacturing group regressions using Kendrick-Grossman Data ($N = 20$)

Regression number	Dependent variable measure	Period	Constant	R & D coefficients[a]		r^2
				ORGRD	USERD	
1.1	ΔTFP	1948–66	2.52	0.194[b] (2.24)		0.218
1.2	ΔTFP	1948–66	1.70		0.872[c] (3.79)	0.444
1.3	ΔTFP	1973–78	0.86	0.001 (0.01)		0.000
1.4	ΔTFP	1973–78	0.82		0.038 (0.07)	0.000
1.5	ΔLP	1948–66	2.54	0.190 (1.64)		0.130
1.6	ΔLP	1948–66	1.85		0.878[c] (2.64)	0.279
1.7	ΔLP	1964–69	1.75	0.210 (1.61)		0.126
1.8	ΔLP	1964–69	1.78		0.359 (0.83)	0.037

a. All R & D variables are divided by 1974 industry group value added; t-ratios are given in subscripted parentheses.
b. Statistically significant in one-tail test at the 0.05 level.
c. Statistically significant in one-tail test at the 0.01 level.

is dominant, whereas *ORGRD* falls to insignificance. Second, strong support emerges for the wrong lag hypothesis. Both variables lose their explanatory power for the 1973–78 period, with r^2 values indistinguishable from zero to three digits. This result, which parallels similar findings by Kendrick and Grossman (1980, pp. 109–111) and Terleckyj (1980), suggests that something went wrong with the linkages between R & D and productivity growth during the 1970s.

To facilitate comparison with later analyses using labor productivity ΔLP as the dependent variable, four additional regressions are presented in table 15.1. For 1948–66, the results are quite similar to their total factor productivity counterparts, except with somewhat lower r^2 values. Regressions 1.7 and 1.8 reveal a deterioration of the relationship when the shorter and more recent wrong lag period used in subsequent analyses is substituted. By 1973–78 (not explicitly reported) the labor productivity results are virtually identical to those of regressions 1.3 and 1.4. The r^2 values are 0.006 for *ORGRD* and 0.000 for *USERD*.

15.4 Disaggregated Data Results

We turn now to the disaggregated productivity data sets BLSIO and BLSPQ. Since one objective is to investigate the links between R & D and the productivity growth slump of the 1970s, it is useful to examine the slump's magnitude in the context of our samples. The BLSIO productivity data are based upon price index-deflated output value statistics. As such, they can be no more reliable than the deflators used. Before the productivity data set was compiled, underlying BLS reports were consulted to distinguish those BLSIO industries for which the price deflators were reasonably comprehensive from those for which they were not. This binary criterion had both a quantitative aspect (whether roughly half or more of industry output was covered by representative deflators) and a qualitative aspect (whether the deflators covered the industry's technologically advanced products). Failure to satisfy either criterion led to a negative judgment. Of course, other things can go wrong in measuring real output, but the BLSIO sample was divided through this analysis into two subsets —fifty-one industries with "comprehensive" deflators and thirty-six with "sparse" deflators. Simple averages of annual labor productivity growth indexes for the full BLSIO sample, its two subsets, and the BLSPQ sample are as follows:

	ΔLP 1964–69	ΔLP 1973–78	Drop
Full BLSIO sample	2.81%	2.03%	27.7%
Comprehensive deflator subset	2.53	1.93	23.5
Sparse deflator subset	3.21	2.18	32.2
BLSPQ sample	2.99	2.54	15.0

Although the BLSIO subsample means are not significantly different from one another for either period, there is at least a suggestion that measured productivity growth fell more in the 1970s, the weaker were the underlying data upon which the measurements rested.

Alternate Technology Flow Measures

Before we turn to the main results, certain further data choice hypotheses must be investigated. For one, it was predicted that R & D dollar measures would explain productivity growth better than raw invention patent counts. Second, R & D dollars flowed out to industries of use were expected to explain productivity growth better than R & D dollars assigned to industries of origin.[12] Third, in constructing "used" R & D indexes, a difficult conceptual problem had to be solved. When there is more than one industry of use, should the invention or its accompanying R & D dollars be treated as a public good, with use by industry j not diminishing the dollars or patents usable by industry k, or should they be handled as private goods, with industry of use values summing to equal origin industry values? Both concepts were implemented, the public goods assumption by letting the industry with the largest purchases have unit weight and normalizing all smaller using industries by the ratio of their purchases from the origin industry to the largest buyer's purchases.[13] Which concept is preferred, public or private goods, was left an open hypothesis. Fourth, for certain component inventions such as new large-scale integrated circuits, one might suppose that the main productivity benefits will accrue not, for example, to the computer manufacturers who buy them but to the computer users who buy the computers embodying the improved components. For all or part of twenty-two component-supplying industries, use vectors were computed incorporating such second-order flow relationships as an alternative to first-order technology flow indexes.

Table 15.2 presents a set of results on the basis of which three of these

Table 15.2
Simple correlations and partial regression coefficient t-ratios for selected technology flow variables, 1973–78; labor productivity growth rate as dependent variable

Variable and description	Simple r, BLSPQ sample, $N = 41$[a]	BLSIO sample, $N = 87$	
		Simple r	t-ratio with $\Delta(K/L)$
ORGRD: R&D by industry of origin	0.238	0.260[c]	2.61[c]
ORGPAT: patent count by industry of origin	0.181	0.161	1.78[b]
USERD1: R&D by industry of use, private goods, with second-order component flows	0.374[c]	0.223[b]	2.35[b]
USERD2: R&D by industry of use, private goods, without second-order component flows	0.385[c]	0.249[c]	2.60[c]
USEPUB1: R&D by industry of use, public goods assumption, with second-order component flows	0.247	0.160	1.92[b]
USEPAT1: Patent count by industry of use, private goods, with second-order component flows	0.238	0.130	1.38

a. Includes four nonmanufacturing industries.
b. Statistically significant in one-tail test at the 0.05 level.
c. Statistically significant in one-tail test at the 0.01 level.

hypotheses were resolved. Listed for six alternative technology flow indexes are simple correlations with 1973–78 productivity growth for both the BLSPQ and eighty-seven industry BLSIO sample, along with t-ratios for the technology flow variables in multiple regressions with a 1973–78 gross capital stock/labor ratio change variable also included.[14] We see that the patent count and public good R & D use variables are dominated by their private good R & D dollar counterparts.[15] Therefore patent count and public good assumption variables will be excluded from further analyses. In the table 15.2 regressions and others, the *USERD*2 variable (i.e., without second-order component flows) weakly but consistently outperformed *USERD*1. However, because the author's a priori conjectures strongly favored them, only variables incorporating second-order component flows will be used in subsequent analyses.[16]

Basic Regression Results

The relative strength of *ORGRD* vs. *USERD* variables in table 15.2 varies with the samples. This ambiguity persists in multiple regressions including both variables, although the relationships are blurred by multicollinearity. A more precise insight is obtained by focusing on the variables *USERD*1 (encompassing both internal process R & D and R & D "imported" through product purchases from other industries) and *PRODRD*, representing originating firms' R & D on products sold to others.[17] This split is implemented in the multiple regressions of table 15.3. Both the correct and wrong lag periods are covered for the BLSIO and BLSPQ samples.[18] The BLSIO sample is also subdivided into groups of industries with "comprehensive" output deflators (BLSIO:C) and "sparse" deflators (BLSIO:S).

Several points stand out. First, in sharp contrast to the results with aggregated Kendrick-Grossman data, there is no clear support for the wrong lag hypothesis.[19] For both full samples and one of the two BLSIO subsamples, R^2 values and R & D regression coefficient values are larger for the 1973–78 period than for the wrong lag 1964–69 period, and for exceptional BLSIO:C regressions, the differences are small. In all four 1973–78 regressions there is at least one significant R & D coefficient. It must follow that the 1970s productivity slump did not result from a deterioration of the marginal productivity $\partial Q/\partial R$ of industrial R & D, or errors of measurement rise sharply when the wrong lag hypothesis is tested.[20]

Table 15.3
PRODRD and *USERD*1 multiple regressions, BLSIO and BLSPQ samples

Regression number	Sample	Number of industries	Time period for dependent variable ΔLP	Constant	$\Delta(K/L)$	R&D variable coefficients		R^2
						PRODRD	*USERD*1	
3.1	BLSIO:A	87	1973–78	−0.142	0.347[c] (3.30)	0.289[b] (2.01)	0.742[b] (1.89)	0.193
3.2	BLSIO:A	87	1964–69	1.90	0.149[b] (2.01)	0.133 (1.05)	0.643[b] (1.84)	0.118
3.3	BLSIO:C	51	1973–78	−0.162	0.400[c] (2.90)	−0.182 (0.54)	1.039[c] (2.53)	0.241
3.4	BLSIO:C	51	1964–69	1.09	0.309[b] (2.27)	0.095 (0.35)	0.741[b] (2.06)	0.260
3.5	BLSIO:S	36	1973–78	0.084	0.310[b] (1.82)	0.431[b] (2.10)	0.096 (0.10)	0.197
3.6	BLSIO:S	36	1964–69	2.94	0.161 (1.52)	0.071 (0.39)	0.049 (0.06)	0.074
3.7	BLSPQ[a]	37	1973–78	−1.50	0.268[b] (2.05)	0.089 (0.46)	0.711[b] (2.03)	0.247
3.8	BLSPQ[a]	37	1964–69	2.43	−0.041 (0.30)	0.051 (0.34)	0.401 (1.42)	0.086

a. Four nonmanufacturing industries (coal mining, railroads, air transport, and telecommunications) are deleted owing to the lack of capital stock measures. Results for the sample including nonmanufacturing, but without capital/labor variables, are similar to those reported here.
b. Statistically significant in one-tail test at the 0.05 level.
c. Statistically significant in one-tail test at the 0.01 level.

In principle, one would not expect to find a significant relationship between *product* R & D and productivity growth unless there are rising price/cost margins associated with innovators' monopoly power and/or systematic mismeasurement. That negative expectation is confirmed for all but two of the regressions in table 15.3. Of the two exceptions, regression 3.5, for the industries with sparse price deflators, is the stronger. Its significant product R & D effect in turn dominates the *PRODRD* coefficient of full-sample regression 3.1, for when the subset of industries with comprehensive deflators is broken out (regression 3.3), the *PRODRD* coefficient becomes negative but insignificant.[21] The sparse deflator subset, it will be recalled, also experienced the sharpest average productivity growth rate drop in the 1970s. These subset results are difficult to reconcile in terms of either a simple measurement bias or monopoly pricing hypothesis. If, for instance, the private gains from product innovation were less well-measured in the turbulent 1970s than in the 1960s, one might expect the correct lag *PRODRD* relationship to be weaker, not stronger.[22] Still it is clear and important that for samples with reasonably well-measured productivity indexes, product R & D conforms to the prediction of having no significant productivity effect.

Even those regressions in table 15.3 with the greatest explanatory power (notably, those using the better-measured productivity indexes) exhibit considerable noise. Nothing like the r^2 of 0.44 obtained with aggregated Kendrick 1948–66 TFP data is obtained. One apparent contributor to the relatively low degree of variance explanation is measurement error associated with the shortness of the time periods over which productivity growth is analyzed. When annual productivity growth over the entire fourteen-year 1964–78 period is taken as the dependent variable, R^2 rises to 0.299 and 0.330 in the analogues of regressions 3.1 and 3.3 despite the inferior lag structure.[23] Evidently, both our dependent and independent variables suffer from considerable noise.

From equation (4), it can be seen that regression coefficients on the R & D variables can be interpreted as steady-state marginal returns on investment in research and development. From the *USERD1* coefficients in particular, the social returns during the 1970s appear to have been quite high: in the range of 70 to 104 percent (regressions 3.1, 3.3, and 3.7). These estimates could be biased downward because of our failure to depreciate R & D.[24] A bias in the opposite direction could intrude because, contrary to the steady-state growth assumption, company-financed R & D/sales ratios declined by about 14 percent between 1970 (whose innovations undoubtedly continued to influence 1973–78 productivity growth) and 1974. Returns trapped as monopoly rents in *PRODRD* may have added as much as 40 percent to the social return total, but on this, the measurement uncertainties are especially severe.

Additional Results

Certain additional results must be summarized more briefly. The R & D covered by *USERD1* includes both internally performed process work and technology "imported" across industry lines. *USERD1* can be decomposed into these two components, *PROCRD* and *OUTRD*. For the full BLSIO sample, the comprehensive deflator subsample, and the BLSPQ sample, the principal coefficient estimates for 1973–78 productivity growth, *t*-ratios (in parentheses), and increases in R^2 relative to the analogous table 15.3 regressions are as follows:

Sample	*PRODRD*	*PROCRD*	*OUTRD*	Change in R^2
BLSIO:A	0.321[a] (2.20)	0.368 (0.74)	1.472[a] (2.04)	0.014
BLSIO:C	−0.154 (0.44)	0.932 (1.60)	1.184[a] (1.71)	0.001
BLSPQ	0.076 (0.38)	0.648 (1.49)	0.874 (1.19)	0.002

a. Statistically significant in one-tail test at the 0.05 level.

The decomposition provides very little new explanatory power; even for the BLSIO:A regression, the incremental *F*-ratio is only 1.45. The estimates are also imprecise. Yet the decomposed coefficient values are both plausible and imply substantial social returns to both internal process R & D and R & D embodied in products purchased from other industries.

USERD1 can also be decomposed in another way—into capital goods R & D outlays and materials-oriented outlays. For the BLSIO sample and especially the comprehensive-deflator subset, this decomposition in 1973–78 productivity regressions led to R^2 increases of between 0.010 and 0.088, depending on the subsample and specification. The capital goods component was clearly the more powerful of the decomposed variables. However, in BLSPQ regressions, the change in R^2 from decomposing

*USERD*1 was minute. A nonlinear form of the BLSIO regression, in which used capital goods R & D levels interacted multiplicatively with new capital investment, yielded positive but weak support for the hypothesis that technological change is directly embodied in new capital goods investment.

Variables estimating the fraction of new investment devoted to meeting environmental pollution, health, and safety regulations were also introduced into BLSIO and BLSPQ regressions for 1973–78. A negative impact on productivity growth averaging between 0.19 and 0.27 percentage points per year was found. However, the regulatory impact coefficients were insignificant, with *t*-ratios of 1.43 or less. Still another variable, measuring used R & D originating from federal government contracts, had characteristically positive but insignificant coefficients.

15.5 Conclusions

An unusually rich new data set has been tapped to explore the relationships between R & D and productivity growth. Without doubt the most important finding is that with disaggregated data the wrong lag hypothesis is not supported: there is no clear indication that the productivity slump of the 1970s resulted from a decrease in the marginal productivity of R & D. Also important is the evidence of substantial returns to *used* R & D, that is, from internal process work and the purchase of R & D-embodying products but not (at least in industries with productivity indexes based on physical output or comprehensive price deflators) to the performance of product R & D. Given the fact that three-fourths of all industrial R & D is product oriented, studies that fail to distinguish between the origination and use of R & D may suffer from appreciable specification errors. Further research using improved R & D and (especially) productivity data is plainly needed, among other things, to clarify the mystery of why estimated R & D–productivity relationships differ for productivity data subsets of varying quality.

Notes

The underlying research was conducted under National Science Foundation Grant PRA-7826526. The author is grateful to numerous research assistants for help. Use is made of line of business data collected by the Federal Trade Commission. A review by FTC staff has determined that individual company data are not disclosed. The conclusions are the author's and not necessarily those of the FTC.

1. For an early recognition of the problem, see Gustafson (1962). For a detailed analysis see Griliches (1979).

2. On the importance of segregating the R & D data by line of business, see Sveikauskas (1981, pp. 278–279).

3. Details of the linking and technology flow procedures are described in Scherer (1981), which also includes an appendix with disaggregated R & D row and column sums.

4. See Kendrick and Grossman (1980). Extensions to 1978 were kindly provided by the authors.

5. Twenty-five observations consisted of one or two four-digit SIC industries. Ten were defined at or near the three-digit level and two at a level broader than three digits. Thus the degree of disaggregation is relatively high. Four nonmanufacturing industries were also included in some analyses, despite the lack of consistent capital stock measures.

6. The original productivity data and a discussion of methodology are found in U.S. Bureau of Labor Statistics (1979a). Nearly matching capital stock data are in U.S. Bureau of Labor Statistics (1979b). Both series were updated to 1978 in computer printouts kindly provided by BLS, although a special effort had to be made to extend the capital stock series.

7. If the R & D stock R decays at 100μ percent per year, the correctly specified coefficient estimate would (ignoring other independent variables) be

$$\frac{\widehat{\partial Q}}{\partial R} = \frac{\Sigma(RE/Q)\Delta LP - \Sigma(\mu R/Q)\Delta LP}{\Sigma(RE/Q)^2 - 2\Sigma(RE/Q)(\mu R/Q) + \Sigma(\mu R/Q)^2}$$

where all variables are centered about their means. Our estimate assuming no depreciation includes only the first numerator and denominator terms. The estimate is downward biased unless the Pearsonian correlation between RE/Q and $\mu R/Q$ is sizable—for example, with $\Sigma(RE/Q)^2$ and $\Sigma(\mu R/Q)^2$ of similar magnitude, in excess of $|0.5|$. A sizable correlation, indicating that R depreciates more rapidly in R & D-intensive industries, could be plausible if one is concerned with measuring the *private* returns to R & D. See, for example, Pakes and Schankerman (May 1979). It is much less plausible in assessing *social* gains that persist even after price competition has eliminated innovators' rents. The latter is our emphasis here. Hence, it seems probable that our inability to measure depreciation leads to downward biases in estimating $\partial Q/\partial R$. I am indebted to a referee for calling attention to this point.

8. See Ravenscraft and Scherer (1982), where the mean lag between R & D and performing firm profitability is found to be four to six years.

9. The peak actually occurred in 1979, although its exact timing is arguable. After January 1979, the industrial production series, which is most closely comparable to our sample coverage, was quite flat.

10. In the unusually unbroken growth period of the 1960s, 1964 was not a peak year. By the Federal Reserve Board index but not by the Wharton index, manufacturing capacity utilization levels in 1964 were similar to those of 1973. See Berndt and Morrison (1981, p. 51). Accepting a difference in initial-year business conditions for the wrong lag period was considered preferable to comparing intervals of unequal length.

11. See Kendrick (1973, pp. 140–143); Kendrick and Grossman (1980, pp. 102–111); Terleckyj (1974, 1980); and Mansfield (1980).

12. These two hypotheses were stated in the proposal dated September 1978 underlying this research.

13. For details, see Scherer (1981).

14. In these and all other regressions that follow, the BLSPQ technology flow variables are divided by 1974 value added, while the BLSIO variables are divided by 1974 gross output value.

15. The correlations for *USEPUB* are 0.028 to 0.051 higher than their private goods counterparts in *BLSPQ* regressions for 1964–69. *USEPAT1* also had a correlation 0.066 higher than *USERD1* in a 1964–69 BLSPQ regression for manufacturing alone, but the relationship reversed when four nonmanufacturing industries were added. These were the main departures from a prevailing pattern favoring private goods dollar-denominated variables.

16. The regressions in table 15.1 are also based upon second-order component flow *USERD* variables.

17. With the eighty-seven-industry BLSIO sample, the simple r between *ORGRD* and *USERD1* is 0.419. Between *USERD1* and *PRODRD* it is 0.222, and between *ORGRD* and *PRODRD* 0.968. The correlation between a variable measuring internal process R & D *PROCRD* and *ORGRD* is 0.514; between *USERD1* and *PROCRD* it is 0.849. All variables are deflated by 1974 gross output value.

18. If K_0 is the beginning capital stock (e.g., in December 1972), I is new investment (e.g., from 1973 through 1977), W is retirements over the same period, and D is depreciation, $\Delta(K/L)$ for the 1973–78 BLSIO regression is

$$\frac{100}{5}\left[\ln\left(\frac{K_{72}+I-W}{L_{78}}\right)-\ln\left(\frac{K_{72}}{L_{73}}\right)\right].$$

All capital stock variables are measured in constant 1972 dollars. Regressions with a *net* terminal capital stock measure $K_{72}+I-W-D$ had slightly less explanatory power. For the BLSPQ regressions, the ending stock is measured as K_0+I. That version of the variable also led to higher R^2 values in BLSIO regressions, presumably because I alone most closely approximates the changes in capital in which new technology is embodied.

19. The change in results does not appear to come from using different data sets. When the 81 BLSIO manufacturing industries were aggregated to twenty two-digit groups, the results were quite similar to those obtained using Kendrick-Grossman labor productivity data. Evidently, support for the wrong lag hypothesis stems mainly from some aggregation effect.

20. Contrast the findings of Griliches (1980, pp. 346–347), who aggregated BLSIO data for 1969–77 to 39 sectors.

21. The average value of *PRODRD* is 2.22 percent for the sparse-deflator subset of BLSIO compared to 0.74 for the comprehensive deflator subset. This is no coincidence. It is hard to maintain good price index coverage in industries with considerable product innovation. For both subsets, the *USERD1* index averages are identically 0.73.

22. However, if competition eroded innovators' profits with special rapidity in research-intensive industries during the 1970s, the high *PRODRD* coefficients observed here could materialize from an estimation bias. See note 7.

23. Because of capital/labor ratio data limitations, no regression analogous to 3.7 was run. However, the simple correlation between 1964–78 BLSPQ productivity growth and *USERD1* was 0.041 higher than for 1973–78. For *USERD2*, it was 0.067 higher.

24. See note 7. A further complication comes from the fact that the BLSIO and BLSPQ R & D variables have different denominators—gross output value and value added, respectively. The former is, on average, roughly twice the latter. Higher denominator values force regression coefficients upward. It is not totally clear a priori which denominator should be preferred. However, with BLSIO output measured in gross terms, the gross value denominator is appropriate unless the omission of a materials input variable biases the R & D variable coefficients upward. This seems improbable, since for the BLSIO sample, used R & D embodied in materials was found to be uncorrelated with productivity growth.

References

Berndt, Ernst R., and Catherine J. Morrison. Capacity Utilization Measures: Underlying Economic Theory and an Alternative Approach. *American Economic Review* 71 (May 1981): 48–52.

Griliches, Zvi. Issues in Assessing the Contribution of Research and Development to Productivity Growth. *Bell Journal of Economics* 10 (Spring 1979): 92–116.

Griliches, Zvi. R & D and the Productivity Slowdown. *American Economic Review* 70 (May 1980): 343–348.

Gustafson, W. Eric. Research and Development, New Products, and Productivity Change. *American Economic Review* 52 (May 1962): 177–185.

Kendrick, John W. *Postwar Productivity Trends in the United States, 1948–1969.* New York: Columbia University Press, 1973.

Kendrick, John W., and Elliot S. Grossman. *Productivity in the United States: Trends and Cycles.* Baltimore: Johns Hopkins University Press, 1980.

Mansfield, Edwin. Basic Research and Productivity Increase in Manufacturing. *American Economic Review* 70 (December 1980): 863–873.

Pakes, Ariel, and Mark Schankerman. The Rate of Obsolescence of Knowledge, Research Gestation Lags, and the Private Rate of Return to Research Resources. National Bureau of Economic Research working paper no. 346 (May 1979).

Ravenscraft, David, and F. M. Scherer. The Lag Structure of Returns to R & D. *Applied Economics* 14 (1982): 603–620.

Scherer, F. M. Using Linked Patent and R & D Data to Measure Inter-Industry Technology Flows. Paper presented at a National Bureau of Economic Research conference on R & D, Patents and Productivity, October 1981.

Sveikauskas, Leo. Technological Inputs and Multifactor Productivity Growth. *Review of Economics and Statistics* 63 (May 1981): 275–282.

Terleckyj, Nestor. *Effects of R & D on the Productivity Growth of Industries: An Exploratory Study.* Washington, D.C.: National Planning Association, 1974.

Terleckyj, Nestor. R & D and the U.S. Industrial Productivity in the 1970s. Paper presented at an International Institute of Management conference, Berlin, Germany, December 1980.

U.S. Bureau of Labor Statistics, Bulletin 2018. *Time Series Data for Input-Output Industries: Output, Price, and Employment.* Washington, D.C.: Government Printing Office, March 1979a.

U.S. Bureau of Labor Statistics. Bulletin 2034. *Capital Stock Estimates for Input-Output Industries: Methods and Data.* Washington, D.C., Government Printing Office, September 1979b.

16 R & D and Declining Productivity Growth

This paper attempts to assemble some pieces of a puzzle. The broad pattern is well-known. The growth rate of private business sector labor productivity, which averaged 3.1 percent per annum between 1947 and 1968, fell in stages since then and in 1977 to 1981 barely exceeded zero. Concurrently, real (i.e., GNP deflator-adjusted) company-financed industrial research and development (R & D) abruptly stopped growing in 1970 and, after a two-year hiatus, resumed its growth at a much slower rate, at least until recently. Had the 6.3 percent annual R & D growth rate of 1960 to 1969 persisted during the 1970s, U.S. industry in 1981 would have performed 38 percent more real R & D than it actually carried out.

Economists have long been persuaded that R & D yields technological advances that in turn foster productivity growth. But the magnitudes involved have been poorly understood, so it has been difficult to say how much of the recent productivity growth slump has resulted from the R & D slowdown. Also, why did R & D growth stagnate? Could it have been because R & D lost some of its power to propel productivity growth? And if so, what are the productivity ramifications?

In this paper I summarize the implications of my own effort to shed light on these questions. Separate research thrusts were directed toward the causes of the R & D slowdown and toward R & D-productivity links. The details are published elsewhere; here integration and interpretation are emphasized

16.1 The Profitability of R & D

Company-financed R & D is without doubt a profit-seeking activity. Using pooled time-series–cross-section PIMS data, David Ravenscraft and I (1982) attempted to measure as precisely as possible the lag structure of R & D-profit links and the biases imparted by applying an improperly specified lag structure. The best-fitting lag was binomial in shape, with peak profits accruing four to six years after R & D spending. For a cross section of business units with the longest time series, we found pre-tax internal rates of return on R & D to be negative for profits realized in 1975, increasing into the 27 to 45 percent range by 1977–78. The increases in estimated profitability are statistically as well as economically significant.

For the early 1970s, the time series are much less complete. However,

Source: *American Economic Review* 73 (May 1983): 215–218.

results with naive same-year lag structures suggest that in at least 1970 and 1971, the returns to R & D were, as in 1975, severely depressed. This evidence is consistent with sample business units' behavior: they cut back their R & D spending relative to sales growth. Through the elimination of low-yield projects, the profitability of R & D then rose in the decade's second quinquennium, inducing (with a lag) spending increases that became evident in 1979. From then through 1982, the real growth rate has been approximately 5.7 percent per year.

16.2 R & D and Productivity Growth

Ascertaining how R & D affects productivity growth poses more difficult conceptual and data problems. One problem stems from the fact that roughly three-fourths of all company-financed industrial R & D is oriented toward the creation of new and improved products which are then sold to other industries. Because competition erodes innovators' rents and because the price deflators used to prepare productivity indexes often fail to capture the superiority value of improved products, a considerable fraction of the productivity benefits from an industry's product R & D is likely to be captured by other industries purchasing its products. Relating R & D in industry i to industry i's own productivity growth will therefore yield downward-biased impact estimates. To measure the productivity benefits more comprehensively, a matrix tracing 1974 R & D from industries of origin to industries of use was estimated (Scherer 1981). Identifying such interindustry technology flows is particularly important in studying productivity growth for nonmanufacturing industries, which do little R & D on their own but "import" new capital goods or materials embodying roughly half of the manufacturing sector's R & D. Within manufacturing approximately 58 percent of used R & D consists of internal process R & D; the rest is imported from other industries. Even for process R & D, however, industrywide productivity benefits may exceed private profit returns because of licensing and/or competitive imitation that lead to reduced end product prices.

Once R & D had been traced to industries of use, a productivity regression could be estimated, following Terleckyj (1974), in the basic form

$$\Delta LP = \lambda + \frac{\partial Q}{\partial RS}\frac{RE}{Q} + \alpha\Delta\left(\frac{K}{L}\right),$$

where ΔLP is the annual percentage change in output per work hour, $\Delta(K/L)$ is the change in the real capital/labor ratio, RE/Q is the ratio of R & D flows to output value, and $\partial Q/\partial RS$ is the marginal productivity of the R & D capital stock (measured as a rate of return on R & D capital). The $\partial Q/\partial RS$ term is of prime interest and was estimated for product R & D, process R & D, and R & D "imported" from other industries using two different disaggregated productivity data sets.

The results are reported fully in Scherer (1982); here only highlights can be summarized. A wrong lag specification tested the hypothesis that the marginal productivity of R & D declined from the 1960s to the 1970s. The hypothesis was not supported; $\partial Q/\partial RS$ estimates for 1973–78 productivity growth were usually higher than, or in one data subset, only inappreciably less than, the corresponding estimates for 1964–69. Estimated 1973–78 returns on product R & D were close to, and insignificantly different from, zero except in one productivity data subset of doubtful reliability. Returns on "imported" R & D were generally higher than on own process R & D, but the differences were not statistically significant. Combining the two into a "used" R & D measure, the estimated $\partial Q/\partial RS$ values imply 1973–78 social returns on used R & D in the range of 71 to 104 percent, except for the productivity data subset of most dubious reliability. Thus the analysis points toward high marginal rates of return to used R & D during the 1970s, and, relative to both the estimated private profitability of R & D and the productivity index-based returns to product R & D, a large divergence between social and private returns.

16.3 Interpretation

We advance now to new ground. The estimated $\partial Q/\partial RS$ coefficients can be used to approximate the R & D growth slowdown's impact on productivity. Had R & D continued to grow at its 1960s trend rate, the 1974 R & D/output ratios would have been 1.37 times their actually observed values. Mean *used* R & D in 1974 as a percentage of sales for my most comprehensive industry sample (covering nearly all of manufacturing plus agriculture, crude oil and gas, railroads, airlines, telecommunications, and electric-gas-sanitary utilities) was 0.73. Multiplying 0.73 by $(1.37 - 1)$, we estimate the 1974 R & D shortfall to have been 0.27 percentage points. For that sample the used R & D $\partial Q/\partial RS$ coefficients ranged between 0.74 and 1.04. Thus the 1978 productivity growth short-fall attributable to lower R & D is estimated to be on the order of 0.20 to 0.28 percentage points per year. Or if the coefficients of a smaller industry sample with particularly well-measured productivity indexes (BLSPQ in chapter 15) are used, the R & D-related productivity growth impairment is estimated to be about 0.39 percentage points. Since the ratio of 1960s trend-extrapolated R & D to actual R & D in the later 1970s continued to lie in the range of 1.37 to 1.42, a drag on annual productivity growth of similar magnitude (i.e., in the range of 0.2 to 0.4 percentage points) can be expected to continue for some time.

These estimates assume, among other things, that the coefficient $\partial Q/\partial RS$ estimates the *marginal* productivity of R & D (e.g., rather than the average return) and that the marginal productivity of R & D remains constant over a rather large change in the amount of R & D performed and utilized. This assumption may be wrong, but the bias from the error is not as obvious as one might suppose. It depends on the particular mechanism inducing a slowdown of R & D growth. To illustrate, two alternative scenarios will be examined.

A central feature in any case must be a fall in the private profitability of R & D. We must also recognize that there is a divergence between marginal social and private rates of return. Based on calculations using the data reported by Mansfield et al. (1977, p. 233), we assume that private returns deviate from social returns by a constant fraction so that the private marginal efficiency of R & D investment schedule $MPER$ intersects the marginal social efficiency schedule $MSER$ at a zero rate of return, with larger absolute departures at higher rates of return. This assumption is also roughly consistent with dynamic limit pricing theory, assuming entry barriers (e.g., patent protection) to be uncorrelated with social rates of return.

In figure 16.1 the initial marginal efficiency schedules are $MSER_1$ and $MPER_1$. With a constant real risk-adjusted cost of capital Oi, the profit-maximizing amount of R & D investment is OR_1^*. If the event precipitating a fall in R & D spending is a parallel leftward shift in $MSER$ (e.g., because the pool of innovation opportunities became depleted or because product characteristics space became more densely packed), the new marginal efficiency schedules will be $MSER_2$ and $MPER_2$. The profit-maximizing level of R & D will fall to OR_2^*, and the net social surplus loss will be the shaded trapezoidal area ZP_1BA. Because of the assumed parallel marginal

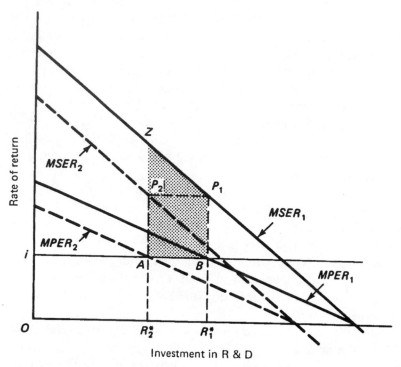

Figure 16.1
R & D reduction owing to a depletion of opportunities

efficiency schedule shifts, the marginal social return on R & D after the market has adjusted will be observed at level $R_2^* P_2$—identical to the preshift estimate $R_1^* P_1$. But relative to the earlier, rich-opportunity situation, a larger social loss $R_2^* Z$ will be incurred at the margin. Using the observed ex post marginal social return on R & D to measure the economy-wide impact, as I have done, will lead to an underestimate by the amount of the triangle $Z P_1 P_2$.

Figure 16.2 provides an alternate scenario in which R & D retains its social productivity and the impetus to declining R & D support is an increasing divergence between private and social returns—such as from intensified research competition, among other things from abroad, or more rapid imitation. The social loss is again measured by trapezoidal area $P_2 P_1 BA$. But now the postshift marginal social return $R_2^* P_2$ will *over*estimate the social loss on foregone R & D projects positioned between R_2^* and R_1^*.

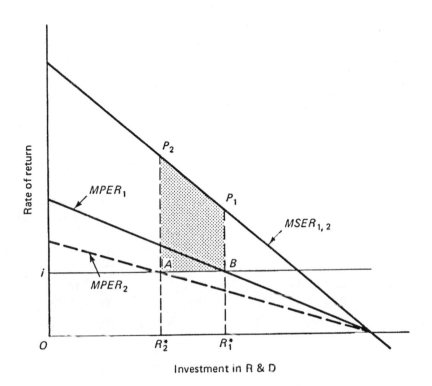

Figure 16.2
R & D reduction owing to decreased appropriability

Evidently, ascertaining more precisely how the R & D slump has affected productivity and economic welfare requires a better understanding
of *why* R & D spending stagnated. And more important, the choice of
appropriate corrective policies, for example, increasing support of basic
research vs. strengthening patent protection, demands such insights. The
increases in estimated $\partial Q / \partial RS$ coefficients between 1964–69 and 1973–78
lend support to a figure 16.2 increasing divergence hypothesis, but the
data are not strong enough to warrant a conclusive inference. The profitability study by Ravenscraft and myself yielded hints that private R & D
returns fell in part because of more intense competitive pressure, but they
were no more than hints. Qualitative observation and some quantitative
research (e.g., on pharmaceuticals) suggests that in at least some fields
of technology there has in fact been a depletion of opportunities (see

Scherer 1977). Nevertheless, much more work is needed before we can have an adequate picture of why R & D spending growth flagged and what its exact connections are to the productivity hammerblow with which it is undoubtedly linked.

If we are to make significant progress on that front, we must have better data. The best disaggregated data on R & D spending come from the Federal Trade Commission's line of business program, covering the years 1974 to 1977. The program's continuation is now in jeopardy. The Canadian Patent Office has since 1978 been collecting comprehensive invention patent origin and use data like those I used to estimate my technology flows matrix. In the United States no similar data development effort exists. And most important of all, our industry productivity series leave much to be desired. I found quite different R & D-productivity growth link patterns in industry subsets whose productivity indexes were based on reasonably comprehensive product price deflators, as compared to those with sparse deflators. While Rome burns, we do little to assemble better information on important fire-extinguishing materials. Perhaps the fire will burn itself out, but in the meantime, appalling losses accrue.

Notes

The research underlying this paper was supported by NSF grant PRA-7826526.

References

Mansfield, Edwin, John Rapoport, Anthony Romeo, Samuel Wagner, and George Beardsley. Social and Private Rates of Return from Industrial Innovations. *Quarterly Journal of Economics* 91 (May 1977): 221–240.

Ravenscraft, David, and Scherer, F. M. The Lag Structure of Returns to R & D. *Applied Economics* 14 (December 1982): 603–620.

Scherer, F. M. Technological Maturity and Waning Economic Growth. *Arts & Sciences*, Northwestern University (Fall 1978): 7–11.

Scherer, F. M. Using Linked Patent and R & D Data to Measure Inter-Industry Technology Flows. Paper presented at a National Bureau of Economic Research conference on R & D, Patents, and Productivity, October 1981.

Scherer, F. M. Inter-Industry Technology Flows and Productivity Growth. *Review of Economics and Statistics* 64 (November 1982): 627–634.

Terleckyj, Nestor. *Effects of R & D on the Productivity Growth of Industries.* Washington, D.C.: National Planning Association, 1974.

Index